Saving Jesus from the Church

Saving Jesus from the Church

How to Stop Worshiping Christ
and Start Following Jesus

ROBIN R. MEYERS

HarperOne
An Imprint of HarperCollins*Publishers*

HarperOne

All biblical quotations are from the New Revised Standard Version.

HarperCollins books may be purchased for educational, business, or sales promotional use. For information please write: Special Markets Department, HarperCollins Publishers, 10 East 53rd Street, New York, NY 10022.

HarperCollins Web site: http://www.harpercollins.com

HarperCollins®, 📖 ®, and HarperOne™ are
trademarks of HarperCollins Publishers

FIRST EDITION
Designed by Level C

Library of Congress Cataloging-in-Publication Data
Meyers, Robin R. (Robin Rex).
Saving Jesus from the church : how to stop worshiping Christ and start following Jesus / by Robin R. Meyers.—1st ed.
p. cm.
Includes bibliographical references (p.).
ISBN 978–0–06–156821–3
1. Christianity—Essence, genius, nature. 2. Christian life—United Church of Christ authors. I. Title.
BT60.M44 2009
262.001'7—dc22   2008051766

09 10 11 12 13 RRD (H) 10 9 8 7 6 5 4 3 2 1

I dedicate this book to all the men and women who have chosen the parish ministry as their life's work, and yet do not wish to be considered harmless artifacts from another age. May all those who labor in the most misunderstood, dangerous, and sublime of all professions be encouraged and inspired by the possibility that one's head and one's heart can be equal partners in faith. Lest the church end up a museum piece whose clergy are affable but laughable cartoons, we must once again dedicate ourselves to this wild calling—one that led us away from more comfortable lives and into the only profession where radical truth-telling is part of the job description. May we fear no man and no creed, save our own timidity, and may we encourage and support one another in pursuit of religion that is biblically responsible, intellectually honest, emotionally satisfying, and socially significant.

CONTENTS

A PREACHER'S NIGHTMARE: AM I A CHRISTIAN?

Am I a Christian?" What a strange question for an ordained minister of the gospel to ask. Born a minister's son and raised in a parsonage, I spent my childhood in the conservative Church of Christ, where no musical instruments are allowed in worship. As a college student, I discovered the Congregational Church and the liberal United Church of Christ, which I was warned to avoid, and then never looked back. The UCC has been my home ever since, a brave and messy denomination that has been speaking truth to power for a long time and insisting that we make more room at the table for those who are forgotten.

Try as I might to be a "normal" kid (as a teenager I once hid copies of *Playboy* in plain sight, lest I be mistaken for a saint), I was a member of a generation that got its marching orders from Bob Dylan and Martin Luther King Jr. When I was at the tender age of sixteen, two of my heroes were gunned down just weeks apart, one on a hotel balcony in Memphis, the other in a hotel ballroom in California. The faint smell of tear gas hung over many college campuses in those days, and the *New York Times* reported that God was dead. The last thing I wanted to grow up to be was a preacher.

As fate would have it, or destiny (if I could figure out the difference between the two), the seeds of the ministry had already been planted in me. A double PK (preacher's kid and professor's kid), I had been invited at age fourteen to offer my first public prayer at the Communion table of the Riverside Church of Christ in Wichita, Kansas. Chances are it was awful. But the dear souls there told me it was wonderful. One woman even went so far as to say, "Robin, that prayer surely found its way straight into God's ear, and you will be a preacher like your father someday."

Now, forty years later, twenty-five of them spent as a UCC minister in my native Oklahoma, I came home one cold January afternoon after serving Communion to my beloved flock and took a nap, which is my Sunday ritual. Parish ministry is tiring in ways most people do not understand, and a Sunday afternoon nap is as sacred to a middle-aged clergyman as the Psalms. Rising before dawn and still fooling with the sermon (or finishing it), many of us preachers are obsessive-compulsive types who believe that no matter how many times we have done this before, this time we will get it right. Preaching is, after all, an audacious and dangerous act.

After the service, we stand in line, listening to "Good sermon, Reverend" a hundred times (all of which can be erased if just one person says, "Good morning, Reverend"), come home, wash off the aftershave and perfume residue from all those handshakes and hugs, sit down to eat, and then lie down to sleep. It's a ritual as old as the priesthood, but there is also something subversive about it. Sleeping at odd times of the day can open the heart to strange dreams, when the ego stands down and the id and superego collide without a mediator. This day was no different, except for the dream. I woke up wondering if I was a Christian.

I had folded myself into a fetal position and drawn the covers over my head. From the other room, I heard the talking heads of TV yelling at one another, arguing over what to do now that we were mired in this hopeless war in Iraq and creating terrorists faster than we were killing them. The morning paper brought the same news we hear every morning—another suicide bomber had done what is unthinkable to those of us who consider our lives worth living. As I drifted off to sleep, I tried to imagine it: a place where human heads roll down the street like apples scattered from a fruit stand, and wailing mothers search for the remains of their children, only to find a shoe and one hand. In my dream I saw a woman holding that hand, grape-colored and dusty like a glove with entrails. If we have become numb to this, then what have we become?

It is not a good idea to think of such things before falling asleep, of course, but this is the world we live in; this is the soundtrack of our lives. We shop frantically while flag-draped coffins bearing the remains of our dead soldiers ("babies," as Kurt Vonnegut called them) get off-loaded in the dead of night like so many burned or broken biscuits from the ovens of war. We hear the droning script of patriotism—members of Congress, all wearing those standard-issue American flag lapel pins, urge other people's children to be brave and "defend our freedom." War is now "outsourced" like everything else, and then we spin the results to hide the reality of a demonic chaos. If Dante came back, his new vision of hell would surely include the Baghdad morgue.

Meanwhile, the music in my dream was provided by right-wing talk-show hosts, crooning like backup singers in a concert of death. TV preachers did the drumming, slicing the world in half with the rhetoric of entitlement. The judgment is coming, they were saying, but instead of sheep and goats, one axis is God's chosen, the other, God's despised. We love Jesus, so we are entitled to kill for the cause; the others are crazy infidels whose resistance to the crusade is inexplicably evil. A preacher smiles and says, "They just want those seventy virgins."

The moment I opened my eyes, with the dream still fresh and vivid, I wondered about the future of the church to which I have given my life. Is it toxic now beyond redemption? Should it be allowed to die, so that something else can take its place, or should we go in search of Jesus one more time? It was as if an animal had curled up on my chest while I slept, bringing with it an urgent message from somewhere east of decency: *if this is Christianity and these are Christians, I must not be one.*

In the dream I had a flashback to Saddam Hussein's execution by American proxies. Rome never does its work without co-conspirators. I saw his neck snapped and torn open, his eyes bulging in death. Someone captured it on a cell phone and in the Bible Belt, where I live, e-mails started circulating that praised God for this righteous act of vengeance. It was as if we had melted the wicked witch of the West with help from an "awesome God." Finally we had an out-of-the-closet Christian in the White House, but what came out of the closet instead was torture. Winking and water boarding, and yet who can be surprised? Mel Gibson had just made a frightfully successful movie in which the One who tortures is God.

In my dream, those in power never took responsibility for anything, nor could they seem to remember anything, especially if it was important. The counsel of Jesus to let our speech be "a simple yes or no" was as foreign as the idea of actually helping the poor. In my dream, the image of Jesus had morphed from a Rembrandt portrait of a sad but radiant face into a bobble-headed doll in the back of a stretch limo. In the landscape of my dream, churches had ceased building sanctuaries and opted for metal auditoriums without steeples or religious symbols. While the band played and the privileged wept tears of self-satisfied joy, young warriors for Christ were taught to love Jesus by hating Darwin and homosexuals. I woke up thinking, *if this is Christianity and these are Christians, I must not be one.*

In this brave new world, Orwell's ubiquitous "telescreens" were everywhere, and the simple truth was treated like a quaint liability. Loyalty counted for more than competence, and the secret handshake in the halls of power was the wink of crony capitalism. There seemed to be fewer and fewer *citizens* now, lost in a stampede of *consumers*. Instead of grand and trembling rhetoric that called us to sacrifice, we heard only advertisements—dazzling new reasons why we should hurry up and act now on our own behalf.

The dream was partly my fault. One should never channel surf before going to bed. There are too many sad spectacles masquerading as ministry out there, religious TV charlatans with cures for "partial hearing loss" or "chronic fatigue." They bring their salvation show to town and the newly "cured" dance a jig in front of the camera to prove that Jesus loves them. Did he not love them when they were crippled? Could he not work an even greater miracle and provide universal health insurance? When they wake up, the pain will have returned, but the crusade will be gone. God loves them, and then leaves them? I woke up thinking, *if this is Christianity and these are Christians, I must not be one.*

Trying to shake off this nightmare, I decided to go for a walk. I went to find fresh air and to gaze at the pink winter sky—to rub my eyes and exhale my troubles. What happened on that walk surprised and unsettled me. I am aware of the ancient belief that dreams are messages from God, but also of the modern case for dreams as extensions of both id and ego. That is, we dream not just to receive answers but to get deeper glimpses of the self swimming in the dark waters of the subconscious. This dream was like a self-confirming interior documentary. The disturbing images did more than just reflect the horrors of our time. They reminded me that we all love to have our opinions canonized. No doubt the world is a mess, but those who make this diagnosis must do more than just enjoy the thought. Everyone has a different list of enemies and "evildoers," and even the liberal clergy can succumb to what the late clergyman and activist William Sloane Coffin Jr. called "spiritual pride."

As it turns out, the real message of the dream wasn't self-confirming. It was self-indicting. Instead of asking, "How can I call myself a Christian now?" a better question might be, "Why haven't I done more to promote biblical literacy and invite others to consider an alternative way of being the church in our time?" It is easier and much more satisfying to rail against the Right than to suggest that we go back to Genesis 1 and study together. Liberals can be just as intolerant as fundamentalists, and we have arrived at a moment in human history when intolerance and hope are mutually exclusive.

I have never believed in the virgin birth as a biological fact, the infallibility of scripture as a test of faith, the miracles as past suspension of natural law demanding current suspension of reason, the blood atonement (that the suffering of the innocent can vicariously atone for the sins of the guilty) as the foreordained mission of Jesus, the bodily resurrection as the only way to understand Easter, or the second coming as a necessary sequel—and I am the pastor of a church that does not define Christianity this way either.

Naturally, people ask, "So what *do* you believe?" They seem puzzled by the answer. I say that we are not "believers" at all, not in the sense of giving intellectual assent to postbiblical propositions. Rather, we are doing our best to avoid the worship of Christ and trying to get back to something much more fulfilling and transformative: following Jesus.

We all know too well the abuses of fundamentalism in our time, and in one way or another we have all been living through a nightmare of bad theology married to bad public policy. But in the liberal church, some of us have failed to work as diligently at *reconstructing* the church as we have at taking secret, self-confirming delight in deconstructing it. As liberal Protestant churches declined and we bought the myth that it was *because* they were liberal (rather than *how* they were liberal), a whole generation has been asked to accept a false dichotomy. Either you believe that Jesus is God or you don't—therefore either you're a Christian or you're not.

Meanwhile, the most urgent question of all goes unasked: *What kind of God did Jesus reveal?* That question has been submerged beneath "battles for the Bible" and bitter disputes over the metaphysics of a Galilean sage. So it has become fashionably iconoclastic these days to ask, "Can I even call myself a Christian now?" Yet perhaps this is the wrong question, at least for those of us still in the church. Instead, we should be asking, "What is the proper object of our worship, and what would it take to make Christianity compelling, even irresistible, again?" How can our faith become biblically responsible, intellectually honest, emotionally satisfying, and socially significant?

Conservatives and liberals alike are caught in confusion and despair about the world in which we live. They wander through the wreckage of broken relationships, broken promises, and broken lives. The evidence abounds that not only do the self-righteous not have the market cornered on "clean living," but they often lead secret, self-destructive lives. In my part of the world (Oklahoma is the reddest state in the union), there is actually a positive correlation between high church attendance and negative social statistics like teen pregnancy, divorce, physical and sexual abuse, and chemical dependency. Where there is denial there is dysfunction, and the more one's faith resembles a fairy tale the sooner the clock strikes midnight.

Obviously, no matter how much preaching we hear to the contrary, fewer and fewer of us actually order our lives around the axis of sin and salvation. Rather, we order it around a search for meaning in a world that often seems meaningless. We are looking for a teacher, not a savior. Does the worship of Christ mitigate such sinful behavior, or just help to enable it through cheap grace?

On both the left and the right there is a growing chorus of voices saying that there must be more to Christian faith than arguments over abortion and gay marriage. Many evangelicals have awakened to the threat of global warming and are rethinking the capacity of Adam Swift's "invisible hand" to reduce poverty. Countless so-called seekers are in exile from the church of their childhood, a mass of refugees from organized religion; these walking wounded cannot return until the church commits itself to both intellectual honesty and an alternative vision for living in a lost world.

Make no mistake, there is a tectonic shift occurring along the old fault lines of the church. Lots of people, including evangelicals, are buying books written by biblical scholars who are not literalists, and they seem willing to consider the possibility that myth and metaphor are not lies, but the most appropriate container for the truth that "passes all understanding." Taking the Bible seriously is not the same thing as taking it literally, and perhaps what we need now is a kind of national "teach-in." Ironic as it may seem, we ought to hold these classes in the sanctuaries of the land—in the church of Jesus the Galilean Jew, the world's most famous missing person—but only if *everyone* is invited.

Among a myriad of fictions in the land today is the one that theology doesn't matter, and that whatever people want to believe is okay. But in truth, our national nightmare is not just political. It is *theological.* Those who would tear down the wall between church and state and have public funds support private faith-based programs are not just dismantling our democracy. They are pushing for a government-supported view of an empire-driven theocracy.

As long as Christianity is the dominant belief system in America, we cannot afford to be biblically or theologically illiterate, regardless of our personal beliefs. To save the country, not to mention the planet, we are *all* called once more to ask the most basic theological questions: "Who *was* Jesus before he was the Christ? What does it really mean to *follow* him as a teacher and not just worship him as a supernatural deity on a rescue mission?"

Organized religion is now so dysfunctional that amateur atheists are writing bestsellers. It's easy—we wrote the script for them. It is no wonder so many mainline churches are dying. They have so long existed in maintenance mode that they have lost their prophet nerve. They have put so much energy into survival that they have forsaken their responsibility to be places of free and fearless inquiry and radical hospitality as well as spiritual sustenance. Alas, the work of rigorous biblical scholarship now takes place in almost complete isolation from the church and in some cases with a palpable animosity toward the clergy, considered by many in the academy to be clods.

Yet the people in the pews are not just reading *The Da Vinci Code, The Secret,* or *The Prayer of Jabez.* They are also reading Marcus Borg, John Dominic Crossan, and Karen Armstrong. They know the arguments for the Bible as both inspired and covered with human fingerprints, but they could use a little help in constructing a meaningful faith in a postmodern and, for many, a postorthodox world. They may not be literalists, but they are not atheists either, and many long to become part of a beloved community. They need help to construct a Christian faith worth having in a community worth belonging to.

Now we have come to a fork in the long and winding road. But this much is clear: we cannot "travel both and be one traveler," as Robert Frost put it. One leads into the undergrowth of endless violence, even nuclear holocaust. This is the road we are on. We should look down it, the poet urges us, "as far as we can." But we must remember "how way leads on to way," lest we pass the point of no return. Now is the time to take the road less traveled.

That road leads away from entitled nation-states and standing armies, away from the fear that is the enemy of the moral life, away from closed religious systems that sanctify the saved and render the lost dispensable, away from faith as a cosmic transaction. The road less traveled is the long and stony road that leads to wisdom and peace.

The first step, however, must be a step backward. We have been traveling down the creedal road of Christendom since the fourth century, when a first-century spiritual insurgency was seduced into marrying its original oppressor. Before there were bishops lounging at the table of power, there were ordinary fishermen who forsook ordinary lives to follow an itinerant sage down a path that was not obvious, sensible, or safe. He might as well have said, "Come die with me."

In the beginning, the call of God was not propositional. It was experiential. It was as palpable as wine and wineskins, lost coins and frightened servants, corrupting leaven and a tearful father. Now we argue over the Trinity, the true identity of the beast in the book of Revelation, and the exact number of people who will make it into heaven. Students who once learned by *following* the teacher became true believers who confuse certainty with faith.

We have a sacred story that has been stolen from us, and in our time the thief is what passes for orthodoxy itself (right belief instead of right worship). Arguing over the metaphysics of Christ only divides us. But agreeing to follow the essential teachings of Jesus could unite us. We could become imitators, not believers.

Those two roads that "diverged in a yellow wood" so long ago looked equally fair, but now one is well worn. It is the road of the Fall and redemption, original sin, and the Savior. The other is the road of enlightenment, wisdom, creation-centered spirituality, and a nearly forgotten object of discipleship: *transformation*. This is the road less traveled. It seeks not to save our souls but to *restore* them.

We know that before that fourth-century fork in the road, there was but one road. The disciples called it "The Way," and it was the only road that did *not* lead to Rome. It took travelers into the heart of God, singing all the way. It welcomed all who would come, especially the poor and the lost, and the only trinity that mattered was to remember where we came from, where we are going, and to Whom we belong.

If we do not go *back* to that fork in the road, we cannot go forward on the road less traveled. If we do not stop traveling down the road we are on, we will not just destroy the planet and everyone on it but continue to betray the heart of Christianity. Our task now is not just to demythologize Jesus. It is to let the breath of the Galilean sage fall on the neck of the church again. First we have to listen not to formulas of salvation but to a gospel that is all but forgotten. After centuries of being told that "Jesus saves," the time has come to save Jesus from the church.

If the door is locked, we will break in through the windows. If anyone forbids us to approach the table, we will overturn it and serve Communion on the floor. If any priest tells us we cannot sing this new song, we will sing it louder, invite others to sing it with us, and raise our voices in unison across all the boundaries of human contrivance—until this joyful chorus is heard in every corner of the world, and the church itself is raised from the dead.

ONE

JESUS THE TEACHER, NOT THE SAVIOR

What has been passing for Christianity during these nineteen
centuries is merely a beginning, full of weaknesses and
mistakes, not a full-grown Christianity springing from the spirit
of Jesus.

—*Albert Schweitzer*

First, I owe a word of explanation to readers. This book is
not about one more attempt to prove why it is wrong to be
a fundamentalist. Nor is it a book meant to prove that Jesus is
not divine—at least in a metaphysical sense—and never walked
on water or raised anyone from the dead. Indeed, I could not
prove such a thing to anyone who wasn't already inclined to
believe it. Instead, it is a book written by a pastor, an invitation
that comes bearing the postmark of the church and addressed
to those who already accept the Bible as inspired, but not infallible. It is not offered as a scholarly argument against literalism
or literalists, nor is it intended to be one more tirade against any
form of ignorance or arrogance. Those in glass houses should
not throw stones.

Rather, it is a word on behalf of those who have walked away
from the church because they recognize intellectual dishonesty
as the original sin of orthodoxy. It is a sermon addressed to
nonbelievers as well as to those who grew up in the church. It

is meant to provide a second opinion for all those who know what they are supposed to believe but refuse to equate miracles with magic or liturgy with history—and yet still fall silent when someone reads the Beatitudes or get goosebumps listening to the parable of the prodigal son. It is not an apologetic but a call to reconsider what it means to follow Jesus, instead of arguing over things that the church has insisted we must all believe about Christ. Doctrines divide by nature. Discipleship brings us together.

Instead of digging deeper trenches, we need to declare a cease-fire and agree to meet around the kitchen table, where people actually live, to discuss exactly what we are fighting about and what on earth it has to do with Jesus. There are countless pilgrims out there who remain fascinated and humbled by his wisdom and by the movement that his life and death unleashed, but who know too much now about the formation of church doctrine, the evolution and redaction of scripture, and the incredible but intransigent cosmology of the church to place much trust in the institution. There is a deep hunger for wisdom in our time, but the church offers up little more than sugary nostalgia with a dash of fear. There is a yearning for redemption, healing, and wholeness that is palpable, a shift in human consciousness that is widely recognized—except, it seems, in most churches.

Strangely, we have come to a moment in human history when the message of the Sermon on the Mount could indeed save us, but it can no longer be heard above the din of dueling doctrines. Consider this: there is not a single word in that sermon about what to *believe,* only words about what to *do.* It is a behavioral manifesto, not a propositional one. Yet three centuries later, when the Nicene Creed became the official oath of Christendom, there was not a single word in it about what to do, only words about what to believe!

Thus the most important question we can ask in the church today concerns the object of faith itself. The earliest metaphors of the gospel speak of discipleship as transformation through an alternative community and the reversal of conventional wisdom. In much of the church today, our metaphors speak of individual salvation and the specific promises that accompany it. The first followers of Jesus trusted him enough to become instruments of radical change. Today, worshipers of Christ agree to believe things *about* him in order to receive benefits promised by the institution, not by Jesus.

This difference, between following and worshiping, is not insignificant. Worshiping is an inherently passive activity, since it involves the adoration of that to which the worshiper cannot aspire. It takes the form of praise, which can be both sentimental and self-satisfying, without any call to changed behavior or self-sacrifice. In fact, Christianity as a belief system requires nothing but acquiescence. Christianity as a way of life, as a path to follow, requires a second birth, the conquest of ego, and new eyes with which to see the world. It is no wonder that we have preferred to be saved.

FROM YESHUA TO JEHOVAH

To understand how a first-century Mediterranean Jewish peasant named Yeshua went from being what historical Jesus scholar Marcus Borg calls a spirit person, a teacher of wisdom, a social prophet, and a movement founder to the Only Begotten Son of God requires a clear and courageous approach to the study of the New Testament. To use Professor Borg's immensely helpful dichotomy, the synoptic gospels (Matthew, Mark, and Luke) provide us not historical accounts but "sketches" by the early Christian community of both a *pre-Easter* man and an emerging *post-Easter* deity.[1]

Jesus is the pre-Easter man, or what biblical scholars have long searched to uncover: the "historical Jesus." Christ is the post-Easter deity that had fully arrived by the time John's gospel was written, even though his evolution from Jewish mystic to supernatural Savior was already emerging in the synoptic gospels. For the remainder of the book, however, I will speak of "Jesus" when referring to the Jewish peasant from Galilee—from his birth through the writing of the synoptic gospels. I will use the exalted title "Christ" to refer to the preexistent divine Savior from John's gospel forward to the writing of the creeds.

This separation cannot be made easily, of course, but the search to distinguish between the two is hardly new. For over two hundred years, biblical scholars have labored to glimpse the Jewish man behind the Christian myths, and Albert Schweitzer made it clear that such a search is ultimately in vain. In his epic work *The Quest of the Historical Jesus*, he solidifies the notion of a "thoroughgoing eschatology" in which Jesus preached an "interim ethic" in what he tragically believed were the last days. Recently scholarship, however, has made this image of Jesus as eschatological prophet a minority opinion.

Even so, it is Schweitzer's closing words that are most remembered—leaving open the possibility that it is only through *discipleship* that we bridge the gap between Galilean sage and long-awaited messiah:

> He comes to us as One unknown, without a name, as of old, by the lakeside, He came to those men who knew Him not. He speaks to us the same word: "Follow thou me!" and sets us to the task which He has to fulfill for our time. He commands. And to those who obey Him, whether they be wise or simple, He will reveal Himself in the toils, the conflicts, the sufferings which they shall pass

through in His fellowship, and as an ineffable mystery, they shall learn in their own experience Who He is.[2]

If this is true, then Schweitzer has both confirmed his belief that the historical Jesus cannot be "found" and confessed that the voice of the Nazarene still beckons. He says, moreover, that it is not in believing, but in *following,* that his identity is revealed. It is ironic that none of those who took issue with Schweitzer's theology and cursed his writings gave up fame and fortune or membership in the highest stratum of German society to live among the poorest of the poor. They prepared their critiques in the comfort of the pastor's study or the university library, while Schweitzer nailed patches of tin on the roof of his free medical clinic at Lambarene by the banks of the Ogoove River. Theologians who sat in endowed chairs took his Christology to task, while he scraped infectious lesions off blue-black natives in the steaming misery of equatorial Africa.

Albert Schweitzer deserves to be remembered as the greatest Christian of the twentieth century, yet he did not believe in literal miracles—the blood atonement, the bodily resurrection, or the second coming, just to name a few. All he did was walk away from everything the world calls good to *follow* Jesus. And in all honesty, his conclusion that the historical Jesus cannot be found is correct—at least not according to the standards of the Western rational tradition. But his work did not close the book on such research, as many thought it would.

There has been a "third quest" for the historical Jesus under way since the 1980s, and, although misunderstood and much maligned, the work of the Jesus Seminar has yielded insights of great value to the church. Moving beyond the work of German scholarship, which sought to extract abiding existential truths from mythological wrappings, the latest generation of historical Jesus scholars has used the tools of higher criticism to isolate two layers, or "voices," in the gospels—a pre-Easter voice that more likely belongs to Jesus and a post-Easter voice that more likely belongs to the Christ of the early church.

One method for doing this, widely reported in the press and mocked as blasphemy by some, was the vote that the members of the Jesus Seminar took on the historical accuracy of the sayings attributed to Jesus. The scholars dropped colored beads—red, pink, gray, and black—in a ballot box to measure the degree of consensus about whether a particular passage is Jesus speaking or the voice of the early church. "A red vote means, 'I'm pretty sure Jesus said that'; pink, somewhere between 'probably' and 'more likely yes than no'; gray, somewhere between 'more likely no than yes' and 'probably not'; and black, 'I'm pretty sure Jesus didn't say that.'"[3]

The idea was not to reduce biblical authority to scholarly hunches, prove that the Bible is "wrong," or suggest that the sayings of Jesus are "fictitious." It was a serious and scholarly attempt to distinguish between the more authentic sayings of Jesus and those created by a witnessing community that had crowned him messiah. The scholarly work of the Jesus Seminar is not done for the benefit of the church, but the church can certainly benefit. We have come to a moment in the life of the church when only the most candid and intellectually honest assessment of the life and message of Jesus can prevent the continued implosion of the church. We should study the Bible with all the tools of higher criticism not to prove that some are "right" and some are "wrong" but to uncover a more authentic reading of the life and ministry of Jesus. Otherwise, the church will quite literally lose its voice. Biblical illiteracy is contributing to theological laryngitis.

The reason that such biblical scholarship is vital has nothing to do with elitism or the intellectual arrogance of separating the blind goats from the enlightened sheep. The quest for the historical Jesus is not ultimately destructive but *constructive*.

Biblical scholars are not myth busters; they work to uncover the truth, whether on behalf of those who still call themselves Christians or those who have given up on organized religion. They have no agenda other than to recover the most accurate and authentic meaning from the text by studying it as literature. They do not presume that facts are the same thing as faith, but they certainly think that faith built on demonstrable fictions advances neither faith nor intellectual honesty.

Anti-intellectualism remains strongly entrenched in many parts of the church, but it is grounded in fear, not in faith. Instead of seeing the benefits of a vital conversation between the academy and the average person in the pew about how a third-millennium man or woman might still follow a first-century Jewish sage, many Christians view scholarship as a threat to church doctrine. They believe that professors who make clever arguments against the virgin birth, for example, are careless vandals poking holes in the dike of faith. To shore up that dike, they believe they need to show "true faith" by accepting uncritically the tenets of their particular tradition without question. Such defiance is captured in a popular bumper sticker: "THE BIBLE SAYS IT, GOD WROTE IT, AND THAT SETTLES IT!"

Ironically, biblical scholars are actually interested in the same "trinity" of ideas, but they put question marks where others put exclamation points. What does the Bible really say? What does it mean to say it is inspired by God? And why do we believe that God's voice is exclusively in the past tense? Perhaps, as my denomination is fond of saying, God is still speaking.

Adoration of the post-Easter Christ so dominates the language and liturgy of the church that the wisdom of pre-Easter Jesus is all but lost. The divine Savior image is now so exclusively the message of evangelical and fundamentalist Christianity that the Sermon on the Mount seems almost superfluous. Sunday school classes have given up the study of the parables, even though the parable was the principal teaching device of Jesus. They are not wrestling with the hard sayings of the Jewish prophets who preceded Jesus. Indeed, instead of being disoriented by divine wisdom, they are "decoding" the salvation "contract" that is presumed to be hidden in scripture, so that true believers can cash in their winning ticket and collect their eternal inheritance. Being a disciple today often means little more than believing stuff in order to get stuff.

Christian education today is often more about spiritual empowerment than about enlightenment. In addition to Christian aerobics and end-times investing, "Bible study" is offered as a series of self-improvement seminars sanctified by John 3:16. Christianity has become primarily a strategy for "victory," but it is an *individual* victory over debt, obesity, or low self-esteem, not a collective victory over injustice, poverty, war, or environmental degradation. Faith has become essentially an individual transaction, and the image of God is that of a personal trainer. Much preaching today is framed as an invitation to God to come into *our* story, but the biblical invitation is radically different. We are being invited into *God's* story.

How can we decide whether to accept that invitation or be prepared for its consequences, however, if we do not understand our own story? Recent studies show that only 40 percent of Americans can name more than four of the Ten Commandments and only half can cite any of the four authors of the gospels. Twelve percent believe Joan of Arc was Noah's wife. Three-quarters of Americans believe that the Bible teaches that "God helps those who help themselves," when in fact Ben Franklin said this. To understand how dangerous this is, just imagine, one scholar wrote, "if 75 percent of American scientists believed that Newton proved gravity causes apples to fly up."[4]

The value of serious Bible study is not to deconstruct the authority of the Bible, one myth at a time, but to use the mind as well as the heart and soul to recover the most accurate possible portrait of what the Bible actually says, not what we assume that it says. If we are going to go to this party, we need to know how to dress, what gift to bring, and whether we will recognize anyone when we get there. A party with strangers is one of life's most awkward situations.

HONESTY AND FAITH

One thing every pastor knows is that knowledge is not redemptive. Indeed, sometimes we can know the truth, and it will *not* set us free. Ask a smoker, for example, if he knows that tobacco is addictive and death-dealing, and he will say yes. Ask a cheating spouse if he or she knows what the affair could cost, and the answer is always yes. Ask a teenager if she knows what drugs and alcohol can do to destroy her future, and she will almost always say, "Yes, I know." Obviously "knowing" is not enough, and one of the great divides in the church could be overcome if we got one thing straight: the truth of which Jesus speaks is wisdom *incarnate,* not intellectual assent to cogent arguments made on behalf of God. Indeed, a quick glance around this broken world makes it painfully obvious that we don't need more arguments on behalf of God; we need more people who live as if they are in covenant with Unconditional Love, which is our best definition of God.

Having said this, it is not the case that faith is more pure when it is uninformed or when it turns away from critical thinking and sound reasoning as threats to the life of the spirit. Science is not the enemy of faith, but rather its handmaiden. More threatening to the future of faith is the fear of what *can* be known as well as the search to know more. In fact, the ongoing suspicion that scientific discoveries or rigorous biblical scholarship will undermine faith is a tacit admission that faith is threatened by knowledge, because it is ultimately constructed on weak or faulty assumptions and, like the proverbial house of cards, needs to be "protected" from collapsing. The horizon, as one preacher put it, is not all there is; it's just the limit of our sight. Faith's impulse is not to provide a substitute for anything less than can be known. Rather, faith wants to trust in more than can be known. Robert Funk, the founder of the Jesus Seminar, puts it this way:

> To be sure, I am not of the opinion that facts of themselves will provide us with the ultimate truth about Jesus, about ourselves, and about our world. But whatever we come to believe about those ultimate issues should be informed by the facts, insofar as we can discover them. I am not an empiricist, much less a positivist, contrary to some of my critics. But the pressure to discover all we can know about our own past, about the history of Jesus, and about the physical universe has a cathartic way of disciplining our imaginations.[5]

Once again, religion at its best should be biblically responsible, intellectually honest, emotionally satisfying, and socially significant. The first half of this formula requires that we fearlessly admit to what higher criticism of the Bible has shown us, recalling that the greatest commandment is to love God "with all your heart, and with all your soul, and with all your *mind* . . . [and] your neighbor as yourself" (Matt. 22:37, emphasis added). After two centuries of intense and devoted biblical scholarship, we can and we should confess to what we now know—and do so fearlessly.

We know that the gospels were written in the last third of the first century, and that they are not historical accounts but testimonies of faith, written to persuade a mostly Jewish audience that Jesus was indeed the long-awaited messiah. Of central importance is the fact that during the forty to seventy years that elapsed between the ministry of Jesus and the written records we call the gospels, his early followers adapted to new circumstances as they blended memories of his teaching with their continuing experience of him as the risen Lord.

We know that Saul of Tarsus, who never met Jesus, became the apostle Paul through a completely mystical experience and seemed to care nothing for the earthly teachings of Jesus, only his "adoption" as the Son of God through the resurrection. Not only did he alter the nature of the gospel from a story to an argument, but his letters and those written by others in his name are the earliest Christian documents we have, written long before the gospels. Almost all scholars believe that Mark was the earliest of the synoptic gospels (or "see together" gospels, Matthew, Mark, and Luke, so called because they share similar material) and that Matthew and Luke drew common material from both Mark and a hypothetical gospel known as Q (from the German *Quelle,* meaning "source").

The *Gospel of Thomas,* a collection of sayings of Jesus discovered in 1945 at Nag Hammadi, is thought to be completely independent of the canonical gospels. It may be similar to the Q gospel, and although it identifies itself as a gospel at the end, it has no overall narrative or biographical framework. There are no descriptions of deeds or miracles and no crucifixion or resurrection stories.[6]

What's more, many other gospels have been discovered that did not make it into the Bible. When historical Jesus researchers sought to chronicle all twenty of the known gospels from the early Christian era, the list looks strange indeed to those who know only the gospels they learned about in Sunday school. In addition to the narrative gospels, the so-called holy four, Mark, Matthew, Luke, and John, there is believed to have been a signs gospel, now lost, which is almost entirely a catalog of Jesus' miracles, intended to prove that he was the messiah.

Scholars group the remaining gospels by categories. Under "sayings gospels" are the aforementioned Gospel of Q and the *Gospel of Thomas,* the *Greek Fragments of Thomas,* the *Secret Book* of James, the Dialogue of the Savior, and the Gospel of Mary. Under "infancy gospels" are the Gospel of Peter, the Secret Gospel of Mark, the Egerton Gospel, and the gospels Oxyrhunchus 840 and 1224. Under "Jewish Christian gospels" are the Gospel of the Hebrews, the Gospel of the Ebionites, and the Gospel of the Nazoreans.[7]

What does this mean? At the very least it means that what we ended up with was a very short, "approved" list of gospels chosen from a large and diverse collection of existing material, and then this "foursome" became a "spectrum of approved interpretation forming a strong central vision that was later able to render apocryphal, hidden, or censored any other gospels too far off its right or left wing."[8] The revelations that come from reading early Christian writings beyond the pages of the Bible provide tantalizing evidence that women held prominent roles in the early church (Gospel of Mary), that Jesus imparted a private revelation to James and Peter prior to his ascension (Secret Book of James), and that the Gospel of Peter may have given us the original passion narrative later adapted in the synoptic gospels.

This simple fact, that the Bible came to us through a process of review and selection by human beings who condensed an enormous amount of material down to four gospels, a pseudo-history we call the Acts of the Apostles, and the letters that complete the New Testament, is remarkably unknown to most Christians. Indeed, part of the controversy over The Da Vinci Code came not just as a result of the question of its plausibility, but as a result of the shock that seems to accompany the realization that other gospels even exist outside the Bible—especially when one of them, the Gospel of Philip, contains a reference to Jesus' companion (also translated "consort") Mary Magdala. It says that he "loved Mary more than the rest of us because he used to kiss her on the ____ [hole in the text]." Perhaps never has a papyrus-eating worm destroyed the final word of a more intriguing sentence!

Regardless of whether this was the holy kiss or something more, we know that Jesus was Jewish and spoke as a Jewish man to Jewish followers. We have no evidence that he thought of himself as the founder of a new religion, and the dark legacy of anti-Semitism is ironically the result of the myth that Jesus was a Christian rejected by "the Jews." In order to put down a growing rebellion that Jesus was inspiring, Rome executed him with the help of Jewish proxies who did not represent the Jews but carried out the orders of the empire. What became the Christian church was originally formed as a movement *within* the life of the synagogue, where it existed for fifty to sixty years before its divorce from Judaism in the late eighth or early ninth decade CE.

This means that Mark and Matthew were written before the divorce and Luke perhaps during the final days. Only John is clearly written after the divorce, and some of its references reveal the bitterness of separation. In Mark, the earliest gospel, Jesus begins his ministry in the river Jordan as a disciple of John the Baptist; in Matthew and Luke he begins life as a divinely conceived infant. But in John, Jesus is preexistent with God and descends into human history from above as the exclusive way to salvation. He supersedes both John the Baptist and Moses and occupies a separate realm in a gospel full of the rhetoric of antitheses: light and darkness, spirit and flesh, knowledge and ignorance, sight and blindness.

In John, Jesus was the Christ before he was born, and those who reject him are children of the devil (8:44). His opponents are called the Ioudaioi, which originally meant "Judeans" but, by the time the gospels were assembled as a collection, came to mean "the Jews" and thus the opponents of Jesus who cry out, "Crucify him!" Only in John's gospel does Jesus appear to disciples who had locked the doors "for fear of the Jews" (20:19). In the progression from the earliest gospel, which records Jesus as saying, "Why do you call me good? No one is good but God alone" (Mark 10:18), to John, whose preexistent Christ visits the earth but lives in a kind of parallel universe as a Gnostic contrarian, we see the evolution of Christianity itself—from Yeshua to Jehovah, from Jesus to the Christ.

After Constantine engineered the merger of Christ worshipers with sun worshipers in the fourth century, the creeds solidified and finalized the view of faith we hold today. Not only was this politically expedient, but it gave the church many elements of Mithraism that survive to this day. Christ is depicted in early paintings as the Sun (with rays bursting from his head), Sun-Day is the day of rest, and Christmas was moved from January 6 (still the date for Eastern Orthodox churches) to December 25, the birthday of Mithra. The ornaments of Christian orthodoxy today are nearly identical to those of the Mithraic version: miters, wafers, water baptism, altar, and doxology. Mithra was a traveling teacher with twelve companions who was called the "good shepherd," "the way, the truth, and the life," and "redeemer," "savior," and "messiah." He was buried in a tomb, and after three days he rose again. His resurrection was celebrated every year.

We know that the manner in which Jesus came into the world is of no concern to Paul or to Mark but becomes increasingly important and supernatural in Matthew, Luke, and John. The conflicts between Matthew's account and Luke's account are irreconcilable from a historical perspective, even as they reveal what each author was trying to accomplish for his audience. Matthew's genealogy is distinctly Jewish, going back to Abraham and tracing the line from David forward through the *kings* of Israel, while Luke goes back to Adam, father of both Jews and Gentiles, and traces the line from David forward through the *prophets* of Israel.

Matthew's Jesus comes out of Bethlehem, where he is born at home, and then moves to Nazareth after returning from the flight into Egypt. In Luke, Jesus' family comes from Nazareth but travels to Bethlehem because of the census; Jesus is born on the road, as a refugee, and finally returns to Nazareth. Matthew's Jesus is attended by wise men who follow a star; in Luke there is neither star nor wise men, but there are shepherds. Matthew tells us that King Herod ordered the slaughter of male infants in Bethlehem, which causes the family of Jesus to flee to Egypt; in Luke there is no slaughter and no flight to Egypt.

We know that the infancy narratives cannot be history any more than the four accounts of the resurrection, all contradictory, can be considered historical. What we really have in the New Testament is a *stylized witness,* a confessing liturgy of believers. It was the Torah of the early church, written finally in the face of an interminable delay in the second coming. To make their case, the early Christian witnesses simply adapted the great themes of Judaism to convert nonbelievers using their own religious experiences and expectations. As the eminent historical Jesus researcher John Dominic Crossan reminds us, just as those in the Homeric tradition would use the *Iliad* and the *Odyssey* to exalt Italy over Greece, so the early Christians used the Law and the Prophets to exalt Christianity over Judaism.

In biblical studies, this is called *typology,* and it opens the meaning of scripture in ways that are both helpful and hopeful. In short, Jesus the Galilean sage becomes Christ the Anointed One through the creative reinterpretation of early Christian believers who went back to read the Hebrew scriptures as divine foreshadowing—no matter how labored and sometimes contorted the process.

Christ is the new Adam, whose sacrifice frees us from the sin of the first Adam; he is the Lamb of God, whose offering in place of a sinful humanity not only mirrors the ram provided in place of Isaac but renders all further sacrifices unnecessary. Isaac, the son of Israel, walked three days to a place where he was to be sacrificed by his own father, Abraham—the same amount of time spent by Christ in the tomb. He also carried his own wood, just as Christ was said to carry his own cross.

Christ becomes the church's Moses figure, leading his people out of bondage and escaping a massacre of the innocents. Both are connected to Egypt, and both are providers of a new law. On the mount of transfiguration, both Moses and Isaiah appear in a dream to hand over the messianic mantle: lawgiver to greater Lawgiver, and prophet to greater Prophet.

Noah saves animals from a physical flood, but Christ saves people from spiritual destruction, and both use the symbolism of water as either life-threatening or, through baptism, life-saving. The obscure figure of Melchizedek, who appears briefly in Genesis 14 and is mentioned in one psalm (Ps. 110), is said to have brought bread and wine with him when he blessed Abram, creating an echo of the Eucharist in the minds of early Christian readers according to the letter to the Hebrews.

In the final round of the plagues in Egypt before the Exodus, the paschal lamb's blood on the doorpost of Jewish homes marked those households to be "passed over" by the angel of death. This experience of the magical saving power of blood would become a template metaphor for the blood shed by the Paschal Lamb of God on the cross, like a doorpost between heaven and earth, to forgive all sins, save all people, and banish death itself.

Jonah spends three days in the belly of a whale before he is "delivered" by God to do his redemptive work among the Arabs, enemies of the Jewish people. The confusion of tongues at Babel is reversed by the translinguistic miracle of Pentecost. Moses is tested in the wilderness; the new Moses likewise. He is said to be born in Bethlehem to fulfill the prophecy of Micah 5:2 and to place him in the same city as the great King David. The baby Jesus is said to have been visited by magi in order to fulfill a prediction in Isaiah 60 that kings will come to "the brightness of [God's] rising" (v. 3, NASB) on camels, from Sheba, bearing gold and frankincense. What about the myrrh? It may have appeared later, to connect the story of another royal visitor, the queen of Sheba, who came bearing truckloads of spices to pay homage to another king of the Jews, King Solomon (1 Kings 10:10). As for a star pointing the way, this was hardly unique. It is part of the "interpretive tradition of the rabbis that a star was said to have announced the birth of Abraham, the father of the nation; another announced the birth of Isaac, the child of promise; and still another, the birth of Moses, the one who most dramatically shaped Jewish consciousness."[9]

BEYOND THE PAPER POPE

The Bible is both inspired and covered with human finger-prints—but the Bible is not what we worship. The God to which the Bible points us is what we worship, and the claim of the first followers of Jesus was not that he was God, but rather that he revealed the fullness of God at work in a human being. For our part, however, the evolution from symbol to idol is inevitable. We are always tempted to make golden calves out of the instruments of revelation, and the result is more than just the sin of idolatry. Jesus becomes the Christ, and then Jesus is lost. We stare across the abyss of adoration at a deity we can worship, but not emulate. Claims of biblical infallibility are identical to claims of the metaphysical divinity of Jesus. Both make idols of the temporal, and idolatry is the mother and father of all sins.

What we learn if we study the Bible carefully is that this library of books, this far-flung and diverse collection of literature, is neither infallible nor inerrant. It is entirely a human product, though one may choose to believe that it is a human response to God or inspired by God. What it preserves is not a formula sufficient for salvation but the repository of wisdom from a particular people living in a particular time and place, elevated through a human process to the status of sacred scripture. As scripture, the Bible is therefore "authoritative" for the community that regards it as scripture, and then that community is shaped by those divine encounters, which continue to spark new encounters with the divine. To use Professor Borg's phrase, the Bible is a "sacrament of the Sacred."[10]

What we are left to decide is whether we will approach the life of faith as a means to an end or as an end in itself. Will we allow the idolatry of any *particular* religious tradition, book, or doctrine to replace the unifying message at the heart of the universal religious impulse? Will we surrender the shared concept of enlightenment, which is present in the teaching of all great religious traditions, to any "closed" system of creeds and doctrines that uses faith in God to divide and conquer?

If it could be proved that there was no star hanging over Bethlehem, where Jesus wasn't really born (or we admitted that what a star is "over" depends entirely on one's point of view), and almost nothing of historical certainty can be known about Jesus of Nazareth, then what should compel any of us to seek out his message or try to emulate his life? If the old image of Jesus as Savior sent on a rescue mission to die for our sins and appease an angry God attracts mostly militant believers rather than honest seekers, then what is left to recommend Jesus to the rest of us? If the scriptures do not contain historical truth, then what sort of "truth" do they contain?

The answer is a very different sort of truth than we expect, arrived at by a process very different from the rational reductionism we have been taught. Readers of the Bible who take poetry less seriously than prose are at a disadvantage when reading Mary's Magnificat, for example, because the deeper the truth, the more uneven the margins. It is, quite unavoidably, a different part of the brain that leads one to "think of Jesus as a poet rather than as the second person of the Trinity."[11]

Even so, the fear remains that the net effect of all higher criticism is a *deconstruction*. Don't we have less to believe after we have finished identifying what is unbelievable? At one level, the answer is yes, but what is exciting about honest biblical scholarship is that, for some, it represents a *reconstruction*. Once we understand the evolution of Jesus the teacher to Christ the Savior, we can *reverse* it and discover the pre-Christian wisdom of the Galilean sage. Our list of things to believe about Jesus becomes something closer to a vision of what the world might look like if God sat on the throne instead of Caesar. Our clues will come not from holding the text under the magnifying glass of modernity, where veracity equals truth and mythology equals falsehood, but rather from what philosopher Paul Ricoeur called a "second naiveté"[12]—the posture of hearing truth in stories that are not and never were intended to be taken literally.

Just imagine listening to Robert Frost read his poem "Stopping by Woods on a Snowy Evening" and then grilling him on the "truthfulness" of the poem. Exactly who *owned* those particular woods? What breed of horse was it *exactly* that "gives his harness bell a shake / To ask if there is some mistake"? And while we're at, Mr. Frost, you don't mean to imply that a horse can actually signal a rhetorical question, do you? Can you verify that it did indeed snow on the night in question? And how will you answer the owner of the property "lovely, dark, and deep," who has filed a complaint for trespassing?

Novelist Saul Bellow said that "science has made a house-cleaning of beliefs," but only if believing means clinging stubbornly to what can be disproved. Better for the future of the human race—and organized religion—is the posture of the Native American storyteller who always began his recitation of tribal creation myths by saying, "Now, I don't know if it happened this way or not, but I know this story is true."

It should be humbling for Christians to remember that great figures were always being called *sons of god* when alive, and more simply *gods* when dead. Gaius Octavius, who became Augustus Caesar, was pronounced a *divi filius*, a "son of the divine one," and virgin births were a dime a dozen—at least among the upper classes. What is utterly remarkable is that a member of the *peasant class,* Jesus, should merit such mythologizing. It was not the *claim* that was absurd, but the *object* of that claim.

As Christians were being persecuted in the late second century, the pagan philosopher Celsus wrote an intellectual attack on this new religion entitled *True Doctrine.* It in, he hardly sneezes at the idea of a virgin birth—how unoriginal! As John Dominic Crossan puts it:

> It is not absurd, in Celsus's mind, to claim that Jesus was *divine,* but it is absurd to claim that *Jesus* was divine. Who is *he* or what has *he* done to deserve such a birth? Class snobbery is, in fact, very close to the root of Celsus's objection to Christianity:
>
> First, however I must deal with the matter of Jesus, the so-called savior, who not long ago taught new doctrines and was thought to be a son of God. This savior, I shall attempt to show, deceived many and caused them to accept a form of belief harmful to the well-being of mankind. Taking its root in the lower classes, the religion continues to spread among the vulgar; nay, one can even say it spreads because of its vulgarity and the illiteracy of its adherents. And while there are a few moderate, reasonable, and intelligent people who are inclined to interpret its beliefs allegorically, yet it thrives in its purer form among the ignorant.
>
> It is not enough, therefore, to keep saying that Jesus was not born of a virgin, not born of David's lineage, not born in Bethlehem, that there was no stable, no shepherds, no star, no Magi, no massacre of the infants, and no flight into Egypt. All of that is quite true, but it still begs the question of who he was and what he did that caused his followers to make such claims. That is a historical question, and it cannot be dismissed with Celsus's sneer.[13]

Perhaps the church itself cannot be dismissed with the scholar's sneer, but not because everyone in it is vulgar and illiterate. The most interesting question that can be asked in the church today is this: *What shall we offer to those who are not believers and yet wish to be followers?* Just imagine that we could take an industrial-size garbage bag and fill it with every discredited myth in the church—the inerrancy of scripture, the virgin birth, the miracles as suspension of natural law, the blood atonement, the bodily resurrection, and the second coming. Twist it, tie it up, and carry it out to the curb. It will be gone in the morning. Now what?

By evening, a crowd will have gathered. People are glad to see that the garbage is gone, of course, but for some reason they do not leave. They linger. They ask about supper. Some want to stay over and have breakfast together. What are they looking for? Don't they realize that when the creeds are gone, Jesus has left the building? Don't they understand that once the stained-glass window of the Savior is shattered, there is nothing left to do but sweep up the shards, build a museum, and give tours?

Before you know it, someone pulls out a pocket version of the Sermon on the Mount and starts reading it aloud. The listeners include a widow, an orphan, a divorcée, a soldier without legs, a high-school football coach, and a gay man who is still in the closet. Standing in the back is a respected local businessman who stopped by on his way home from the motel; when he touches his face, he can still smell the adultery on his hands. There is a drunk, a confused teenager in dark clothing, and a university professor who was just denied tenure. Not a single one of them is into angels or demons or worries about being "left behind." They just can't believe their ears.

Blessed are those who hunger and thirst after more than food? Blessed are those who are not popular because they do the right thing? Let's hear it for salt and light, and for those who are reconciled to one another before they go to church? You can commit adultery in your mind? Divorce is actually condemned? Turn the other cheek? Pray for your enemy, but don't do it where people can hear you and compliment you on what a fine prayer it was? Fast in secret? Don't store up treasures on earth? Don't serve two masters? Don't worry? Don't judge? Ask, search, and knock before you give up? Not everyone who talks about Jesus a lot will enter the kingdom?

They all sit down to eat a simple meal, and around the table there is no discussion whatsoever about what anyone "believes." A motion is made and seconded to meet again and take turns reading, listening, and discussing this utterly fantastic document. The group agrees that such meetings are both important and dangerous, and it would be wise to move them around to a different location each time. Those who are more affluent are instructed to share out of their abundance, giving to anyone in need. It is assumed by everyone, without a word spoken, that what Jesus taught cannot be separated from how Jesus lived— or how we ought to live. The questions are all ethical. None are theological. How can we do the will of God?

No one thinks to write a creed.

TWO

FAITH AS BEING, NOT BELIEF

To be or not to be: that is the question.

—Hamlet, *Act 3, Scene 1*

In the practice of religion today, faith is so uncritically joined at the hip with the idea of "believing" that any attempt at separating the two seems radical. In fact, just the opposite is true. Not to separate them is both unbiblical and, paradoxically, unfaithful. A Galilean sage evolved over time into a divine Savior because a new way of *being* in the world gradually morphed into a new way of *believing* in the world. Jesus of Nazareth was not the first Christian, nor did he come bearing a list of theological propositions. Peter is reported to have been the first to identify him as the expected messiah, and then the conviction of the community that he had been raised from the dead and would come again started the process by which following Jesus would ultimately be replaced by worshiping Christ.

Ask almost any Christian on the street today what it means to have "faith," and that person will surely recite a list of things that he or she *believes* about Christ. The longer the list, the more evidence has been offered that proves "faithfulness." The more stubborn and resolute the level of certainty, the more implacable and obstinate, the more obvious it seems that the believer is a man or woman of "deep faith." If the "believer" is not even willing to discuss his or her beliefs and resents any challenge to them, we call such a person a "true believer." What does this have to do with being a follower of Jesus? According to the earliest Christian documents we have, including the gospels, it means almost nothing.

Yet this definition of faith dominates Western Christianity and requires those who would describe themselves as "faithful" to hold a set of "beliefs" that certain statements about the Bible, Jesus as the Christ, and church doctrine or dogma are true. We take this definition so much for granted that when people first learn that the early church had no creeds and followers referred to the early Christian movement as "The Way" or to its disciples as those following "the path," they suspect that *this* is the fiction—a secular humanist plot to destroy "the faith."

In Britain to this day, the word "believer" is synonymous with the word "Christian." The question "Are you a believer?" means "Are you a Christian?"[1] It is just as common today to assume that this definition of faith—faith as *intellectual assent to propositional statements,* or faith as a "head trip"—is as old as Christianity itself. To have "faith" is to believe the things that the church has taught us about the Christ, not the things that Jesus first taught his disciples about God. The only problem with this idea is that it's false, and no amount of "faith" can make it true.

The word "faith" is crucial in the New Testament, of course, as a means of healing for Jesus ("Your *faith* has made you well," Matt. 9:22), a means of justification for Paul ("by grace . . . through *faith,*" Eph. 2:8), and a defining mark of the people of God, beginning with Abel and ending with Jesus ("the pioneer and perfecter of our *faith,*" Heb. 12:2). The best-known single text in the New Testament is the same one that makes its omnipresent, albeit subversive, appearance at major sporting events—John 3:16: "For God so loved the world that he gave his only begotten son, that whosoever *believeth* in him should not perish, but have everlasting life" (KJV). The problem is that the original meaning of the word translated as "believeth" is lost.

Marcus Borg reminds us that there are four meanings of the word "faith" in the history of Christianity, and only one of them, *assensus,* has anything to do with intellectual assent, or faith as a "head trip." This idea developed after the Reformation, when the meaning of "orthodoxy" shifted from "correct worship" to "right belief" and continued to grow in urgency after modern science challenged the biblical worldview. Only in the past two hundred years has faith come to mean believing things that are increasingly easy to disprove.

What have been lost in our time are the other three meanings of the word "faith." They expand the idea of faith beyond believing things you may secretly doubt are true in order to get rewards you fear may be unavailable to more honest doubters! They are faith as *fiducia* (radical trust in God), as *fidelitas* (loyalty in one's relationship to God), and as *visio* (a way of seeing creation as gracious).[2]

This is not to say that what one believes is entirely incidental, or that one can believe anything and still call oneself a Christian. It means that the idea of faith so narrowly defined has probably done more than anything else to drive thoughtful people out of the church. Sadly, the idea of faith as a way of "being" in the world, instead of a loyalty oath sworn to creeds and doctrines, remains largely unknown to those who have left the church and find no compelling reason to return. If the church does not succeed in restoring the idea of faith as "being," and not "believing," then the gospel story of Jesus as the heart of God in the flesh will wither and perish.

In the end, to say one "believes" something like the virgin birth as biological fact or the miracle stories as literal suspensions of natural law requires *nothing* in the way of a changed heart or a self-sacrificing spirit. For that matter, neither does saying that one does *not* believe in these things. Whether one assents to the implausible as a sign of faith or refuses to do so as a sign of the capacity to think critically, the world does not change. No one even breaks a sweat, much less takes up a cross to follow. Faith as *assensus* is "relatively impotent, relatively powerless. You can believe all the right things and still be in bondage."[3]

In fact, faith as mere agreement or disagreement allows the "faithful" to reverse the message of the incarnation, which is that the love of God became flesh in the life of Jesus, not in a disembodied argument for God. It is the incarnation that forms the most compelling and distinctly Christian teaching of all, and it carries with it a verdict: when the doors to heaven open before you, walk through. Don't form a committee to assess the identity of the doors, how long the doors will remain open, or who gets to close them to protect those on the inside from those on the outside.

The word became flesh, and the flesh became wisdom, and the wisdom became radical freedom in order to *transform* the world, not to correct it or put it to the test. The first word was an oral/aural event, between teacher and student, not a text, or a theological argument, or a school of thought on the blood atonement. It was enfleshed in the body of a Jewish man whose brief and tragic life was a metaparable and living proof that St. Irenaeus was right when he said, "The Glory of God is a human being fully alive."

ON BEING JEWISH AND A DISCIPLE OF JOHN THE BAPTIST

My only daughter was recently married, and she enthusiastically agreed to be married by a rabbi who is a dear family friend. She requested that I be the father of the bride, not the minister in charge of the ceremony, and I happily complied. For one thing, I would never have made it through the ceremony. But some of my colleagues were a bit scandalized and, upon hearing the news, asked the first question that came to mind. Was my new son-in-law Jewish? "No," I replied, "but Jesus was."

This always brings nervous laughter, of course, but not much wisdom. The real point gets lost in the assumption that I am just trying to be iconoclastic or play the role of a typical liberal clergyman. The truth of the matter is that I had more confidence in the rabbi to perform a dignified and authentic marriage ceremony than I would have had in most of the Christian ministers I know. It was not the faith of the rabbi that mattered to us, but our *relationship* to him. He has been our family rabbi (every minister needs one) for twenty-five years and had watched all our children grow up.

My congregation had formed a covenant with the rabbi's Reformed Jewish temple over two decades ago, and we have worked and worshiped together on behalf of progressive religious values. When he read Psalm 100 at my daughter's wedding, originally thought to be composed for a wedding, he spoke each line in flawless Hebrew and then translated the blessings into English—moving back and forth in a kind of bilingual call and response. The sound of it was remarkable, as if the ancients were also present in the room. As the father of the bride, I had walked my daughter down the aisle to stand before a representative of my ancestors, my mothers and fathers in faith. Having a rabbi bless this sacred covenant struck me as preferable to taking a chance that some preacher might make a joke about the odds against a successful marriage or, worse, launch into a diatribe against the evils of fornication.

This fact remains both obvious and yet somehow scandalous: Jesus was a Jew. Born a Jew, he died a Jew, and his only scripture was the Hebrew Bible. He spoke as a Jew to fellow Jews and all his first followers were Jewish. So were all the authors of the New Testament, with the possible exception of the author of Luke-Acts. It is easy to forget how strange this sounds to Western Christians. A familiar bumper sticker says, "My boss is a Jewish carpenter." Upon seeing it recently, a fundamentalist friend of mine objected, "Mine is a Christian king!"

It is not within the scope of this book to explore all of the ramifications of the Jewishness of Jesus, but a substantial and growing body of scholarly work should be on every minister's reading list.[4] As Amy-Jill Levine, author of *The Misunderstood Jew: The Church and the Scandal of the Jewish Jesus,* points out, the pervasive belief that Jesus was "against" the law, "against" the Temple (as opposed to its first-century leadership), and "against" the people of Israel but in favor of Gentiles has contributed much to the sad history of anti-Semitism—as has the deadly fiction that the Jews (rather than the Romans) killed Jesus.

Less obvious perhaps, but just as harmful, is the popular notion that, because Jesus practiced social justice, spoke to women, taught nonviolence, and cared for the "poor and the marginalized," he was an exception to the Jewish rule. That is, he becomes a "negative foil: whatever Jesus stands for, Judaism isn't it; whatever Jesus is against, Judaism epitomizes the category."[5] The divorce of Jesus from Judaism does a disservice to both. The claim of the church that Jesus of Nazareth (not Jesus of Cleveland, or Jesus of Mexico City) is the incarnation of God in the flesh means that the "scandal of particularity" requires an understanding of the way in which a Jewish man born into a time and place can be understood fully only "through first-century Jewish eyes and heard through first-century Jewish ears."[6]

According to history's best guess, Jesus of Nazareth was born just before 4 BCE to Joseph and Mary in a tiny hamlet. He was perhaps the firstborn, but more likely not, and had at least six siblings. The rest is etiology and myth, adapted to convey important interpretive responses by Matthew and Luke to his remarkable life, written fifty to sixty years after his death. A beautiful, but obviously contrived, tale is the virgin birth, which may have been used to cover a scandal. Matthew seeks to ground his story in the Hebrew scriptures and offers a Greek translation of Isaiah 7:14, which had nothing whatsoever to do with biological virginity. As Bishop John Shelby Spong put it, "Birth stories are always fanciful. They are never historical. No one waits outside a maternity ward for a great person to be born."[7]

There are no reliable stories about Jesus before about age thirty, although legends abound.[8] It is believed by many scholars that Joseph, if he is not a fictional character altogether, died before the public ministry of Jesus began, in part because he is not mentioned at all during that ministry, even though Jesus' mother and siblings are. The idea that he was an old man when he married Mary is pure invention, created perhaps to add plausibility to a later tradition about her perpetual virginity.

It is reasonable to assume that Jesus went to school in the synagogue in Nazareth to study Torah and became a woodworker (in Greek, *tekton*), which is not exactly what we think of today as a carpenter, but rather one who made wood products like doors, roof beams, furniture, boxes, and so forth. More important, this places him at the lower end of the peasant class, among those who had lost their land. And in the Greco-Roman world, the great divide was between those who had to work with their hands and those who did not. There was no middle class, and peasants who lived at the subsistence level, barely able to support their own farming efforts, were required to send two-thirds of their annual crop to support the upper classes.

So long have we exalted Jesus as the Christ and robed him in purple prose, that we forget the simple fact that he was *dirt poor,* living just a notch above the degraded (outcasts) and the expendables (beggars, day laborers, and slaves). Likewise, so long have we studied the record of his remarkable teachings, especially the parables, that we assume he was literate. But 95 to 97 percent of the Jewish population was illiterate at the time of Jesus, so "it must be presumed that Jesus also was illiterate, that he knew, like the vast majority of his contemporaries in an oral culture, the foundational narratives, basic stories, and general expectations of his tradition but not the exact texts, precise citations, or intricate arguments of its scribal elites."[9]

If his family was reasonably devout, Jesus would have been raised in the practices of "common Judaism." Faithfulness for this young man would have consisted of learning the stories, singing the hymns, celebrating Jewish holidays, traveling to Jerusalem to observe the pilgrimage festivals (Passover, Pentecost, and Tabernacles), and, on a regular basis, observing the Sabbath and praying the Shema (Deut. 6:4–5) upon rising and before going to bed.

Like any child growing up in a religious tradition, he would have soaked it all up uncritically, never imagining a world outside his own or questioning the efficacy or authenticity of his own faith tradition. But as with most young visionaries, there must have come a time for differentiating, questioning, and answering the call to nonconformity and rebellion. One day, without question, Jesus left home to became a follower of the most famous, most eccentric, most apocalyptic wilderness preacher of his day—John the Baptist.

All four gospels attest to this. Luke's account of the miraculous births of both Jesus and John against the odds connects Jesus to the most powerful and successful evangelist of the day; Luke then establishes the primacy of Jesus over John and thus all of his ancestors in one Jordan River "moment." Luke's message is clear. "John is the condensation of and consummation of his people's past, but Jesus is far, far greater than John."[10]

More fascinating to contemplate, however, is what effect John the Baptist must have had on Jesus when it came to his understanding of God and the meaning of faith. Author Frederick Buechner captures the essence of the Wild One:

John the Baptist didn't fool around. He lived in the wilderness around the Dead Sea. He subsisted on a starvation diet, and so did his disciples. He wore clothes that even the rummage sale people wouldn't have handled. When he preached, it was fire and brimstone every time. The Kingdom was coming all right, he said, but if you thought it was going to be a pink tea, you'd better think again. If you didn't shape up, God would give you the axe like an elm with the blight or toss you into the incinerator like what's left over when you've lambasted the good out of the wheat. He said being a Jew wouldn't get you any more points than being a Hottentot, and one of his favorite ways of addressing his congregation was as a snake pit.[11]

Could it be that Jesus attached himself to this extraordinary firebrand for reasons analogous to those that caused some young African American men in the 1960s to be more attracted to Malcolm X than to Martin Luther King Jr.? John's preaching must have seemed electric—religion stripped of its usual domestic impotence and rabbinical droning. Here was a real "turn or burn" man as stark and reckless as the desert is indifferent and deadly. After all, Jesus is reported to have said about him, "Among those born of women, no one has arisen greater than John" (Matt. 11:11; Luke 7:28).

Yet this is not unusual. Which one of us cannot name a teacher or a mentor who turned our lives in a new direction? In the biography of any notable human being, credit is invariably given to the influence of some other human being whose charisma and conviction at a formative moment made him or her into a role model. Which begs the question: What did the arrest and execution of John mean to Jesus? In Mark's gospel, Jesus' public ministry begins with John's arrest. With his own teacher now in prison, did the Nazarene need to step in and start teaching the class?

What's more, it is intriguing to wonder if John's execution was traumatic and disorienting, leading Jesus to reconsider and rethink John's message. Consider the differences. John worked out of town. Jesus took his gospel into the city. John preached grim justice and pictured God as a "steely-eyed thresher of grain." Jesus preached a God of love and forgiveness and compared him to a father who throws a party for a prodigal son. John said the hour is growing late. Jesus said it is never too late. John baptized as a sign of conversion from darkness to light. Jesus moved in the shadows, healing the sick and restoring the broken as if faith is a compassionate verb, not an intimidating noun.

John Dominic Crossan speculates that the death of John caused a shift in the preaching of Jesus from an apocalyptic to a nonapocalyptic understanding of the kingdom of God. It is an educated guess to be sure, but commensurate with a later story in which two of John's disciples are sent to ask on behalf of their imprisoned teacher, "Are you the one who is to come, or are we to wait for another?" (Matt. 11:3).

ON BEING WISE

The ultimate defining characteristic of Christianity is the incarnation, the mystery of God's presence in a person. When Christianity is "personal" (though not to be confused with "individual"), it is at its best. Other approaches to the life of faith have important prophets, of course, and the record of their teachings and the sacred canon of their scriptures. But what began as a fledgling movement in first-century Palestine occurred among people who responded to a *human being*. He seemed transparent to God and opened the heavens to reveal an approach to faith they had never known. The Word became flesh, as John put it (1:14), and *lived* among us.

The incarnation gives the faith its form and content, bringing God "nearer to us than our jugular vein," to quote the Qur'an (50:16). But it also brings with it the risks of idolatry, in which the messenger becomes the message, and eventually a divine rescue mission trumps that wisdom, even destroys it. Yet peculiar to Christianity is that at the heart of everything there is not a text, or a single commandment, or even a new Torah—but rather flesh and bones and breath and the remarkable response of Jesus' followers to both his brief public ministry and his brutal execution.

Our scriptures matter, of course, because they bear witness to this incarnation. And the mystery of God matters, because Jesus was a spirit person who lived in relation to that Mystery. But none of it ultimately matters more than the wisdom of Jesus himself. We work to recover a portrait of his life and essential message because our confession of faith is centered in the wisdom of his *life* and the new relationship it makes possible with God—not in the Bible's inerrancy or in some definitive theological statement about the nature of God or salvation.

This means that when there is a conflict between what the scriptures say in particular and what we have come to expect from the wisdom of Jesus, *his wisdom wins.* We hold the Bible accountable to the message of Jesus, not Jesus accountable for everything in the Bible. When it comes to what the church decided much later to add to that message or to layer on top of the earliest voices (or by the fourth century to convert into creeds that deified him), we are all responsible for *going back,* as much as possible, to the earliest and most authentic record of his message. Even when we know that the words attributed to him have been altered by the gospel writers over time, there is still something remarkable about comparing the earliest voices of his followers to the later voices of Christendom.

One very helpful way to understand this is to pull down from your shelf, if you still have one, an old "red-letter" edition of the New Testament—so called because everything Jesus is reported to have said is set off in red type on the page. It will probably be a King James Version or the New International Version,[12] but don't let that stop you. Now read through all four gospels, saying aloud only those things in red, attributed to Jesus. By a process of omission, you will have given yourself a crash course in how a marginalized Jew became the Savior of the World.

First, you will notice that even those words attributed to Jesus change dramatically in character from the earliest gospel, Mark, where the Galilean sage says humbly, "Why do you call me good? No one is good but God alone" (10:18), to the last gospel, John, where the preexistent Christ figure declares, "I am the way, and the truth, and the life. No one comes to the Father except through me" (14:6). You will also notice little things that chart his evolution from an enlightened teacher to a deity. In Mark, Jesus has to heal a blind man twice after the first effort falls short and the man sees people, but they look like trees (8:22–26). But by the time we get to John, this preexistent Christ heals a man blind since birth using the same mixture of mud and saliva, but only after announcing first, "As long as I am in the world, I am the light of the world" (9:5). Now only one attempt is required.

When Mark tells the story of Jesus' rejection in his hometown, which Matthew repeats (13:54), Mark's explanation is that "Prophets are not without honor, except in their hometown, and among their own kin, and in their own house" (6:4), and we are told that "he could do no deed of power there, except that he laid his hands on a few sick people and cured them. And he was amazed at their unbelief" (6:5–6). By the time John writes his gospel, these hometown failures have been contracted—from a rationalization by Jesus to a parenthetical aside from John (4:44), and the line about failing to heal many people is dropped altogether.

Jesus as the divine Savior, the preexistent, metaphysical Son of God sent to die for our sins will not pass even the "red-letter" test. From the earliest layers of the tradition, in which nothing is said that indicates messianic self-identity, to the later material, which includes Holy Week predictions of suffering and the emerging idea that his death was a "ransom" for many, there is still nothing that comes close to the fully formed doctrine of the blood atonement. The earliest record indicates that he was a means to an end, not an end in himself. His message was *theocentric*, not *Christocentric*—centered in God, not centered in messianic proclamations about himself.[13]

Ours is a time of astonishing biblical ignorance, yet we are constantly urged to read the Bible by people who ignore the heart of it or invent a message that is simply not there. What does the red-letter test tell us about the views of Jesus concerning homosexuality? Nothing. About gay marriage? Nothing. About being born again as a nonmetaphorical legal requirement for salvation? Nothing. About prosperity as a sign of God's favor? Nothing (to the contrary, we are warned against it). About the need to believe in the bodily resurrection or the second coming? Nothing. About the proper manner of baptism? Nothing (Jesus baptizes no one we know of). About justification by faith or works? Nothing. In fact, the life of Jesus renders this distinction meaningless.

What the earliest layers of the gospel record reveal, and to some extent the later layers as well, when sifted through a higher Christology, is that Jesus was *wise*. He was charismatic, a gifted speaker, and a teacher of wisdom. He taught the "narrow way" as opposed to the broad way of convention and tradition. Both his life and his message were subversive and modeled the metaphor of death and resurrection as a way of life. Discipleship was not about knowing new things or subscribing to certain theological statements or positions, but about the never-ending process of dying to an old self and being reborn into a new one. The evidence for this rebirth was not a clever argument or allegiance to a certain rabbinical school. It was made obvious by a new way of *being* in the world. Good Friday and Easter are therefore not isolated events. They are the twin polarities of wisdom—as we constantly die to the bondage of blindness and are reborn to the light.

This way of "being" was open to the mystical, or the "sacred," and was so grounded in pure compassion that Jesus could not be around the sick or the broken without attempting to heal them. Because such wisdom can make the scales fall from our eyes, it often produces what French philosopher Jacques Lacan calls *la douleur de voir trop clair* ("the pain of seeing too clearly"). Opening oneself to this disparity between the world as it is and the world as God intends it to be leads either to despair or to the calling of a prophet—a greatly misunderstood vocation in our time. There are many latter-day "prophets" who secretly enjoy the attention they get, decrying the mad hypocrisies of our time while sacrificing nothing. They make headlines, but they make no changes. The kingdom of God is not a press conference, or a resolution, or a short course in how to be eloquently indignant. It is a table, laden with grace, at which the social maps are all redrawn. The guest list comes straight out of *One Flew over the Cuckoo's Nest.*

Indeed, to this day, we often mistake wisdom for a kind of sedimentary traditionalism, most apparent in the elderly. But in Jesus it seems to have been marked by a rather brash intimacy, as when he dared to address God as Abba (in English, "Papa"), in contrast to the rabbinical reverence that forbids even saying God's name aloud and requires the omission of the vowels in the spelling of God's name (YHWH)—lest we get too familiar with the "Holy One, Blessed be he." Vowels, after all, are the soul of words.

What's more, the wisdom of Jesus was an alternative wisdom, not a conventional one. Contrary to the path of practicality and prosperity that passes for wisdom in most cultures, what Jesus taught was *subversive* wisdom. Like Lao-Tzu and the Buddha, who were both teachers of a world-subverting wisdom, Jesus led followers away from convention and "grasping" to enlightenment and compassion. Socrates, like Jesus, was executed not for leading a rebellion but for an insurgency of ideas—"corrupting the youth of Athens." Clearly some ideas are too dangerous to ignore, especially when they are fused with the life of the one who teaches them. Today, it is monks who threaten military governments most, because nonviolence is more dangerous to the principalities and powers than brute force.

Being wise for Jesus meant teaching subversive ideas in a subversive manner. It was not new information that he shared; instead, he used new ways to entrap listeners inside their own instincts for the truth—forcing them to appropriate it through a struggle to reduce what psychologists call "cognitive dissonance."[14] His use of aphorisms, or short wisdom sayings, is one example, but the supreme example is the parable, which was his primary teaching device. Parables are also thought to be, by virtue of the way stories can hang together over time in the oral tradition, the most authentic material in the New Testament.

It should come as no surprise that Mark, the earliest gospel and the most "historical," has an entire chapter of parables and includes a line indicating that Jesus did not even speak to his disciples "except in parables" (4:34). By the time we get to John's gospel, however, and Jesus has become the preexistent Christ, there is not a single parable to be found. The teacher of alternative wisdom of the synoptic gospels has become the self-proclaimed messiah. The invitational rhetoric of the teacher ("Suppose one of you has a friend, and you go to him at midnight," Luke 11:5) has been replaced by the self-declarative rhetoric of a Savior ("I am the light of the world," John 8:12).

Although it is clear that the gospel writers adapted the parables to suit the needs of their particular community, and stories are always being adapted by storytellers to changing circumstances, it is this *method* of teaching that is so instructive. Wisdom is acquired only through personal struggle. It is not a spectator sport, any more than faith is a list of ideas about what to believe or how to behave. The parables of Jesus are confounding, sometimes even maddening. But they remind us that wisdom is a process of disassembling and reassembling. Before students can be *reoriented,* they must first be *disoriented.* Before the seeds of an alternative wisdom can germinate, the hardened soil of conventional wisdom must be broken up, so that those seeds can be dropped into fertile soil.

BEING FEARLESS

It should come as no surprise that some people thought Jesus was crazy. The best-known reference is in Mark 3:21, in which his family hears of his fame at casting out demons and the disruptive crowds who followed him and "went out to restrain him, for people were saying, 'He has gone out of his mind.'" It might be more accurate to say that, given what we now know about the resistance of conventional wisdom, or what one scholar calls "life under the superego,"[15] Jesus only *appeared* to be mad. In fact, so does any human being who is both fully alive and radically free.

What is meant here by "radical freedom" is not the shedding of all social or personal responsibilities or living a life of reckless abandon because "freedom's just another word for nothing left to lose," as Janis Joplin put it. It is a life lived outside of the straitjacket of fear and anxiety that controls most of us. It is a way of being in the world that is so fully connected to another Source of wisdom and worthiness that the person appears to be "missing" something—and indeed he or she is.

What is missing is the despair that Danish philosopher Søren Kierkegaard called the "sickness unto death," that gnawing angst that shadows all our days. We try in vain to secure ourselves against our own insecurity, and thus we never become a "self." We are finite, vain, and consumed with the fear that if we do not stay busy micromanaging the chaos of life, it will overwhelm us, which of course it does. Or to put it in the vernacular: no matter how clean and well organized our garage, we still die.

Henry David Thoreau put it best in *Walden:* "The mass of men lead lives of quiet desperation. What is called resignation is confirmed desperation." It is the second half of that famous quote, less well known, that intrigues me with regard to teachers of alternative wisdom. They appear mad only because the conventional wisdom of their time is so fully and uncritically accepted by everyone that any challenge to it is what appears desperate; in fact, it is that mass resignation that is the true desperation, according to Thoreau.

Conventional wisdom is like the water of the culture in which we swim. It is the air of "common sense" that we breathe. It's what "everyone just knows" to be true. In the time of Jesus, it was centered in the Torah and in the folk wisdom of Proverbs. It was both practical and based on a system of rewards and punishments. Hard work and righteousness will make you prosper. You reap what you sow, and good things happen to good people. The corollaries were just as obvious: laziness and immorality will prevent you from being prosperous, and bad things will happen to bad people.

What's more, life itself is *hierarchical* by design, and people need to "know their place" and "stay in it." Our tribal ways become our religious ways, and God is not just "man writ very large," as philosopher Friedrich Nietzsche put it, but the ultimate endorser of our tribal wisdom. God shares my definition of beauty, of worth, of the natural superiority of men over women and the need to preserve peace through strength. Such a God is "awesome," because we have a penchant for mindless superlatives. This is the God of the warrior, thanked by football players in the end zone after catching a touchdown pass.

This God is also a kind of superparent, making rules, enforcing them, and handing out rewards and punishments appropriately. Life is a stage, said Shakespeare, and our lives are often reduced to a kind of "performance principle."[16] The reviews come in many forms: grades, wealth, social status, notoriety—and, ultimately for some, the assurance of personal salvation. But the focus is always the same. It's all about *me*. We are encouraged, in a million ways, to leads lives of profound selfishness.

It is no wonder, then, that when Jesus began to teach and preach an alternative wisdom, he appeared to be insane. Samaritans were often the heroes of his stories, even though they were considered heretical and impure. Pharisees were often exposed for hypocrisy and empty faith, even though they were the keepers of the faith. Parties were given for prodigal sons who did not deserve them, and God heard the agonized prayer of a tax collector above the rote prayer of a religious professional.

The Beatitudes, or "blessings," of the Sermon on the Mount turned the world upside down, and in the language and symbol of sacred paradox a true king rides a donkey to his coronation. At the dinner table, which was the ultimate social map in those days, if the invited guests made excuses and didn't show up, then God would invite bums in off the street to sit at the messianic banquet. Mustard seeds and the weeds they produce are apparently tenacious enough to carry the hope of a redeemed future within them. Leaven in bread is a corrupting force, just like the reign of God. Those day laborers who don't show up until the eleventh hour will be paid the same wage as those who have labored all day—proving that God is God, not the Chamber of Commerce.

Reversing the categories of pure and impure, Jesus lifted up women (impure), leaven (also impure), and children (neither pure nor impure, just invisible). Most disturbing of all, he ate with outcasts, criminals, and prostitutes—proving that if we are known by the company we keep, then it is no wonder they called him a drunkard and a glutton. Now we call him "precious Lord," without even thinking.

He did this in an utterly brief public ministry (only a year according to Mark, perhaps three to four years according to

Matthew and Luke) as if "possessed" by a desire to upend the very tradition in which he was raised and bring down the judgment of the very faith he sought to reform. He did it *fearlessly* and counseled his followers to "fear not." Fear is the enemy of the moral life, and yet which one of us could imagine attacking the sacred cows of our time or challenging the conventional wisdom in American society?

If you think "family values" is a potent idea today, just imagine how fixed the centrality of the Jewish family was in the time of Jesus. It was the center of social, material, and spiritual identity. Yet consider that Jesus, who called people out of their families and into an itinerant existence, actually spoke of "hating" one's own kin as the measure of an even higher loyalty.

Wealth was seen as a sign of God's favor in those days (as it is today), and yet Jesus warned that it could be spiritually debilitating and that money was a primary object of idolatry. "It is easier for a camel to go through the eye of a needle than for someone who is rich to enter the kingdom of God" (Mark 10:25).[17] He ridiculed the high and mighty and upended the purity system of his time with acts of pure provocation. He is reported to have gone ballistic in the Temple one day, turning over the tables and driving out the money changers with a whip. Today he would be arrested as a public nuisance and ordered to take anger-management classes.

In the wisdom of the Galilean, life is seen as a joyful return from the exile of law and judgment to the unconditional love of a recklessly gracious God. This love is a given, not something we earn, putting us on a par with the birds of the air and the lilies of the field. It also drove his critics to fear that the very foundations of society were being destroyed and the advantages of the righteous were being mocked. Is there no judgment at all?

There is perhaps nothing more frightening to fundamentalists than the idea that there is no final judgment. The very foundation of morality is tied up in rewards and punishments, and if sinners are allowed to sin without consequences, then what's the point of being good? Doesn't that mean that they "got away with it"? There are passages in the New Testament about a final judgment, of course, with eternal consequences. But they are believed to be largely the redactions of Matthew, who remained most tethered to Mosaic law, which Jesus would "complete" but not "destroy." Ironically, when Jesus brings up such final judgments, it is to *subvert* commonly held assumptions about those judgments, such as how much better Gentiles will fare than the self-respecting crowd he is addressing.[18]

Make no mistake. Such subversive wisdom is always a threat to law and order, to the religious establishment, and to the social hierarchy that creates and preserves wealth. Jesus undercut the power and purpose of religious professionals, excited the poor and empowered the powerless, and quickly attracted large crowds in an occupied territory that was smoldering under Roman occupation. Then, as now, the solution to this problem was simple.

THREE

THE CROSS AS FUTILITY, NOT FORGIVENESS

> Roman crucifixion was state terrorism. . . . Its function was to deter resistance or revolt, especially among the lower classes; and . . . the body was usually left on the cross to be consumed eventually by the wild beasts.
>
> —*John Dominic Crossan*

To his credit, John Dominic Crossan admits that few things could be more painful to consider than the likelihood that Jesus' corpse ended up as food for wild dogs or grim pickings for birds of prey. But the truth is, only one crucified skeleton has ever been recovered, even though there were thousands of crucifixions, for exactly this reason: there was seldom a body left to bury.

The cross sits at the center of Christian consciousness, and yet its sheer horror has been kept from us in numerous ways. It is ironic that what was originally an instrument of torture is now shaped into jewelry—earrings, belly-button rings, and enormous, expensive bling worn by rappers. A symbol of evil is now worn as personal adornment and the lengths to which love will go has been sentimentalized into a kind of perfumed rack where some unpleasantness did indeed occur, but it was all part of God's plan for the redemption of the world. As messy as it must have been, the faithful can always imagine that Jesus was not only writhing in pain but also gazing toward heaven and winking at the Father.

One of the most common misconceptions among contemporary Christians is that executions on a cross were rare, as befits this extraordinary victim. In fact, they were remarkably widespread in antiquity; whether they were used to kill military officials, slaves, violent criminals, or the unruly element in rebellious provinces, their chief purpose was to act as the supreme deterrent. Usually having been flogged or subjected to other forms of torture, the naked victim was displayed publicly in a prominent place to serve as a constant reminder of his "crime" or the utter futility now associated with his "cause." Because victims of crucifixion were seldom taken down and buried, the bones were ultimately picked clean, and the humiliation was complete. "What it meant for a man in antiquity to be refused burial, and the dishonor which went with it, can hardly be appreciated by modern man."[1]

Rome had three methods for punishing its enemies: the cross, fire, and beasts. What made all three gruesome was not just the method of execution but also the ultimate indignity of no proper burial. In the ancient world, the treatment of corpses was of supreme importance. One of the greatest fears of any soldier was not that he might die in battle but that his corpse would be left unburied to rot and become food for scavengers. That such an indignity would have befallen Jesus of Nazareth is not only unthinkable but, for many, sacrilegious.

Serious study of the Bible reveals that no crucifixion story even existed for at least forty years after Jesus' death, and yet we continue to read the gospel accounts as if they are the work of eyewitnesses and view the crucifixion itself as if it is the unfolding of a divinely ordained drama. All we can know with certainty is that it happened—that Jesus was killed (both the Jewish witness Josephus and the pagan Roman witness Tacitus attest to it). This is hardly insignificant, since Christianity is the only major religious tradition whose founder was executed by established authority.

More intriguing is to speculate on the reasons why. Was the "final straw" the triumphal entry into Jerusalem during the heightened tensions of Passover, or is this yet another etiological script to fulfill the prediction of Zechariah 9:9 that the true king will make his triumphal entry riding on an ass?

Was it perhaps the Last Supper and the self-declared institution of a new covenant in the body and blood of Jesus that was heretical? Serious doubt exists as to whether such self-awareness can even be established. And there is no consensus in the earliest records that Paul's understanding (1 Cor. 11:23–26) coincides with other sources like the *Gospel of Thomas* and the Q gospel, since they are silent concerning any Last Supper tradition. The *Didache* describes only "a communal and ritual eating together, from the second half of the first century, with absolutely no hint of Passover meal, Last Supper, or passion symbolism built into its origins or development."[2] Did Jesus simply leave the idea of the open table behind, and then did certain disciples create the Last Supper as a ritual to make sense of both his life and his death?

Or was his fate sealed in that strange and little-understood moment when Jesus was said to have entered the Temple in a rage to drive out the money changers and sellers of sacrificial animals with a whip. Unfortunately it has been called the "cleansing" of the Temple, which may have caused countless Christians to mistake an actual *attack* upon the Temple for an anger-management problem or, worse, a concern for cleanliness. The Temple was the center of religious life, for Jews the house of God, and Mark's gospel combines this incident with the cursing of the fig tree and its withering—leaving little doubt that Jesus was doing more than just "acting out."

By the time we get to John's gospel, the same incident is reinterpreted again not as an attack upon the Temple itself but as an allegory in which the body of Christ is the Temple, raised up only three days after its destruction. Yet even with these unfolding redactions, there is good reason to believe that such an incident would have been unforgettable and is therefore likely to be historical. It puts Jesus directly and violently at odds with his own faith tradition and would surely have been one of the most remembered and repeated tales in the oral tradition. Was this the "last straw" that led to the arrest and execution of Jesus? We will never know. But Mark gives us a strong hint that perhaps a combination of unacceptable acts was to blame: "And when the chief priests and the scribes heard it, they kept looking for a way to kill him; for they were afraid of him, because the whole crowd was spellbound by his teaching" (11:18).

FIRST THERE WAS NO STORY

For those of us who grew up in the church, listening to the rich and familiar details of the crucifixion story, it is easy to assume that those passion narratives contain historical or at least quasi-historical details. In fact, an entire generation passed without any written record of the events leading up to the death of Jesus. Because Paul's writings are the earliest New Testament material available, his account of the cross is both revealing and utterly spare: "For I handed on to you as of first importance what I in turn had received: that Christ died for our sins in accordance with the scriptures, and that he was buried, and that he was raised on the third day in accordance with the scriptures" (1 Cor. 15:3–4).

That's it. That is the "totality of the only written story of the cross that Christians had until the eighth decade CE."[3] Although Paul speaks often of the death of Jesus and the meaning of the cross, there is no crucifixion story placed in the week of Passover, no familiar and beloved passion narrative:

There is no account of the betrayal, no visit to the Garden of Gethsemane, no arrest and no trial before the chief priests, . . . no mention of Pilate, no recollection of the accusations made against Jesus and no record of the pressure from the Jewish crowd to have him executed. There is no story of his being beaten, no mention of a crown of thorns, no narrative of his having to bear his own cross and no mention of a hill called Calvary. There is no account of the soldiers who drove the nails, or of the thieves who were said to have been crucified with him. There is no mention of the darkness at noon and no reference to any word Jesus was said to have spoken from the cross to anyone.[4]

Paul does say that the death of Jesus was "for our sins in accordance with the scriptures." So it is clear that twenty-five years after the crucifixion, both the saving nature of this death and its "prediction" in Jewish scripture were established. He also adds, in this one-line account, that "he was buried." Perhaps this was essential to establish in order for anyone to take the resurrection seriously, since resurrection could only be understood as a bodily resurrection and thus required the burial of a body!

Scholars have speculated about what this means, wondering if perhaps Paul knew more but didn't care for the details, or if in fact this was all he knew because there was no crucifixion story. We know that three years after his conversion he went to visit Simon Peter and remained with him for fifteen days (Gal. 1:18). Is that where he learned about the death of Jesus? Did he forget most of the story, or is this the entire story that Peter had to pass along?

Before Mark wrote his gospel in the early 70s, both Paul and Peter had apparently died, and the single most important event in early Christian history occurred in 70 CE. Roman legions, under the command of Titus, broke through the walls of the city and laid waste to Jerusalem, even destroying the Temple. It was in this traumatic context of defeat and humiliation that the first gospel was written; this was the lens through which Mark looked at the life of Jesus and the meaning of his death and resurrection. Had Jesus predicted the destruction of the Temple? Was this a sign from God that his teachings were vindicated? What would now rise in place of the Temple, and did the early Christian movement need its own written record now more than ever—its own Torah?

Cataclysmic events have both an intensifying and a distorting effect on those who suffer through them. Just consider the modern example of September 11, 2001. The destruction of the twin towers, a symbol of American power, led to both a reappraisal of the threats we face and an intense desire to restore what had been lost, to "raise up" something redemptive out of the ashes. The president stood on the smoldering wreckage of the symbol of our economic power and used a bullhorn to issue a kind of fatwa. The identity of the enemy was now clear, as was the enemy's evil intent. So let us as "victims" recommit ourselves to doing what must be done to restore what has been destroyed. Thousands of young people responded by enlisting in the armed forces; others, by asking the question, "Why do they hate us so much?" It was a crack in time.

Likewise, one can only wonder what effect the destruction of the Temple had upon the early followers of Jesus. Surely it would also have had a similar effect—to both intensify and distort the meaning of the life and death of Jesus. His message concerning the leadership of the Temple had been unmistakable. After the war, there followed an intense period of Roman hostility toward the Jews, particularly the Jerusalem religious leaders. So what did this tragedy mean in relation to the radical message of Jesus?

Was the cleansing of the Temple a foreshadowing of the actual destruction of the Temple, or did Mark just write the

story that way to make Jesus appear prophetic? In the crucifixion of Jesus, had people just accepted the fact that "might
makes right" and that Rome had done what it needed to do to
keep order? Or did the destruction of the Temple bring home
an entirely different reality—namely, the shock of realizing that
violence can never save, that it can only destroy?

We will never know, but about this we can be fairly certain:
the first followers of Jesus knew almost nothing about the details of his crucifixion, death, or "burial." Those details would
come decades later, not as "history remembered but as prophecy
historicized."[5] It would be Mark's job to compose a story that
made sense of the death of Jesus long after the fact, with the
Temple now in ruins and this deeply disturbing question hanging over the whole smoking mess: *How could God's Chosen One
have been so treated, and if he had been so treated, could he still be
God's Chosen One?* Perhaps no single argument for the existence
of the "historical Jesus" is more persuasive than this: if the Jews
were going to make up a story about how the messiah would
look, act, and die—this would not be the story.

THEN THERE WAS MARK'S STORY

The first gospel ever written has been called "a passion narrative with a long introduction."[6] Mark arranges his whole narrative around the final events of the life of Jesus and prefaces
the passion narrative with multiple examples of a healer and
prophet who tells everyone to whom he reveals himself that
they should keep quiet about it. The reason for this "messianic
secret" in Mark is debated by scholars, some of whom think it
provides cover for the fact that so few believed, and others of
whom think that Mark's real message is that the messiah's true
identity can be known only at the end, and then only by confronting the Mystery, as did the three women who ran frightened from the empty tomb. What a marvelous way to end a

gospel (the shorter ending of Mark)—even if later scribes didn't think so and felt compelled to write their own postscript (the longer ending of Mark).

In Mark's passion narrative, which may have been developing in worship for a long time but now took on new urgency with the destruction of the Temple, the events of the death of Jesus are placed in the season of the Jewish observance of Passover. It may indeed have been the case that Jesus was arrested during the Passover festival and that his disciples did indeed flee for their own safety, but Mark's permanent appropriation of the symbolism of Passover and its connection with the death of Jesus changed the course of human history—and our understanding of what the death of Jesus ended up meaning to all of Christendom.

Putting quill to scroll, Mark produced not only the foundational synoptic gospel but also a template for Matthew and Luke. The original autograph is lost, of course, rendering the claim of its inerrancy meaningless. What we have, as biblical scholar Bart Erhman reminds us, are copies of copies of copies, in which all the mistakes, both accidental and intentional, have been multiplied exponentially over the centuries. In fact, there are now more known differences among our manuscripts than there are words in the New Testament.[7]

Even so, Mark's gospel is the baseline for the written accounts of Holy Week, and its appropriation of both the Paschal Lamb and the Exodus is obvious. Just as the children of Israel understood themselves first and last to be those freed from the bondage of slavery in Egypt by the hand of God, so the followers of Jesus saw themselves as delivered from the "bondage" of sin by his death and resurrection. It would be unreasonable to assume that the writer of Mark's gospel came up with this all by himself. Surely the nonpeasant, literate followers of Jesus had been searching the scriptures for some time to understand their past, reclaim their present, and envisage their future. The clues must be found in the text, of course, for the Jews were, first and last, the People of the Book.

The question is, what were they looking for in this period that preceded the writing of the first gospel? Surely it would have been passages that "show death not as end but as beginning, not as divine judgment but as divine plan, not as ultimate defeat but as postponed victory for Jesus."[8] If Jesus was the new Lamb of God, how did that relate to the Jewish understanding of the Day of Atonement?

The answer is found in Leviticus 16:7–10, 21–22, the story of two goats—one driven out into the desert carrying the sins of the people (the scapegoat) and the other presented as a blood sacrifice to atone for the sins of the people in the Temple. Which one was Jesus? Any observant Jew who had actually participated in this ritual would know that the scapegoat had a scarlet wool placed on its head and would actually be abused by the crowd as it was hurried toward the desert—recalling Isaiah 1:18, in which God promises, "Though your sins are like scarlet, they shall be like snow; though they are red like crimson, they shall become like wool."

A deeper look at Isaiah 50:6 explains how, just as the sins of the people can be transferred to a doomed animal, they can also cause a true prophet to suffer: "I gave my back to those who struck me, and my cheeks to those who pulled out the beard; I did not hide my face from insult and spitting." If this is beginning to sound familiar, then the adoption of Jesus as the suffering servant and the Paschal Lamb will make perfect sense.

People actually spat their sins onto the scapegoat and poked and pierced it on its way out of town—not to be cruel, but because the ritual required it. So was Jesus to be seen as the scapegoat, or the goat sacrificed in the Temple for the sins of the people—or both? Leviticus 16 also tells the story of Aaron being commanded to change his garments, bathe, put on vestments, and prepare the burnt offering of the people for atonement.

The change of garments reminds us of Zechariah 3:3–5, in which Joshua the high priest is imagined as having his clothing changed from filthy to clean by an angel—providing a metaphor to explain the transformation of a man dishonored on the cross to one radiant and triumphant at his second coming. By the time we reach the twelfth chapter of Zechariah, the image of the "Pierced One" is thought to foreshadow the passion of Jesus and set the stage for his triumphant return:

> And I will pour out a spirit of compassion and supplication on the house of David, and the inhabitants of Jerusalem, so that, when they look on the one whom they have pieced, they shall mourn for him, as one mourns for an only child, and weep bitterly over him, as one weeps over a firstborn. (12:10)

Clearly the layers of tradition were in place to create a "prophetic passion" that linked the death of Jesus with the hope for his return at the end of the world. But the emphasis on resurrection came years later, when Mark fused these elements of scapegoat and sacrificial goat with other literary traditions of the mockery of the pseudo-king (*Epistle of Barnabas* 7) that add a theatrical mime with throne, crown, robe, and scepter. What one might end up with is not only the first gospel but a new "narrative passion"[9] that will sound remarkably like Mark 15:16–20:

> Then the soldiers led him into the courtyard of the palace (that is, the governor's headquarters); and they called together the whole cohort. And they clothed him in a purple cloak; and after twisting some thorns into a crown, they put it on him. And they began saluting him, "Hail, King of the Jews!" They struck his head with a reed, spat upon him, and knelt down in homage to him. After mocking him, they stripped him of the purple cloak

and put his own clothes on him. Then they led him out to crucify him.

Here is the journey from life to death to life—from bondage to liberation. Mark's passion narrative is preserved for future generations as the familiar imperative of the Exodus story to *remember* (Exod. 12:14) combined with Paul's version of the Last Supper, to do this "in remembrance of me" (1 Cor. 11:24). But most important of all, both focus on the death of one called the "lamb of God." Just as the blood of the unblemished young male lamb spread over the doorposts of the Hebrew households would spare those inside as the angel of death "passed over," so now does the blood of the unblemished young male representative of his people shed on the cross (now seen as the doorpost of the whole world) save us all from sin and death itself. Jesus is the new Paschal Lamb and thus the Christ.

As if we needed more evidence that this is liturgy, not history, consider the way in which Mark organizes his passion narrative to take place over a period of twenty-four hours. Because the observance of Passover was normally a three-hour ritual that revolved around a common meal, Mark gives us a Christian story that stretches over three eight-hour segments but also revolves around a common meal.

It begins "when it was evening" (14:17), or sundown, and, just like the Passover observance of three hours, ends with the singing of a hymn (14:26). The disciples go with Jesus to the garden of Gethsemane, and they cannot stay awake, leading to the question, "Could you not keep awake one hour?" (14:37), a lament repeated twice more (or two more hours), bringing us to the bewitching hour of midnight. The darkest moment in human history would therefore take place at the darkest hour.

All of his disciples are said to have fled, a memory so painful and counterintuitive that it is widely regarded as historically accurate. "A movement does not tend to introduce negative stories about its founders, but it is also unable to suppress a searing historical memory that is so vivid it is incapable of being forgotten."[10] Jesus is given a mock trial and is condemned to death. Does this happen at three in the morning, when he is alone, given the Torah law forbidding anyone to sit in judgment except in the light of day? Probably not, but liturgy is concerned with divine drama, not with journalism. The watch of the night between three and six in the morning was called "cockcrow," and so it is no surprise that the story of Peter's threefold denial is inserted here—one for each hour until daybreak.

The condemned Jesus is then led before Pilate, where a form of Roman plea bargaining occurs, and when no fault is found in the accused, it is suggested that Barabbas be substituted. But the crowd wants the death of one man, as if it is inevitable. The torture, mocking, and scourging play out the familiar drama of the scapegoat, and Jesus is crucified at the "third hour," or nine in the morning (15:25). Simon of Cyrene is said to have carried the cross, and wine mixed with myrrh is offered as a final insult. Two robbers are executed also, but in Mark they are silent observers.

When the sixth hour, or "noon" (15:33), comes, an apocalyptic darkness covers the whole earth and lasts for three hours, or until three in the afternoon. This is when Jesus utters his anguished cry, "My God, my God, why have you forsaken me?" (15:34; Ps. 22:1). It is mistaken by the crowd for a call for Elijah to come, which introduces into the liturgy a connection to the great prophet, the one for whom a place is set at the table of the Passover meal by Jews to this day. The veil of the Temple, which separated the Holy of Holies from the people, is torn in two, symbolizing the access of all people to God, and even a Gentile soldier recognizes Jesus as the Son of God (15:39).

The last watch of the vigil takes us from three to six in the afternoon and completes the liturgy of a single day in the redemption of the world. This is when, Mark tells us, Jesus is buried and the figure of Joseph of Arimathea is introduced (or perhaps created). The tomb is made ready, the body is wrapped in a linen shroud and laid in the tomb, and a stone is rolled against the entrance. Sundown on Friday has arrived, and with it the holy Sabbath. The liturgy is complete, and Jesus has now indeed died "in accordance with the scriptures." All who could read or hear Psalm 22 and Isaiah 53 might be persuaded that his death was predicted in scripture:

> Surely he has borne our infirmities and carried our diseases; yet we accounted him stricken, struck down by God, and afflicted. But he was wounded for our transgressions, crushed for our inequities; upon him was the punishment that made us whole, and by his bruises we are healed. All we like sheep have gone astray; we have turned to our own way; and the LORD has laid on him the iniquity of us all. (Isa. 53:4–6)

SO WHAT IS OUR STORY?

Once it becomes obvious that the crucifixion narratives are not history but liturgies designed to interpret the meaning of the death of Jesus by appealing to the "prophetic" authority of existing scripture, it becomes imperative that we ask the obvious question: *What meaning can the cross have for us today?*

Intellectual honesty demands that we not pretend to be first-century Jews, living in a three-story universe, who still practice animal or human sacrifice to atone for sins. Once these first premises are removed, especially the idea that the suffering of the innocent can vicariously cleanse the guilty and appease an angry God, then the rest of the argument collapses, and faith as assent to such doctrines collapses.

That is, unless *we* interpret the meaning of the crucifixion and the mystery of the resurrection *for our own time,* relying not on ancient cosmologies but on the transcendent nature of the gospel message. In the decades following the brutal execution of a Galilean peasant, killed because of his politics, because of his passion for God's justice, the early Christian movement preserved his memory—even as it added layers of meaning to that memory. Caught between the chilling reality of his death and the transforming memory of his life, the first disciples surely believed that it could all be explained as part of God's plan for salvation. The result is that today we say, "Jesus died *for* our sins." The truth may be closer to this: Jesus died *because* of our sins.

There were other teachers of wisdom in his time, other wise ones who taught and healed and sought to reform the religious practices of their time. But there must have been something remarkably different about Jesus. Few scholars believe that he thought the purpose of his life was to die; rather, it was what he *did* that marked him out for death. We know that those who challenge the status quo and do so with both conviction and charisma are at risk of being killed. In our own time, both Mahatma Gandhi and Martin Luther King Jr. were killed as a result of what they did. But we do not regard their deaths as the purpose of their lives.

Several interpretations of the meaning of the death of Jesus emerge from the New Testament itself and demonstrate that it was open to debate from the beginning. One says the authorities rejected Jesus, but God vindicated him (Acts 2:36). Another says that behind the Roman rulers in Judea were "principalities and powers," and these were systems of domination built in human institutions.[11]

A more modern approach is to see the cross as the death of an old way of being in the world, so that we can be raised to a new way of being, as when Paul speaks of the death of his old self and the resurrection of a new self, one with Christ (Gal. 2:19–20). Another view is that the death of Jesus is primarily to be understood as a revelation of God's love, as expressed in John 3:16, "For God so loved the world that he gave his only Son, so that everyone who believes in him may not perish but may have eternal life."

Finally, the most prominent understanding is that his death was sacrificial, even though the fully formed doctrine of the blood atonement did not appear until just after the first millennium, or about nine hundred years ago. Yet this idea now dominates popular Christianity and must be rejected if the church is to survive.

According to this dominant view, we are born with original sin, damned, and helpless to overcome that sin and gain eternal life unless an adequate sacrifice is made. This can't be an animal or even an imperfect human but must be a "perfect" sacrifice provided by God in the form of a perfect human being (the Christ). He is the substitute victim who takes on the punishment deserved by humanity that is required for restoration and forgiveness by a "loving" God. This raises an obvious and deeply disturbing question: "Is God so implacable that he demands a victim and so unjust that he does not mind that the victim is innocent?"[12]

Forget for a moment that we no longer believe in the idea of blood atonement. Think what this view says about God. First, God must not be both all-powerful and all-loving, or God would not require such a sacrifice in order to be restored to his own creation. Second, if this "had to happen," then we are dealing with a deity who not only must play by our rules but is, at best, capable of being bribed or, at worst, guilty of divine child abuse.

If we can get behind the doctrine of the blood atonement, however, to the original meaning of "Jesus is the sacrifice for our sins," we will find something very different and, for our purposes, very promising. That confession, when first uttered, was not substitutionary in nature, but utterly *subversive*. Because it was believed that the Temple had a monopoly on forgiveness of sins, and because forgiveness of sins was a prerequisite for entry into the presence of God, Temple theology also claimed an institutional monopoly on *access* to God. Therefore, to say that Jesus is "the sacrifice for our sin" was to "deny the temple's claim to have a monopoly on forgiveness and access to God. The temple franchise had been circumvented. Using the metaphor of sacrifice, it subverted the sacrificial system. It meant: God in Jesus has already provided the sacrifice and has thus taken care of whatever you think separates you from God."[13]

This is why the first followers of Jesus ceased the practice of sacrifice. Doing so was a radical statement that no further sacrifice was required, and one that endangered their lives— marking them as defectors from the Temple system, which Rome permitted as a form of social control. Taking Jesus at his word, "I desire mercy, not sacrifice" (Matt. 9:13), the first followers of The Way saw Jesus as standing against sacrificial thinking and in favor of compassion. When he entered the Temple to turn over the tables and drive out the money changers, he was challenging the very purpose of the Temple, which is to be not a house of sacrifice but a "house of prayer for all the nations" (Mark 11:17). Just as Abraham's near sacrifice of Isaac signals the end of human sacrifice, the death of Jesus on the cross signals the end of *all* sacrifice.

How ironic that this statement of amazing grace would by the fourth century begin to claim for *itself* an institutional monopoly on access to God! Jesus comes to preach and teach the kingdom of God and pays the ultimate price for it. His followers believe that he has opened the heavens and revealed a God who does not require sacrifice but is repulsed by it. Then by the time his later followers get married to the Roman Empire, the church itself is set on a course to become, by doctrine and the sword, the new House of Sacrifice.

This is what is meant by the idea that the cross is ultimately about *futility,* not about forgiveness. This is why the idea that the body of Jesus may have been ravaged by wild dogs or picked clean by crows is not the same thing as saying that the death of Jesus is meaningless. It means that even if he was born in obscurity and died alone, forgotten and abandoned by his disciples, the ways of Rome did *not* have the last word. It means that as horrifying and powerful as state terrorism can be, built on fear and funded by the principalities and powers, violence is effective only in the short run. It can proficiently kill bodies, but it is ultimately impotent when it comes to slaying the spirit.

We are accustomed to hearing the death of Jesus and events leading up to it described as his "passion," and we assume this refers only to suffering. But it is more accurate to say that his passion had to do with the revelation of God that consumed him. Justice was his passion. Healing was his passion. Gathering up the last, the least, and the lost and helping them to stand up straight in a world that kept them permanently bent over was his passion.

For this passion he suffered, of course, and yet we must never assume that such suffering was part of the plan and purpose of God, lest we give divine sanction to all violence. In fact, if Jesus came only to save us by dying for us, then for what purpose did he teach his disciples? What good is the Sermon on the Mount or the parables? Why heal a few people when you can hurry up and die to heal them all? Docetism, which asserts that Jesus was not a man at all, but merely God masquerading as a man, is the dominant heresy in the church today. Yet when Jesus ceases to be human and becomes only Christ the God Man, we can choose to believe it or not to believe it, but we cannot follow. We can admire, but we cannot emulate. We have turned "the iconoclast into an icon."[14]

We think that the way to exalt him is to deify him, and by speaking of him as "just a man" we render him powerless. But the opposite is true. If he is a metaphysical alien, then his miracles are nothing—they are what you would expect from the supernatural. If, on the other hand, he was born and died a human being, then the stories of his miraculous deeds are testimony to the miraculous effect that he had on his followers. As one South African scholar puts it, "Jesus is a much underrated man. To deprive him of his humanity is to deprive him of his greatness."[15]

Likewise, to see the death of Jesus as a ransom payment in blood to a God whose love and forgiveness can only be purchased in pain is to turn the redemptive idea of the cross on its head. Instead of a verdict on the ultimate futility of violence, it actually commends it and sends a chilling message to the human species: *violence saves*.

Nor can we assume that this death is noble, as in the Greek and Hellenistic notions of martyrdom. Dying for religious, political, or military honor is a constant theme in the ancient world, but the difference here is striking. Martyrs give last speeches and die for their city, their people, their religion, or their comrades—but not for their enemies.

Those who defended their religious and political turf killed Jesus. The cross is a symbol both of the cruelty of the state and the violent envy of religious hierarchies. Far from being a great blessing in disguise, it was meant to be just one more gruesome blip on the radar screen of human violence. Got a problem with somebody? Get rid of the body. Want to deter future troublemakers? Hang the offending corpse along a busy highway. Want to snuff out the first stages of a peasant rebellion? Snuff out the peasant rebel.

This will always work. The Roman recipe is guaranteed. Kill them over there, so you don't have to kill them here. Mop up, do the paperwork, close the file, and return to your gated neighborhood. You will sleep well far from the sound of weeping. Then you will be promoted.

Except that every once in a while, for reasons known only to God, the plan will go astray. The corpse will rot, but the hearts of those set free will not. The birds of prey will swoop down to peck out the vowels of the parables, but in some upper room they are being repeated and reinterpreted. While Antipas sips his wine and has his bath drawn, he fails to notice in the cup the ringed vibrations of a distant, otherwise imperceptible tremor. His wife says he looks tired.

Meanwhile, in a gospel not yet written, the wife of Pilate will report having trouble sleeping because of bad dreams. She knows, in the way that women know, that the deed will be undone by three of her sisters, who go looking for the living among the dead.

FOUR

EASTER AS PRESENCE, NOT PROOF

Emmaus never happened. Emmaus always happens.

—*John Dominic Crossan*

So it all comes down to Easter, does it not? Isn't the whole of the Christian enterprise left stone cold and wrapped in a shroud if the body of Jesus was not raised from the dead? What else can vindicate this shameful treatment of God's chosen? What else can truly reward those who profess to believe it, save the resurrection of their own bodies—or the bodies of all believers at the end of time? Take the shout of Easter morning away, and what remains to rouse the faithful from their sleep? Leave the rock unmoved, and what is there to move us to do battle with the ultimate enemy? If he did not "get up" on Easter Sunday, then why should we get up on any Sunday?

Is the resurrection not the good news, the nonnegotiable verdict of a God who turned death into life and defeat into victory? Or is it just the final fiction about the end of Jesus' life, a mythical bookend to match the miraculous infancy narratives? Isn't the guilt-induced presence of those who come to church only on Christmas and Easter a sign of the last vestige of belief in the supernatural Jesus, or what one might call "airport theology"—the life of Jesus reduced to an arrival and a departure? Take this away and what is left? If the empty tomb is a metaphor and not a description of the resuscitation of a corpse, then shouldn't all the crosses in the world be turned in and melted down for scrap? Shouldn't all the churches be razed and an amnesty program implemented to allow everyone to turn in their Bibles without sanction?

Besides, haven't the gospels told us the truth about what happened after the death and burial of Jesus, if indeed he was buried at all? Doesn't the Bible say, plainly and consistently, that on Easter morning the tomb was found empty, and that by Easter evening the risen Christ had appeared to his closest followers as proof that he was back? As one scholar puts it with obvious sarcasm, "Friday was hard, Saturday was long, but by Sunday all was resolved."[1]

First, we must ask ourselves whether these are three literal days or three liturgical days, like the six days required by the God of Genesis to create the universe. Second, we must ask whether an Easter faith requires us to believe in the resuscitation of a corpse. And third, if the answer is no, then the next question is obvious: To what can the church point as proof that Jesus was indeed the Christ? Is it possible to rise from the dead *without* one's body, and if so, how would this be verified? Is Easter a molecular event or a spiritual one?

The great New Testament scholar Rudolph Bultmann wrote, "Jesus rose into the kerygma"—that is, into the faith of the first believers.[2] In other words, the conviction of the followers of Jesus that he was still with them was *itself* the resurrection. To ask the question of whether the resurrection is true, and to mean by this that only a resuscitated corpse constitutes such proof, is to impose the standards of the modern mind upon a prescientific culture of myth and magic. The dualism of body and soul was a Greek idea, so for the Jews there could be no resurrection without a resurrection of the body. How could one "rise" without a body to rise in? What we refer to as the "inner voice" would have to have come from the clouds in the first century. The nonspatial "interior life" is a modern, psychological concept. The ancients simply located the mysteries of the spirit in the movement of objects. Something was not "known" unless it could be described as something "happening."

All that the early Christians needed to know was that Jesus died for our sins, was buried, and was raised on the third day, all in accordance with the scriptures. This was the original "kerygma" (the first faith of the believers). Oddly enough, the arguments over the validity of this claim would have centered on the scandal of Jesus as the *object* of that claim, not on the idea that someone had been raised from the death. That claim was made all the time, but only about those of noble birth or institutional power.

Today we stumble over the claim because we find it incredible, missing the real scandal of saying about Jesus, "He is risen!" The church has failed generations of would-be followers of Jesus by confusing the transrational with the irrational. They come to Easter service believing that they must believe the impossible in order to feel the implausible. Before they can sing the "Hallelujah Chorus," they must check their brain at the door. God's "yes" to Jesus is assumed to be a "no" to the laws of the physical universe. Tears of joy are then, by definition, the counterfeit symbols of sentimentality. Why not say it as plainly as the renowned biblical scholar John Dominic Crossan: "I do not think that anyone, anywhere, at any time brings dead people back to life."[3]

What can be known with certainty is that the Jesus movement in Judea did not cease after the execution of its leader under Pontius Pilate—but expanded. By the early decades of the second century it had reached all the way to Rome. Because there was neither a crucifixion nor a resurrection *story* until around 70 CE, it is obvious that after the death of Jesus his followers did not cease being his followers. That is, they went right on healing and teaching and hosting the open table that was the centerpiece of his kingdom. Jesus was a figure of the present, not simply of the past. As the angel in the story puts it, "Why do you look for the living among the dead?" (Luke 24:5). You won't find Jesus here. He has been raised into the land of the living—resurrected in his disciples, who have all the proof they need: hearts that burn within them.

What could possibly explain this empowerment and courage? How is it that the death of their teacher did not mean the end of their own course in miracles? In the early *Gospel of Thomas* we read nothing about resurrection or atonement, but only about an abiding *presence* that sustained his followers like the wisdom of God on earth. In fact, to explain this physical absence but spiritual presence, the only title in *Thomas* for Jesus is "the living Jesus."[4]

Fundamentalist Christians would quickly assert that what sustains them is their certain knowledge of his *bodily* resurrection, followed by his *bodily* appearances, and all on the same weekend! Don't we have the empty tomb stories and a rash of postresurrection appearances—all before the first gospel was written? And besides, we have Paul's word on it, right? Sometime around 53 or 54 CE, didn't the great missionary apostle tell us in no uncertain terms that the bodily resurrection was both real and essential?

> If there is no resurrection of the dead, then Christ has not been raised; and if Christ has not been raised, then our proclamation has been in vain and your faith has been in vain. (1 Cor. 15:13–14)

As a Pharisee, Paul believed in the resurrection of the dead, and certainly he believed that Jesus had been raised from the dead. But the question Paul goes on to ask is, "With what kind of body do they come?" His answer is remarkable and seldom gets heard in the debate about the resurrection of the body:

So it is with the resurrection of the dead. What is sown is perishable, what is raised is imperishable. . . . It is sown a physical body, it is raised a spiritual body. If there is a physical body, there is also a spiritual body. . . . What I am saying, brothers and sisters, is this: flesh and blood cannot inherit the kingdom of God, nor does the perishable inherit the imperishable. (1 Cor. 15:42, 44, 50)

Whatever sort of vision Paul claims to have seen on the road to Damascus, it had nothing to do with a body. This "disembodied" vision does not occur until 34 or 35 CE, or three to four years after the death of Jesus. If he had been raised physically from the death, this begs the question: Where was he during this long interval and what was he doing? In fact, Paul has no empty tomb story to tell, and even decades later Mark has not a single postresurrection appearance story to tell. A decade later Matthew is ambivalent, combining two resurrection narratives, one involving women at the tomb, the other involving the disciples in Galilee, which is more like a vision.

It is only when we get to Luke-Acts and John, or the late ninth to early tenth decade of the common era, that the Easter story depicts the resurrection of a *physical* body walking out of the tomb. Before this, Paul does not even recognize Jesus; neither does Mary; neither do the two men walking down the road to Emmaus; neither do the seven when he appears on the shore of the sea (Acts 9:5; John 20:14; Luke 24:16; John 21:4). It is the *elusive* Jesus that is standard fare, because he was *not* a mass of molecules. But as time passed and the tradition grew, these visions lost their luminous quality and took on flesh and bones.

FROM APPARITION TO ANATOMY

The irreconcilable differences between the gospel accounts of the resurrection are well known to any student of the New

Testament. In Mark's earliest account three women go to the tomb—Mary Magdala, Mary the mother of James, and Salome—and find it empty. The large stone has been rolled away and inside they find a young man in a white robe who advises them that Jesus has been raised. They are to go tell the disciples to precede him to Galilee, where he will appear (as promised), but they are fearful and don't tell anyone. The risen Jesus appears to no one.

In Matthew, written about a decade later, there are only two women, Mary Magdala and another Mary—Salome has disappeared. An earthquake signals the arrival of a heavenly messenger, who has rolled away the stone and now sits on it. The instructions are the same as in Mark, but Matthew adds the tremor (perhaps to explain how the stone got moved) and a description of the angel's glistening white robe. Also, as the women hurry away from the tomb to report the news to the disciples, Jesus meets them and repeats the angel's instructions: "Go and tell my brothers to go to Galilee; there they will see me" (28:10). This may well be "a defensive move on Matthew's part to cover the flight of the disciples and to provide official permission for something they have already done."[5]

Matthew also adds a new scene, in which guards report what has happened at the tomb, and the priests and elders offer a bribe to the soldiers if they will tell everyone that the disciples came at night while they slept and stole the body. The risen Jesus appears to the Eleven on a mountain in Galilee, where some worship him and others are dubious. The Great Commission is given, believed by many scholars to be the work of Matthew, not the words of Jesus.

In Luke and Acts, the number of women grows to include Mary Magdala, Joanna, Mary the mother of James, and an unspecified number of other women who come to find the stone rolled away and the tomb empty. The number of angels present grows as well; *two* heavenly messengers remind the women of Jesus' own predictions of his death and resurrection.

This larger delegation of women goes to tell the Eleven, who do not believe them. The impetuous Peter runs to the tomb to have a look, finding nothing but the shroud. In a first appearance, Jesus appears as a stranger to two travelers on the road to Emmaus and is only recognized later in the breaking of bread. Then he appears to the Eleven and the others assembled, and he is now "human" enough to be hungry—requesting something to eat. He is given a piece of grilled fish, and yet some are still terrified and think they are seeing a ghost. Luke wants to prove this is not a ghost, but a famished being. A ghost would not show his hands and feet, inviting the skeptical to touch them. A ghost would not lead them to Bethany and then float up into the sky, showing those below the bottoms of his feet.

In the first chapter of Acts, Luke develops the story further by having Jesus exit the world not by dying again (which did not succeed in taking him "out" of the world) but by *rising* into the sky, as Elijah does (2 Kings 2)—not in a fiery chariot, but with two men dressed in white robes who interpret his departure and also predict his second coming. More than any other writer, it is Luke who shifts the resurrection narrative decisively from vapors to entrails.

Finally, in the last gospel, John, which probably ended at chapter 20 (chapter 21 may have been added later as an appendix), the evolution from *apparition* to *anatomy* is completed. Mary Magdala goes to the tomb and finds it empty and the stone rolled away. She runs to tell Peter and the "disciple whom Jesus loved" (the unnamed one), and the men have a footrace to the tomb, which the other disciple wins—even though Peter enters the tomb first. They find the tomb empty and describe the strips of burial cloth left behind, including the odd detail about the one that wrapped the head of Christ "rolled up in a place by itself"

(20:7). Such details add emphasis to the physical nature of the resurrection and beg the question: Who else but the risen Christ could have removed his own head bandage on the way out?

Meanwhile, Mary is hanging around outside the tomb, and two angels ask her why she is crying. She responds that someone has taken her Lord away, and she then turns to see someone she thinks is a caretaker. She recognizes the Resurrected One when he calls her name, and she reports this to the disciples. That evening, when the disciples are locked into a room "for fear of the Jews" (20:19), Christ appears, but he displays different parts of his anatomy (hands and side rather than hands and feet). He commissions them and *breathes* the Holy Spirit on them in what may be a kind of mini-Pentecost scene.[6]

The entire scene is then repeated for Thomas, who represents all of us who were either absent or "untimely born" or still stubbornly refuse to believe. The doors remain locked, as John writes in the heat of the Christian-Jewish divorce, and Thomas is invited to *touch* the hands and side of the risen Christ—now far removed from the crucified Jesus. Thomas will be persuaded *only* if the proof is entirely anatomical: "Unless I see the mark of the nails in his hands, and put my finger in the mark of the nails and my hand in his side, I will not believe" (20:25).

In the appendix to the gospel of John (chapter 21), the beautiful story of the appearance of the risen Christ to seven disciples on the shore of the Sea of Tiberias is told. After the disciples fish all night and catch nothing, a familiar voice from the past urges them to cast their nets to the right side of the boat. As in the walk to Emmaus, it is another *Jesus memory* that triggers recognition—either table fellowship or advice on how to fish. The unnamed disciple who won the footrace to the tomb recognizes the risen Christ, while, true to form, Peter leaps into the sea to greet him first.

Think how far we have come now, from Paul's earliest vision of a *disembodied* voice heard only by him to this final chapter in which a body walks out of the tomb to eat, drink, walk, talk, teach, and expound on scripture. What was an ecstatic inner vision at first has now become a tangible physical form. Christ is said to be *standing* on the beach, using a *voice* that is audible to all—followed by a narrative that includes peculiar mathematical details. The disciples drag their nets full of fish to shore, "about a hundred yards off" (21:8), and empty their catch of exactly "a hundred fifty-three" large fish (21:11). The narrative is concrete, and some of the elements seem to add nothing to the story except an unmistakable *physicality:*

> When they had gone ashore, they saw a charcoal fire there, with fish on it, and bread. Jesus said to them, "Bring some of the fish that you have just caught. . . . Come and have breakfast." Now none of the disciples dared to ask him, "Who are you?" because they knew it was the Lord. . . . This was now the third time that Jesus appeared to the disciples after he was raised from the dead. (21:9–14)

Here is the resurrected Christ cooking and serving a postresurrection Communion meal at the dawn of a new day, in contrast to the evening shadows of the Last Supper. No one doubts his identity, because all they have to do is *look* at him and *listen* to him. He *gives* them the bread and the fish, and what follows this sacramental breakfast is a poignant and real-time *dialogue* with the ever-recalcitrant Peter.

This is reported by John almost as a playwright would; it is a scene of give-and-take occurring in time and space. When breakfast is *finished,* Christ asks Peter a direct question and then *repeats* it twice more to drive home a point—that Peter's authority is restored, and humanity's own recalcitrance is again lamented. When will we get it?

When asked, "Do you love me?" Peter offers a quick and easy response. Christ responds, "Feed my lambs." Then the question a second time, as if he didn't get it, and a second imperative, which widens the flock, "Tend my sheep." But when the question is asked a third time, Peter is "hurt," and we hear John's familiar theme of separation and misunderstanding. "Lord, you know everything; you know that I love you" (21:17). To which the risen Christ says a final time, perhaps while poking at the dying embers of the breakfast fire, "Feed my sheep." The "triple statement of love from Peter to Jesus" and the "triple statement of mandate from Jesus to Peter" are apologetic in tone, restoring Peter and putting him in charge of the entire flock. "Peter is a *specific leader* given authority over both a *leadership group* and the *general community*."[7] Now we know what appearance stories were truly meant to accomplish.

THE POLITICS OF APPEARANCES

Just as there are irreconcilable anomalies in the birth narratives and the accounts of the resurrection, so it is impossible to trace the postresurrection appearance stories without becoming entangled in contradiction. That is, unless one understands the appearance stories as *political,* rather than historical. In fact, the strange and often baffling accounts of Jesus sightings have more to do with conferring authority on certain disciples or leadership groups than they do on persuading the audience to believe.

Once again, the pattern holds. As times passes, a Jewish boy born in obscurity becomes the preexistent Son of God. Then, after a brutal but routine execution, the ecstatic visions of his followers (which are common in all religious traditions) evolve into physical encounters with resuscitated corpses. Then as the early church begins to organize itself after the long delay in the second coming, it must produce stories that can mediate disputes over the pecking order in the apostolic community.

For years, the first generation of witnesses had their bags packed and sitting by the door. He would come as "a thief in the night." They died waiting, and then a second generation waited and grew old. It became obvious that the bags should be unpacked. The beloved community of Jesus followers would need to organize itself into a community of worshipers with a written record. The evolution from folding chairs to pews had begun, and the inevitable hierarchies emerged, as did arguments over authority and status. Who better to promote some while demoting others than the risen Lord himself? What more powerful endorsement on a disciple's resumé than to have been the *first* to see him?

Remember, in Mark (the first gospel) there are no appearance stories at all. But something must have happened in the decade before Matthew and Luke took up the quill and then John gave us the Gnostic Christ who hums in a parallel universe. What began as "luminous apparitions"[8] and was then replaced by a material body may actually be the result of an ongoing conflict with the Gnostic tradition.

Near the end of the first century, the Gnostics began to claim only one form of revelation (their own, of course) to be normative. It was the bright light accompanied by some heavenly communication. As Robert Funk points out, this led "not only to different types of appearance stories, but to different kinds of gospels. The so-called Gnostic gospels incorporate the instructions Jesus gives the insiders in a dialogue between Jesus and his intimates—they are, in other words, revelation gospels."[9] But in what would become the orthodox tradition, the instructions given to the disciples are moved *back* inside his life, prior to his death and resurrection. "This move had the effect of restricting the circle of insiders to those who knew Jesus during his lifetime; that of course excludes Paul."[10] Hence, Paul must make it clear that he is one "untimely born" and received his gospel by direct revelation.

All told, the risen Lord appears to *individuals* (Peter, Mary Magdala, James, and Paul); to *groups* (the Eleven, the Twelve, all the apostles, seven disciples at the Sea of Tiberias, and five hundred at the same time); and to various *others* (two on the road to Emmaus, a second, unidentified Mary, two soldiers, a centurion, some Judean elders, and unspecified witnesses). These accounts are so varied and so impossible to locate that we are obviously dealing with legendary expansions meant to convey the kind of authority only a coveted appearance could bestow—especially if you were the *first* to see the Risen One, or the *protophany.*

According to Paul and Luke, that would be Peter. But according to Matthew, that would be the two Marys (one of whom was Mary Magdala). In John, it is definitely Mary Magdala. Only in a fragment of the *Gospel of the Hebrews* is James said to be the first to see the Risen One. How interesting that when Paul provides us with his list of those to whom the Risen One has appeared in 1 Corinthians, he doesn't even mention Mary! If she was the *protophany,* she would be preeminent among the leaders of the Jesus movement. But she was a woman, and so in that society she did not qualify.

As to that strange footrace in John 20, what one scholar calls an "Alphonse and Gaston act,"[11] Peter and the unnamed disciple stumble over each other to be first. The other disciple wins the race, but Peter enters the tomb first. John tells us, however, that the other disciple is the first to believe. Confused? It is the clearest indication we have that a *rivalry* has developed in the early church. The story is an obvious attempt to give a place of honor alongside Peter to the "disciple whom Jesus loved."

Again, if one is reading literally, then the whole enterprise collapses. Who would be expected to believe, for example, that, as Matthew reports, at the moment of the crucifixion tombs were opened and "many bodies of the saints who had fallen asleep were raised" (27:52–53) and came marching into Jerusalem? Talk about an unforgettable parade! But if the New

Testament can be seen for what it is—the unfolding, metaphorical witness of a community unalterably changed by the life, death, and abiding presence of Jesus, then it all represents an act of supreme devotion. In the community of his followers, this remarkable and unforgettable human being has become the Anointed One, and the integrity of their witness is to be found not in its objectivity but in its passion. What's more, it can be recovered and brought forward as our gospel too, using new metaphors.

The Bible is covered with human fingerprints, and what the gospels reveal is the "gospel truth" about both enlightenment and the pride of authorship: *what is born in revelation is invariably corrupted by pride.* What startled the world when it first appeared in the flesh, with its wild-eyed countercultural ferocity, gets slowly tamed by being turned into a bloodless doctrine. The doctrine is well meant, to preserve the revelation for all those who missed it and to leave a record of this astonishment, so that every generation of those "untimely born" might come to believe. The problem is that no one ever falls in love with a doctrine.

It's a little bit like staring over the edge of the Grand Canyon for the first time and then trying to explain this bluish gash of prehistory to a friend over the telephone. You can talk about height, depth, width, and the luminous Bright Angel Canyon as a "showcase of the forces of erosion," to quote the brochure you picked up in the gift shop. But it just won't do the trick. In frustration, you will add, "You've just got to see it for yourself." Perhaps this is why Paul always felt like an outsider—like a tourist who arrives at the canyon at sundown, just after the last mule ride, and has only the box camera of his heart.

To be a witness was to be an authority; so the gospel writers used appearance stories to *commission* their first officers—beginning with Peter, then James, then all the apostles, and then Paul—so that the Jesus movement could spread beyond

Jerusalem and Judea. Paul in fact reports his own ecstatic commissioning, and it may well be that the appearance to "the five hundred" represents the establishment of the Christian community at Pentecost. Whether the appearance is "to the eleven" or "to the twelve" (which may be the same group), the purpose was to authorize the *true* apostles and establish their successors. If you witnessed the resurrection, you were given special power in the ancient church, and the shape and substance of that community would be altered accordingly.

Biblical scholar Elaine Pagels insists that the doctrine of the resurrection cannot be understood solely on the basis of *content* but must be seen as a practical and political act. Note that by the second century, Tertullian was labeling everyone a heretic who did not accept the doctrine of the bodily resurrection and said that only believers could expect the resurrection of their own bodies. This was not just a theological position, argues Pagels, but an organizational and ecclesiastical one. The bodily resurrection "legitimizes the authority of certain men who claim to exercise exclusive leadership over the churches as the successors of the apostle Peter."[12]

In the apostolic flowchart we begin with Jesus, who is commissioned at baptism and in the transfiguration. He hands over the keys of the kingdom to Peter, because he is the first to believe in the resurrection—even though he had "competition" at first—from Mary, James, and even Paul. But only Peter, as an original follower, had primacy. Only Peter could pass down this authority to all his successors, the bishops, and ultimately to the head bishop—the pope.

There were other appearances, of course, to Stephen and Paul, but they were clearly secondary. Then the ascension shut down the whole appearance business. Someone needed to turn out the lights and drop the curtain on the appearance scene—to put a period at the end of the Easter story. So with the ascension, the gospel writers officially "closed" the appearance canon.

This did not change the fact, however, that the first appearances did *not* depend on believing in a resuscitated corpse. They required only that one be open to ecstatic revelations, which became the Gnostic gospel. For this reason, the Gnostics didn't need Peter for anything. They had direct access to the Risen One for perpetual instruction and inspiration. This independence was an obvious threat to orthodoxy, and so it should come as no surprise that by the second century Tertullian would find a simple way to close a different sort of canon—that of all "false" views of the resurrection. He declared all Gnostics to be heretics.

THE SCANDAL IS JESUS, NOT RESURRECTION

Sadly, the church has been declaring all those who do not believe in the bodily resurrection of Jesus to be heretics ever since. This includes thoughtful, committed Christians who do not believe that Easter has anything to do with the resuscitation of a corpse or believing things you know are not true in order to get rewards you secretly doubt are available. We don't live in a three-story universe anymore, and the disappearance and reappearance of corpses should be left behind with the ideas of demon possession, slavery, and the subordination of women.

Remember, the concept of resurrection as the resuscitation of a corpse by divine action, or as the giving back or recreation of the body by God after death, is not found in the pagan traditions of the first century, although multiple ideas existed with regard to life after death. In Judaism, the concept of resurrection evolved, moving away from a disembodied to a more embodied understanding of resurrection. It meant not "survival" of death, however, as if one might simply transition from death to life, but a *redescription* of death by some reversal in the future. Even so, Jewish beliefs about bodily resurrection in the time of Jesus ran the gamut, from denial of it (Sadducees) to insistence on it (Pharisees).

Like so many other Christian doctrines that developed late and are now assumed to be central to the faith and unequivocal, the resurrection of the body, or its transformation into a new body, is but one idea among a myriad of resurrection concepts so varied as to be maddening.[13] We may be reading back into the gospel stories a concept the New Testament writers never intended, or one that developed during the period of the Maccabees to preserve God's justice, as Crossan argues.

Anglican bishop N. T. Wright would have us believe that *only* a belief in the resurrection of the body can ultimately explain the transformation of the disciples, but this break from the spectrum of Jewish ideas about life after death is more easily explained. It is more likely that we have Paul (the Pharisee) to thank for the emphasis on resurrection, and the ultimate divorce from Judaism to blame for a doctrine that could set Christians apart from those like the Sadducees, "who deny the resurrection of the body," and thus support a post-Temple Pharisaic Judaism.

Those who have left the church today and will not return until they are allowed to think for themselves can follow the argument so far, and any atheist can do so with delight. But this is a book meant not to do further harm to the church—rather, to help *reconstitute* it. What is tragically less obvious than the arguments against Easter are the arguments for it. Easter may have nothing to do with a corpse and yet everything to do with the mysteries of human existence and our hope for the redemption of the world. The church has expressed this distinction between the irrational and transrational in one parabolic afternoon: "Emmaus never happened. Emmaus always happens."[14]

The stories of resurrection are acts of devotion, because "those who believed in Jesus before his execution *continued* to do so afterward. Easter is not about the start of a new faith but about the continuation of an old one. That is the only miracle and the only mystery, and it is more than enough of both."[15] It is a "terrible trivialization," Crossan writes, "to imagine that all Jesus' followers lost their faith on Good Friday and had it restored by apparitions on Easter Sunday. It is another trivialization to presume that even those who lost their nerve, fled, and hid also lost their faith, hope, and love. It is a final trivialization to mistake stories about competing Christian authority for stories about inaugural Christian experience."[16]

Almost all biblical scholars agree that the abandonment of Jesus by his disciples at the darkest hour is historically accurate, because it is a negative assertion made about people who are otherwise meant to be exalted. Just as certain, however, is the belief that those same disciples experienced something remarkable and life-changing after the execution of their teacher and Lord. Even if Jesus died alone, something brought his disciples back and empowered them to take up the cause and face persecution and martyrdom. "They never wavered. The strength of their conviction was such that no threat or fear could now separate them from the God they believed they had met in Jesus."[17]

The church now faces the fundamental challenge of *recovering* that view of God and the empowering way of life that Jesus taught and for which he died, while *abandoning* the creedal claims of the institutional church that separate the saved from the unsaved based on intellectual assent to discredited propositions. The former brings life; the latter bring division in the church and misplaced priorities. What must be celebrated at Easter is not a particular view of resurrection but the integrity of a first-century act of devotion. There is simply nothing unique about claiming that some *notable* person had been raised from the dead.[18] What was utterly uncommon and turned human history on its axis was the claim that *Jesus* had been raised from the dead. It reset all the clocks in the Western world. Easter was God's "yes" to a peasant revolutionary, and God's "no" to the Roman Empire.

The refrain of every apostolic song was the same. "Death cannot contain him. . . . We have seen the Lord. . . . He is risen!" These lyrics are not metaphysical. They are confessional. Easter is God's vindication of The Way, not a statement about the blood atonement. It is a daring and dangerous statement that says that when you live the way of Jesus, you will see God. And that when you dare to live in the radical freedom that is authentic faith, you need fear nothing at all—not even death.

To see the "human face of God," as New Testament scholar John A. T. Robinson puts it, was an experience so liberating that it required a new Sabbath day on which to worship and turned the early church into a beloved community of "resident aliens."[19] But unlike the claims of orthodoxy, Jesus did not come to die, rendering his life and teaching secondary. He died *because* of his life and teachings. He was killed *for* the things that he said and did. Then the claim of his first followers and his first community is that God raised him from the dead to undo the injustice done to him and to place a divine stamp of approval on his words and deeds.

This may not sound like such an important distinction, but it is the Continental Divide that separates a dying church, on the one hand, from the possibility of a church reborn and freed from the American empire, on the other. Placing all the emphasis on the saving effect of the death of Christ as a cosmic bargain negates the life of Jesus. It not only gives us movies like Mel Gibson's *The Passion of the Christ* (an anti-Semitic, sadomasochistic spectacle truncating the life of Jesus and reducing it to a feature-length act of divinely sanctioned torture) but actually *legitimizes* violence in a world already saturated with it.

In that movie, rated R for violence but attended by children as young as twelve whose parents know "good violence" when they see it, the life of Jesus and his message are reduced to a few "flashbacks" as he dies on the cross "for our sins." The life is optional, but the death is not. It is no wonder that so many high-profile Christian fundamentalists have such a taste for torture and extraordinary rendition. After all, sometimes even an "awesome" God must do what "must be done"—inflicting pain to get good intelligence and accomplish a larger purpose. No pain, no eternal gain.

Again, think how far we have come from the noble death of Jesus, who was raised in the heart of the beloved community, to the "necessary" death of the divine scapegoat, who "pays the price" for all sin and appeases an angry Father, who can be satisfied only by the foreordained torture and death of his only son. In the former, access to the kingdom is unbrokered; Jesus never appoints anyone to anything. In the latter, God is the ultimate Broker, and death can be seen as the ultimate bargain. In the former, there is no hierarchy of privilege; true leaders are those who serve and make themselves slaves of all. In the latter, there is a perpetual pecking order, whose upper members are assumed to have the power to save souls and who have the utterly corruptible hubris to act as gatekeepers between heaven and hell.

To raise Jesus is to recover the liberating quality of the gospel, freeing it from precisely the obligatory rituals that have always been confused with righteousness. For Paul, circumcision, dietary laws, and other aspects of Mosaic law have given way to a new covenant and a new reality: "There is no longer Jew or Greek, there is no longer slave or free, there is no longer male and female; for all of you are one in Christ Jesus" (Gal. 3:28).

Sadly, we have replaced one form of legalism with another. To insist that "Jesus was God" (the dominant American heresy) and that the only true resurrection is the bodily resurrection is not even biblically honest. What's more, it reverses the inclusionary model of Jesus and cuts us off from all those generous and compassionate latter-day gnostics for whom Easter is a spiritual, not a molecular, event.

It is easy to understand why "eternal life" is such a powerful and appealing idea. Not only are we terrified by death, but we are sustained by the belief that good people (like us) will be re-warded and the evildoers (like them) will get what is coming to them. Surely if God is just, the afterlife will reflect that justice. The idea of a final judgment, with its separation of the sheep from the goats, is drawn from this universal human longing. And yet, strangely enough, there is more evidence to suggest that this was *not* the message of Jesus.

He was remembered as talking about the kingdom *here* and *now*—a way of being in right relationship to God and to one another that could be both present and future tense. It was both now, in his wisdom, and yet to come, when that wisdom would rule the whole earth. In his parables he sought to *reverse* human expectations of rewards and punishments, and he audaciously proclaimed that the first would be last, and the last first. Insiders would be outsiders, and the rewards of faith would be intrinsic, not extrinsic.

In the end, what right do human beings have to expect eternal bliss for being good—or on the cheap, for just *believing* the right things? And what single idea is more shameful or horrific than to project our human longing for vengeance upon God by claiming that in God's infinite mercy God has made and maintains a place of eternal torment? It is no wonder that so many good people avoid the word "Christian" like the plague. It has become synonymous with hypocrisy, mean-spiritedness, and conspicuous consumption.

Yet some churches do not just celebrate Easter; they live it. There are Jesus followers who live as Easter people every day and provide more proof of the resurrection than any literalized metaphor of an empty tomb. They are all "untimely born," but they have no need to boast of an ecstatic vision or cover their doubts by touching wounded hands or pierced sides. They accept the laws of nature yet refuse to live in a universe devoid of mystery or stripped of all enchantment. By *following*, not by believing, they remain open to the possibility of resurrection in this life, not just in the next.

A woman in my own congregation spent more than a decade despising me—or at least I thought she did. I was too liberal, and I had persuaded the deacons to remove the American flag from the sanctuary and place it in our fellowship hall. My explanation about any symbol of a nation-state in a "house of prayer for all people" could not be heard above her certain belief that I did not honor veterans, including her husband. Sunday mornings became an elaborate ritual of avoidance, including extraordinary measures to avoid passing in the hallway. If she saw me coming, she turned and went the other way. It was "her church," but I was not "her pastor."

When I greeted her, there was no response. She only communicated through surrogates, and near the end of her life she issued an ultimatum. If I did not insist that the congregation sing "Battle Hymn of the Republic" within six weeks, she would resign from the church. Needless to say, we did not sing that hymn in the required period of time, and she made good on her threat. She disappeared for several years, and I enjoyed her absence.

Then word came that she was dying. She was in intensive care in a hospital near my house, and I knew what I was supposed to do—go see her. But I didn't want to. I reasoned that she was no longer a member and that I was the last person on earth she would want to see anyway. I joked with my wife, Shawn, about what the real impact of a visit might be—would I make her worse? What if she died when I entered the room?

Shawn persuaded me that a visit was the right thing to do, because about such things she is almost always right. "To what oath are you bound, Robin?" she asked me. "Visiting only the people you like?" I headed for the hospital, feeling vaguely as though I was about to be the first minister ever to kill someone by making a hospital call.

I approached the nurse's station and decided to send advance notice to her room. That way, she could send word that she could not be bothered. After all, I had nothing good to report about our prospects for singing the "Battle Hymn of the Republic," and I knew she was going to ask me. The nurse returned from her room and said, "Go right in."

I turned the corner and from the corridor I saw her lying on her deathbed, with tubes running out of her nose and mouth and into numerous ports in her body. This is so often the soundtrack of death, the clicking and wheezing of artificial life support. I hesitated at the door, only to have her raise her arm and motion me to the bedside.

Before I could say a word, she lifted herself up in defiance of all those tubes and all that misery. She wrapped her arms around my neck and kissed me on the mouth. "I'm so glad you came," she said.

We talked for two hours, catching up on children, the church she no longer attended, and the sad state of the world. She died the next day.

Some people would argue that this is not a resurrection story and has nothing to do with Easter.

That's unfortunate.

FIVE

ORIGINAL BLESSING, NOT ORIGINAL SIN

> This then is salvation: to marvel at the beauty of created
> things and to marvel at the beauty of their Creator.
>
> —*Meister Eckhart*

G. K. Chesterton once wrote that certain "new theologians dispute original sin, which is the only part of Christian theology which can really be proved."[1] All you have to do, he argued, is open your eyes to see that original sin is self-evident and validated by all of human history. When St. Augustine, bishop of Hippo from 396 to 430, solidified the notion that we sin because we are born to sin, that we are the children of sin, that sin is in our DNA, passed down to us from the disobedience of Adam and Eve, he created the first major premise of orthodox Christianity.

Although the concept was not original to Augustine, it was his enormous influence on early Christian theology that gave us the fully developed notion that we are "fallen" by birth, trapped by the sin of our first parents, and can only be "saved" from that sin by Jesus. There is no doctrine of original sin in Judaism, and none in the biblical story of creation, except as the myth of Adam and Eve is "literalized."[2] In effect, the church has created the ultimate spiritual franchise, a kind of salvation monopoly. We are pronounced bad by birth and given only one possible cure by the same entity that provided the diagnosis!

Because of the doctrine of original sin, countless Christians have long considered sin to be a condition, not a choice. We are not sinners because we sin; rather, we sin because we are sinners. Sin is in the human gene pool like any other physical trait we inherit; nothing else can explain how a perfect God could have created such an imperfect species.

Although it is obvious that human beings sin and seem to do so pathologically, it is one thing to say we sin because we can't help ourselves. It is entirely another to say that our sins are the result of the *choices* we make—separated from God, from each other, and from creation itself. What's more, if we are born "infected" with sin, then sin is really an STD, a sexually transmitted disease. Augustine called it "concupiscence"—when people had sex and conceived a child, they brought home more than just a bundle of joy. They brought home a bundle of sin, hardwired to rebel, a baby bearing the seeds of guilt and shame.

More than any other Christian theologian, Augustine wrenched body and soul apart as a result of his own struggles with the flesh, laid bare in the world's first autobiography, *The Confessions*. An absent father, a hovering mother who begged him to convert, and his own hedonistic lifestyle drove Augustine to see human sexuality as the battleground for the soul. For nine years Augustine had belonged to a sect called the Manicheans, which preached dualism, asceticism, and determinism and believed that life was a pitched battle between the forces of light and the forces of darkness. They also believed that evil existed independently of a good God, who was powerless to stop it.

Augustine converted to Christianity at midlife, famously after hearing a child singing "*Tolle, lege*" ("Take it up and read") in his Milan garden, after which his Bible fell open to Romans 13:14— Paul's warning to "make no provision for the flesh, to gratify its desires." Augustine believed that this was the sign he had been looking for, and Western theology would be changed forever.

Although Augustine left the Manichean sect, it would seem that Manichaeism never completely left Augustine. In his thinking, the sins of the flesh became the principal arena of the battle between darkness and light. Evil was considered an autonomous force stronger than God, which manifested itself most fully in an all-consuming sexual dualism. It was this fear and loathing about human sexuality and the idea of the body as betrayer of the soul that led the church to label sex as a necessary evil, a regrettable and dangerous obligation strictly for the purposes of procreation. Eros could not produce joy, intimacy, and spiritual union, not even in marriage—just sinful children.

It meant that the tiniest babies were tiny sinners, and if they died before they could be "saved" through baptism, then they went to a place called "limbo"—created by the Catholic Church to "spare" the smallest of heathens from burning in hell, while not allowing them to taste paradise either. The same fate reputedly befell all those babies who had the misfortune to be born before Jesus came. No word yet on how this spared grieving mothers.

When limbo was abolished by papal decree in 1992, the obvious question became a standard joke among my Catholic friends: Where did all the babies in limbo go? Perhaps a better question to ask is this: *When are we going to graduate from the Middle Ages?* The answer: when we reject once and for all the disastrous doctrine of original sin and replace it with the idea of original blessing.[3] The former is about shame, helplessness, and entrapment. The latter is about joy, connection to creation, and personal responsibility.

IMAGO DEI, NOT EXEMPLARY SIN

It seems ironic that the church urges people to study the Bible critically and view the scriptures as normative for faith and life, while at the same time requiring them to believe nonbiblical or postbiblical concepts like original sin, the Trinity, and the blood atonement as gospel. No one can blame Augustine for wondering how a perfect God could have created such an imperfect world, but the very same dilemma confronted the very first author of the Bible, the Yahwist (or J) source, in the ninth century BCE. The answer he came up with, however, was very different. The biblical answer is found in an apologetic mythology. It says that creation is good, but that when given a choice, humans will often make the wrong one, especially if they have been told exactly what *not* to do.

In the poetry of Genesis, two different creation stories followed by the account of the first sin and its punishment are examples of inspired metaphor and pure *etiology*. Although "etiology" is normally a medical term dealing with the search for the causes of disease, in biblical studies it refers to the process of explaining the current human situation by creating a story and placing it into the divine drama retroactively. The Hebrew poet must have looked around at the world, as we all do, and wondered what could possibly explain the selfish and rebellious behavior of the human species. How could Yahweh be responsible for this deeply flawed creature who sins compulsively and destructively? If God is perfect, then what can explain the deeply imperfect state of God's creation?

At least three possible answers come to mind. (1) There is no God, and so human beings are simply what they are, animal in nature and wired to survive. (2) God is imperfect or limited, and human beings reflect that imperfection as the defective product of a defective Creator. And (3) God is perfect and created a perfect world, but human beings rebelled, turned their backs on God, and introduced the world to sin, guilt, and shame. Once we occupied a garden of bliss, unaware of our nakedness, but now we have been expelled from paradise and must live forever "East of Eden."

The Hebrew poet chose the last option by creating the myth of the first humans and the first sin. In an oral culture, such stories functioned to establish identity and provide a narrative to explain how we turned out this way. God could remain perfect while the imperfection of creation is given a human cause. Life in the *present* tense has been explained by divine action and human rebellion in the *past* tense. The story also provides answers to some of the oldest and most perennial of human questions.

For example, if we are born innocent, then why do we "fall" from that innocence by telling our first lie or being drawn into the commission of the very sins we have been warned not to commit? Why are we ashamed of our own bodies and our sexual urges? Why do we tend to blame others for our mistakes, as Adam blamed Eve, who blamed the serpent?

The story of Adam and Eve's expulsion from the garden is a metaphor for the fundamental separation of human beings from God, and when God's sentence is handed down—that women shall give birth in pain and men shall work by the sweat of their brow and then die—it serves etiologically to explain why both realities are with us still. After all, what sort of God would design a world in which childbirth was agonizingly painful, even deadly? Or sentence men to toil in barren soil, choking on the dust to survive until the day they died?

The Genesis answer: not the God *we* worship. Yahweh created paradise, and human beings created sin. God provided everything we need, but we incessantly wanted more, including the power to be as God and to worship ourselves. God gave us companionship and the abundance of the natural order, but we chose to lust after what is unattainable and thus destroy the shameless bliss that came before we knew we were naked.

As a myth, the story of Adam and Eve and their expulsion from the garden is profound. As a myth, it is not history, and yet it is "true"—contrary to the continued insistence that a myth is a lie. As the renowned mythology professor Joseph Campbell taught us, a myth is about a truth so large, so important and mysterious that it cannot be contained by mere facts. Myths do not just explain the meaning of life but help us to understand the experience of being alive. We are creatures who need symbols and stories to represent the stages of life. Across cultures and traditions, the myths we make are remarkably similar. They involve the hero's journey, temptation, testing, transformation, and return. Myths are frequently built around initiation ceremonies that move us from childhood to adult responsibilities. As such, the myth of Adam and Even and their expulsion from the garden is an initiation story on a grand scale.

A myth, Campbell says, "is the secret opening through which the inexhaustible energies of the cosmos pour into human manifestation."[4] The details of the myth are not *meant* to be taken literally. When they are, not only is the power of myth and metaphor weakened; bad theology can be the result.

Augustine knew this when he wrote about his struggle to interpret some Old Testament stories metaphorically, saying, "When I understood literally, I was slain spiritually."[5] Yet this rule apparently did not apply to the story of the Fall, proving that even bishops can practice selective literalism. Ironically, what never happened became the basis for the formulation of a doctrine about what always happens. Working from the consequences of fictional events involving fictional people, Augustine confused symbolic truth with historical truth to justify etiology as history and mythology as dogma.

To claim, as Augustine did, that we are permanently infected by Adam's sin and that this condition is incurable, save by profession of faith in the atoning sacrifice of the new Adam, Jesus Christ, is to declare that creation is inescapably bad, but selectively redeemable. Yet the biblical account of creation says something entirely different—that we are made in the image and likeness of God, expressed by the beautiful Latin phrase *imago Dei*. It says that we are born inescapably *good*, as part of a good creation, and yet we lose our way by making bad choices. We do so not because we are carriers of sin, but because we are deluded by ego, trapped by fear, and paralyzed by insecurity. We may make mistakes, but we are not a mistake. This truth lies slumbering within us, as Socrates understood, and must be mined by a teacher, not cancelled or covered over by a savior.

Although it was once widely believed that sin was passed down from generation to generation like red hair or left-handedness, new understanding of both human development and genetics has rendered this idea unbelievable to most people. Thus, the idea that people should be punished for a "crime" they did not commit is unethical and unacceptable.

A literal reading of the myth of Adam and Eve also makes it possible to pin the blame mostly on Eve and has thus helped to create centuries of bias against women. A popular bumper sticker reads simply, "EVE WAS FRAMED." But this is, once again, an example of the danger of reading the Bible literally. In the church, too many clergy have failed to teach their congregations what they have been taught. What, then, is the purpose of their seminary education? If they assume that people can't deal with concepts like sacred myth and etiology, then they deprive their flocks of the richness and wisdom of biblical stories that could ignite the imagination and open the eyes of the heart. To teach that the Bible is inerrant and infallible would appear to represent the most exalted relationship of the reader to the text, but it defies the nature of scripture itself. What is meant to convey reverence and spark a conversation with God becomes a spiritual straitjacket.

In the case of Adam and Eve, the deeper truth is that it never happened, but it is *always* happening. It never was, but still is. It is both primitive and postmodern. The Bible is a Metaphor made up of metaphors, and the point is not to organize a search party to find a garden that never existed or Noah's ark on a mountain in Turkey, so that we can "prove" that the Bible is true. Our calling is to graduate from a definition of truth that is too narrow and embrace the reading of scripture as sacred, normative poetry—not ancient journalism or objective history. This does not mean we stop "believing" the Bible. In this case, just think how timeless is the message of an archetypal woman duping a clueless, archetypal man and then passing the buck down to a talking snake!

The truth is, we all grow up and get kicked out of the garden, because we are all tempted by the very fruit we are warned not to eat. We are seldom satisfied with the life we have, always looking for a better garden than the one we live in. But treating the details of such a myth as if they were history and then expanding them into doctrines that seal the separation of humankind from both Creator and creation alike is the true definition of sin. Pronouncing the whole of humanity to be incurably sick and then claiming a monopoly on the cure limits the power of God, makes excuses for the inexcusable, and invites absolute power to corrupt absolutely.

The doctrine of original sin gives the church a permanent clientele in a salvation enterprise with no competition. You are born a hopeless sinner and sentenced to eternal damnation unless you "purchase" the only "product" that can save you. But there are no other choices. Recall the lines from Annie Dillard's *Pilgrim at Tinker Creek*, in which an Eskimo asks a priest, "If I did not know about God and sin, would I go to hell?" The priest responds, "No, not if you did not know." To which the Eskimo replies, "Then why did you tell me?"

THE DEADLY LEGACY OF DUALITY

If we can read the Bible as sacred myth, poetry, and pseudo-history, we can move beyond the questions that still preoccupy much of the church, shaped by a Western, rationalist perspective that came with the Enlightenment. What is true is not reducible to "what really happened" any more than "what really happened" is an adequate representation of the truth. Even so, we humans crave fixed, absolute categories, especially when it comes to religion. We are not just featherless bipeds. We are *binary* thinkers with on-off switches in the brain.

Dualism is deadly, however—whether in biblical studies, human relationships, or foreign policy. The tendency of human beings to see life as a simple choice between opposing and irreconcilable states is, at best, falsely comforting. At worst, it is apocalyptic. Perhaps we like things to be simple because real life is not. It is difficult, confusing, even terrifying. Although we speak of death as the great enemy, it may be despair that haunts us even more—the idea that life itself means nothing. Macbeth put it memorably: "[Life] is a tale / Told by an idiot, full of sound and fury, / Signifying nothing."[6]

This much we know. The more frightened we are, the less secure we feel. The more anxious we are about the world and our place in it, the more we seek simple answers to complex questions. Whether it is about sin and salvation, human sexuality, or the cosmic battle of good versus evil being waged for our souls, we are addicted to the easy answer. Ambiguity is frightening, and "situation ethics" (as if there is any other kind) smacks of moral relativism. It is no wonder that in times of fear, we follow leaders who talk tough and appeal to nostalgia. When thinking, deciding, and doing become too painful, we surrender our lives to authority figures who have all the answers.

For the same reason, we want the Bible to give us simple answers, not richly textured metaphors, songs, poetry, prayers, dreams, and maddening parables—but marching orders. We turn biblical symbols into theological propositions and dazzling metaphors into dreary ecclesiastical mechanisms. Biblical wisdom is replaced by doctrinal armor. Hearts "strangely warmed" become bony fingers writing new commandments. Bethlehem is now ablaze with floodlights, and the garden of Gethsemane is a tourist trap. Or, as Kierkegaard put it, "Something true when whispered may become false when shouted."

We want our government to keep us safe by any means, because no matter how advanced we think we are, we are still profoundly ethnocentric, expecting others to become more like us to prove that they have made "progress." The term "axis of evil" (and its unstated corollary, "axis of good") is such a rich example of our addiction to dualism as to raise suspicion that a sophist made it up, instead of just a presidential speechwriter. Here is dualism immortalized in the State of the Union speech as a prelude to war. It reminds us that the way we use language is a moral issue, and life is linguistically constituted. "Be careful how you describe the world," said one physicist. "It is that way."[7]

Just as we want a blue pill to make us thin and a red one to make us happy, we want church doctrine to clear up the Mystery, not deepen it. We want the process of enlightenment to be translated into "strategies for success," because faith as a transaction is simple, while faith as *transformation* is both complicated and costly. We want to fortify the self, not shatter the illusions by which it lives. We want to put on the "whole armor of God" and do battle with the infidels, not stretch ourselves out across the pain of the world as if nailed to a cross.

In trying to explain this swirling chaos that is life, the church has unwittingly participated in creating what might be called, for lack of a better term, "terminal false dichotomies" or "radical either/or-ness." Whether it is the battle for the Bible (Do you believe it or not?), the existence of evil (Do you believe in Satan or not?), or the reason we sin (Do you believe in original sin or not?), it's all or nothing. One is lost or found. One is fallen or saved. One must "turn or burn."

The appeal of such simple choices is enormous, but so are its consequences. We are absolved from doing serious Bible study, which is hard work; absolved from considering that the enemy may be more like us than different from us; and absolved from caring for the earth itself and all living things because we have falsely interpreted the word "subdue" in our creation myth to mean us (humans) against them (the forces of nature). Our planetary house is now groaning from abuse, and this is a rallying cry that could unite the whole church across all its divisions. As theologian Matthew Fox put it prophetically thirty years ago, Mother Earth is dying.[8]

"Are you with us or with the terrorists?" This question divides the world like a machete dropped on a watermelon. Original sin cuts the same way. It tells us that we are both helpless when it comes to our condition and undeserving when it comes to our cure. Life is a battle to win or lose, not a journey toward wisdom. Original sin says that each of us is really born in the enemy camp, and the battle for our souls began with our first breath. We cannot help what we are, but to be "saved" from this inherited doom will require someone *else's* sacrifice. Thus every human is in a state of total spiritual dependence. We are lost at birth, with only one hope of being found, so "salvation" becomes a closed system, a cosmic bargain initiated to save the helpless from being hopeless.

The language of the church reinforces guilt and shame by reminding us constantly that we are sinners. A common Protestant confession is

> We poor sinners confess unto thee, that we are by nature sinful and unclean, and that we have sinned against thee by thought, word, and deed. Therefore we flee for refuge to thine infinite mercy, seeking and imploring thy grace, for the sake of our Lord Jesus Christ.

Although we know that confession is good for the soul and that pretending we do not sin is a form of delusion, the making of *inherited* sin into a self-loathing form of theological entrapment is one of the saddest legacies of the church. It has turned Christianity into a series of propositions that substitute for the life of faith and turned worshipers into those who "recite and receive." Take a look at much of the church today, and you will come to a sad but inevitable conclusion. Faith for millions really is about *believing stuff in order to get stuff.*

Many Catholics must still make a confession first in order to receive the Eucharist. What is biblical about this? For the rest of us, sin is offered as the reason for the incarnation. Because we are born in sin, Jesus had to be born as God in the flesh and sent to die, according to the plan and purpose of that same God, in order that our sins might be forgiven. We continue to sing about, pray about, and confess to believing in having been "washed in the blood of the Lamb," even though the assumed premise of the blood atonement is something most people no longer believe—at least outside of the church. Why, then, do we pretend to believe it when we are sitting in a pew?

The closed loop of original sin and exclusive salvation through Jesus (born bad/only way out) is a deadly false dichotomy. It suggests that sin is not just pervasive but inevitable, and that salvation is not a rebirth but a rescue. What we cannot save ourselves from, the church will save us from, and all we have to do is confess to believing in a set of postbiblical propositions that were not finalized until the early Middle Ages. Offering the only hope for the hopeless certainly solidified the power of the church, but it defies a much older tradition of creation spirituality. That tradition is older than the Hebrew poets who wrote the biblical accounts of creation and the wisdom literature of Proverbs and the Prophets, older than patriarchs and other "royal persons," older than the ministry of Jesus with its focus on compassion or Paul's talk of a "new creation" and the cosmic Christ motifs of Colossians, Ephesians, Galatians, and Philippians.

Salvation meant originally not that we are saved *from,* but that we are saved *to.* Having "the same mind in you that was in Christ Jesus" (Phil. 2:5) is a new way of *being* in the world that recognizes our kinship to Jesus as our teacher, not our indebtedness to him as a savior. The English word for "salvation" comes from the root word "salve," which is a healing ointment. Salvation originally meant to be healed of what was wounding us. In the New Testament, salvation is about transformation in this life, not a change of destination in the next.

It is one thing to say that creation is flawed, but quite another to say that we are a mutant strain, a defective product, a bad seed. In so doing the church has sanctified helplessness, made all humanity victims, and built an inherited lack of responsibility into every waking moment. "The devil made me do it" is part of the vernacular of original sin. So are songs about wretchedness, loathsomeness, and humans as lowly worms. So are prayers urging that a deeply disappointed Father God "take pity" on and "show mercy" toward children who are a chronic disappointment. What else can we be? We were born to disappoint!

The pervasiveness of sin should not be confused with the inevitability of sin. The answer to the age-old question of whether people can change is yes, they can—but not because they confess to believing in theological propositions. Rather, change occurs when people are born again to their own goodness. It may take a convulsive event, since suffering often brings with it a redemptive clarity, but the verdict of all the saints and mystics is clear: we are not rotten to the core but made in the image of God.

Whenever someone says that real change is impossible, the late George Wallace comes to mind. Former governor of Alabama and once the embodiment of resistance to the civil rights movement, he espoused a holy trinity full of hate: "I draw the line in the dust and toss the gauntlet before the feet of tyranny, and I say, segregation now, segregation tomorrow, segregation forever." He ran for president in 1972 and won nearly ten million votes in a campaign in which he vilified blacks, students, and people who called for an end to the war in Vietnam. That campaign ended in a parking lot when Arthur Bremer tried to assassinate him. The bullets paralyzed him from the waist down, and he spent the rest of his life in a wheelchair.

He also realized that he had been wrong about race all along and returned to public life as an integrationist. Earlier he had literally tried to block the schoolhouse door; he turned state troopers with dogs, whips, and tear gas loose on peaceful black demonstrators in a scene that shocked the nation and helped galvanize passage of the Voting Rights Act. But in his later days, he locked arms with the same human beings he had once vilified and learned to sing "We Shall Overcome."

In the end, it is a very strange business indeed, this born-bad-but-saved-by-Jesus treadmill. We are said to be without a choice with regard to our condition, but free to choose our only means to salvation. This choice is not a choice to be good (which we obviously cannot be if we were born "bad"), but a choice to believe something about Jesus that renders us, not changed, but forgiven. After professing to believe this, we go on choosing to sin, of course, but are now absolved by the choice we have made! If this sounds like a convoluted version of free will, just remember that this comes courtesy of the same institution that only recently apologized to Galileo for being right about the solar system and still practices exorcism.

Original sin is a theology of entrapment, not liberation; it is a "recent" theological exception, not the rule; it is an interruption, a detour, an artificial formula, not the timeless flow of creation spirituality that preceded it and will succeed it. Long before the church created a sickness for which it alone had the cure, mystics, poets, and wise ones all agreed on this: we are not apart from nature, and nature is not our enemy. We are part of an insurgency of life whose arc is long and whose future is mysterious. We did not drop from the sky to do battle with our fallen nature; rather, we have crawled up out of the sea to work the garden, to protect our young, and to contemplate the gifts and obligations of higher consciousness. What does it mean to be human, to ask questions, to solve problems, to make art, and ultimately to discover the most sublime gift of all—love?

ON BEING WORTHY, NOT WORTHLESS

A preacher tells the story of a certain student, in middle school, in what used to be called "homeroom." It was the first day of class—a tender, frightening moment when adolescents sit in awkward proximity to other adolescents and wonder why they can't think of a single thing to say that doesn't sound stupid.

Class begins with the reading of the roll, a seminal moment when individual identities are established by a godlike voice that speaks them into existence. Out of the teacher's mouth comes the sacrament of sound, joining names and faces for better or for worse. All a good teacher has to do when she reads an unusual name is say, "I like that." All she has to do, if the student is plain or shy, is to see something beautiful and name it.

This particular teacher, however, knew her subject, but little else. When she arrived at the name of one particular student and called it out, the young woman responded, "Here!" The teacher stopped, peered over her glasses, and said to the young woman, "Is so-and-so your father?"

"Yes, ma'am."

"And is so-and-so your uncle?"

"Yes, ma'am."

"Well, I sure hope you're not like them."

You see, the father and his brother had been arrested recently on drug charges, and both were now serving time in prison. The class fell silent. The girl said nothing. And for some reason, for some inexplicable reason, no one called the police to have the teacher arrested. They should have, for if this is not child abuse, then what is? "Sticks and stones can break your bones, but words can never hurt you." That's cute, but there's one small problem. It's not true.

Over a lifetime of ministry, I have come to believe one thing without reservation: most of the dysfunctional things we do are *compensatory*. Whether we realize it or not, we are always trying to prove something to someone. As a child we try to please our parents (some adult children never outgrow this). In our intimate relationships we try to prove that we are worthy of being loved by a partner, so at first, instead of being authentic, we try to appear irresistible. Because the act cannot be sustained, eventually we appear to be fraudulent.

At work we struggle to please the boss, to be singled out as the employee of the month, or to be voted the man or woman most likely to succeed. In other words, our worthiness is dependent on what others think of us, and we depend on external recognition to measure internal value. If we are never certain of our own inherent goodness, then we will never be satisfied with the verdict rendered by others, no matter how frequent or exalted. Rabbi Harold Kushner wrote a book once entitled *How Good Do We Have to Be?* The answer seems to be: we are never good enough.

In a capitalist society, where money measures the value of almost everything, no one ever thinks that enough is enough. In a society that elevates competition to the level of a sacred spectacle, we are always being reminded that we fall short of someone else's prowess and expertise. In a celebrity culture, most of us are peons. In an entertainment culture, most of us are spectators. In a consumer culture, we are all just "three easy payments" away from rock-hard abs, easy salad preparation, or a lucrative career in real estate.

Meanwhile, we wake up feeling unworthy; we go to bed feeling unworthy; and on Sunday morning, if we go to church, the preacher will render a similar judgment! So will the liturgy, the prayers, and many of the hymns. When we start from the doctrine of original sin, "one is old before coming into the world," as Matthew Fox put it. The late psychologist Eric Fromm once wrote, "Those whose hope is weak settle for comfort or for violence."

Imagine what might happen to the church in our time if we took seriously the praise of the Psalmist, who locates us, even in our brokenness, "just a little lower than the angels" (8:5), or the words of the Ephesians letter that we are "God's masterpiece" (2:10, NLT). What shape would ministry take if we "accepted the fact that we are accepted," to quote philosopher and theologian Paul Tillich? What if we truly believed that we had nothing, ultimately, to prove to anyone? What if faith could become again what it once was, a radical *trust* in God and the essential goodness of creation? Would this not be the ultimate form of liberation? Isn't the end of all striving the true definition of freedom?

Since the word "religion" itself (from the Latin *religare*) means to "bind us back" to our source, the first question we must ask is not about our destination but about our origin. Where did we come from? Why is there anything? Does creation have intentionality, or is it a grand but fantastic accident? Why is there matter, and does it matter? Or, as Albert Einstein put it, is the universe a friendly place or not?

These are more than just basic philosophical questions. They force us back to a mysticism largely lost in the Western world. Since the Enlightenment, we have gotten very good at explaining things, even as Newton's clockwork universe is being challenged by chaos theory and quantum mechanics. Yet we seem reluctant to move beyond cause-and-effect models to embrace reverence. We weigh and measure; we observe and analyze; we collect data and hypothesize. Now if we could only remember how to be astonished.

When Apollo astronauts snapped the most important photograph ever taken, on December 24, 1968, of the earth rising over the moon, the modern environmental movement was born. But it was more than just a photograph. It was also a call to a new cosmology. No wonder it inspired the poet Archibald MacLeish to write these words: "To see the earth as it truly is, small and blue in that eternal silence where it floats, is to see riders on the earth together, brothers on that bright loveliness in the eternal cold—brothers who know now they are truly brothers."[9]

Rabbi Abraham Heschel calls it "radical amazement,"[10] and Matthew Fox calls it "deep ecumenism flowing from a morality of reverence for all creation."[11] But whatever you call it, creation-centered spirituality represents a return to our religious roots without the sacrifice of either the intellect or the legitimate place of reason and science in the modern world. We need this move now, more than ever before, because time is running out—for the earth and for the church. Fox says, "The universe itself, blessed and graced, is the proper starting point for spirituality. Original blessing is prior to any sin, original or less than original."[12]

The endless arguments over evolution versus creationism are a symptom of this sickness. Evolution attempts to tell us *how,* but not *why* or *wherefore.* Science makes no presumptions with regard to theology, and theology should make none with regard to science. The two should be partners in pushing back the frontiers of an enchanted universe. Believing in evolution and believing in God are not mutually exclusive, but neither is it intellectually honest to pretend that a literal interpretation of Genesis should be passed off as science. To do so mocks both science and the poetic power of Genesis.

It is often assumed that faith and science are enemies, but they are not. The enemy of both is fundamentalism, which is driven by two forces: fear of women and the need to feel chosen. In both cases, men fear most *not* being chosen—either by women or by God. Nature is seen not as a parent, but as an adversary. To be victorious over nature or over a woman, men become warriors, and the outcome is a zero-sum game. Either we win, or nature destroys us. Either the woman chooses us, or she becomes the property of another warrior.

In the church, the language of war persists in the language of salvation, and ours is an ecclesiology of conflict. We are at war with our sinful nature, at war with the enemies of God, at war with the principalities and powers that seduce us with delusions of grandeur. Someone wins only if someone else loses. Someone is right only if someone else is wrong. Someone is saved only if someone else is lost.

Ours is a theology of entitlement, not communion. Ours is a culture of irresponsibility, not responsibility. Ours is a strategy for victory, not a journey toward wisdom. If we continue to believe that we did not come up out of the earth, but were dropped from the sky, then Jesus will continue to be understood likewise as an invader—a harpoon shot from God's bow to reel in the perishing. He will be not a teacher but an elevator operator. He will bring us not wisdom but self-aggrandizement. He will not give us an assignment but deliver a certificate.

Faith as a *corrective,* as a means of slaying the insatiable appetite of the self, has become a form of neutral energy in our time. Whatever it is we are up to, we simply add Jesus to our tank, like STP, to get wherever we are going faster and with fewer knocks. But no one seems willing to ask: *Where are we going?* Our presses turn out countless books with the word "soul" in the title, but as integral theorist Ken Wilber puts it, what this really means is the "ego in drag." What we are doing in the name of "spirituality" or "care of the soul," he writes, "means nothing more than focusing intensely on your ardently separate self . . . just as 'Heart' has come to mean any sincere sentiment of the self-contraction."[13]

Christianity is now so fundamentally associated with the formula of fall and redemption, so focused on beliefs *about* Jesus instead of invitations to *follow* Jesus, that a new Reformation is needed. It will deal not with matters of doctrine and church order but with a recovery of the concept of transformation through the imitative wisdom of discipleship. It will reject once and for all the illusion that knowledge alone is redemptive and seek to restore the ancient truth that creation is blessed, not fallen. Augustine said, "The soul makes war with the body," but Meister Eckhart said, "The soul loves the body."

When Martin Luther sparked the original Protestant Reformation by nailing to the door of the Wittenberg church in 1517 a list of ninety-five grievances he wished to debate, he questioned not the premodern cosmology in which the church was born but the inconsistencies and corruption of the institution. The new Reformation will be about the very life and death of Christianity itself. We must first recover the original message and then be willing to interpret it for a new age. It will be a return to faith as *praxis,* grounded in trust, not intellectual assent, grounded in doctrine. Christianity was once, and must be again, about following Jesus, not about worshiping Christ.

SIX

CHRISTIANITY AS COMPASSION, NOT CONDEMNATION

Professors of faith are great prattlers and talkers and disputers but do little of anything that bespeaks love to the poor or self-denial in outer things. Some people think religion is made up of words, a very wide mistake.

—*John Bunyan, in* Pilgrim's Progress

For a double PK, John Bunyan's words hit close to home. As a preacher I stand in the pulpit every Sunday to talk about the good. As a professor of rhetoric in the philosophy department at Oklahoma City University, I talk to my students about how to talk about the good. As an author, I write books full of words about the good for good people to read and talk about. Sometimes I even talk to myself about talking to myself!

I *am* one of those "professors of faith," and my life is awash in words—words about the Word, words about the words used to express the Word, and words about the limitations of words. My hypereducated European tribe loves to *metacommunicate* (talk about talking), and sometimes we even engage in the ultimate linguistic nonsense: we talk about the value of silence.

The danger here is both obvious and insidious. As People of the Book, we are so oriented toward the value of expression that we confuse concept with capacity. Søren Kierkegaard spent the whole of his eccentric life trying to shatter this illusion—reminding us through irony, parable, and prose that talking about the good, the beautiful, and the true is not the same thing as being good, creating beauty, or living truthfully. My favorite Kierkegaard parable alludes to this danger. It is called "The Man Who Walked Backwards":

> When a man turns his back upon someone and walks away, it is so easy to see that he walks away, but when a man hits upon a method of turning his face towards the one he is walking away from, hits upon a method of walking backwards while with appearance and glance and salutations he greets the person, giving assurances again and again that he is coming immediately, or incessantly saying, "Here I am"—although he gets farther and farther away by walking backwards—then it is not so easy to become aware. And so it is with the one who, rich with good intentions and quick to promise, retreats backwards farther and farther from the good. . . . As a drunkard constantly requires stronger and stronger stimulation—in order to become intoxicated, likewise the one who has fallen into intentions and promises constantly requires more and more stimulation—in order to walk backward.[1]

Kierkegaard was particularly hard on clergy, who agree to be on display every week as an example of what the gospel actually *does* to a person. We are paid to talk about virtue all the time, but a kind of "virtual virtuosity" sets in. "The performance becomes the product. We must be a caring person, we think to ourselves—after all, we are always recommending it. We must be sensitive, patient and kind, because we just finished a sermon series on all three, and lots of people have requested copies."[2]

It is sobering to remember that one does not become gracious by reading a good book on grace. What's more, the incarnation itself argues against it, since by definition our claim is that theory and praxis were brought together in the pure compassion of one who wrote nothing down. Our faith is "commissional," not rhetorical. We are commanded to "go and *do* likewise," not to go and *talk* likewise. Disciples are empowered to heal and forgive sins, not to apply for endowed chairs or publish and debate papers on the Q gospel—important as these may be. The life of the mind is not the problem, unless of course our life begins and ends there. Words can be a form of action, but they can also be a substitute for action. According to Luke, the first sermon of Jesus wasn't a problem as long as it didn't get personal: "All spoke well of him and were amazed at the gracious words that came from his mouth" (4:22). Then he dared to do what precious few preachers are willing to do. He told an audience of locals who wanted to pat this fine young man on the head, like a member of the youth group, that they were hypocrites. Words are not enough when people are starving and lepers are ignored. What followed, according to Luke, was an attempted assassination (4:29).

Yet even this explanation is a risky exercise, since it is primarily an intellectual activity mediated to the reader through words. Most thoughtful people would agree that we need to do more than just "talk the talk," and yet here we are talking about it! Ministers can joke that after their first sermon no one tried to kill them—because they were all asleep. Of course Christianity is about compassion, not about theories of compassion. Of course we should be taking action to save a dying world, not just talking about how awful it is that the world is dying.

What has changed dramatically in our time, however, is that we are quite obviously running out of time. We can no longer afford the luxury of a church that is bent over its writing desk but cannot find its boots and gloves. We cannot just go on decrying the hypocrisies of our time, like sheep getting together at annual meetings to pass resolutions against the wolves. No matter how often we say "Whereas" and "Therefore," the world is changed not by those who condemn but by those who act.

The disciples are sent out to heal the sick, not to collect data and issue a report on the long-term effects of too many sheep without a shepherd. "The harvest is plentiful, but the laborers are few," says Jesus as he first defines their work and then names them (Matt. 9:35–38). Think about it. First there is a job description, and only then are there disciples. The assignment precedes the naming, followed by the "sending out." Their identity comes from their commission, and his compassion defines their compassion. This is not a teaching moment. Notice the conspicuous absence of theology in Matthew's description of the mission of the Twelve:

> As you go, proclaim the good news. . . . Cure the sick, raise the dead, cleanse the lepers, cast out demons. You received without payment; give without payment. Take no gold, or silver, or copper in your belts, no bag for your journey, or two tunics, or sandals, or a staff; for laborers deserve their food. Whatever town or village you enter, find out who in it is worthy, and stay there until you leave. As you enter the house, greet it. If the house is worthy, let your peace come upon it; but if it is not worthy, let your peace return to you. If anyone will not welcome you or listen to your words, shake off the dust from your feet as you leave that house or town. (10:7–14)

When I was a kid growing up, the message "Jesus is the Answer" was ubiquitous—painted on barns, outcroppings of rock, or as the final installment of a Burma Shave sign. The message, however, is distinctly unbiblical. The message should be "Jesus is the Assignment."

Considering our current obsession with what my boyhood church called "sound" theology (correct theology, as opposed to

"unsound," or incorrect, theology), I was led to believe that the
Bible was a kind of encyclopedia of theological propositions. It
was somewhat shocking to discover how conspicuously absent
are theological systems in the earliest strands of the gospel.
Mostly illiterate, uneducated peasant laborers are recruited and
sent out to practice spiritual healing without a license. They
are told that in the *practice* of such healing and in the radical
freedom they will experience by moving unencumbered from
house to house, giving freely and taking nothing, the windows
of heaven will open. But let's be honest. What would you do if
such a motley crew showed up on your doorstep?

Sadly, to worship Christ in our time is to believe that the
healing was made possible by the supernatural quality of the
healer. Following Jesus in our time would only require that
you believe in the power of love to heal a broken world. What's
more, the tone of much preaching today is not invitational, but
condemnatory. It lashes out rather than binding up. "I have
condemned, therefore I am" is not the maxim of the Galilean
sage. Neither is "Be it resolved the world is a mess." Condemnation feels good, and it is now a staple of religion, politics, and
the media (both left and right), but it changes nothing. Compassion, on the other hand, changes everything.

The gap between rich and poor is widening. Food riots are
increasing around the world. Polls show that young people view
organized religion with suspicion, even contempt, but have a
compelling interest in the ways of Jesus. High-profile fundamentalists have exploited our growing fears of living with less
or reaping the whirlwind of terrorism, while high-profile liberals
have exploited our hatred of fundamentalists. TV preachers on
the right tell us to get saved and then wait for the rapture, while
change agents on the left mock the sea of abysmal ignorance in
which we are drowning and fund lifeboats for the chosen.

In Oklahoma, the more overtly "Christian" politicians claim
to be, the more likely they are to pass mean-spirited legislation,

especially with regard to our treatment of the stranger. Anti-immigrant and English-only fever is running high, all in the name of Jesus. Among the more progressive crowd, a fatal flaw continues to paralyze the work of those who believe that, in the end, logic and eloquence will usher in the reign of God or "honking for peace" will end the war. I have grown equally weary of prosperity gospel preachers and Gucci hippies, for each group is trying to have its ideological cake and eat it too.

The Chamber of Commerce crowd pretends to back the rule of law when it comes to undocumented "aliens"—only to discover that there is no one left to clean our houses, manicure the broad lawns of the narrow-minded, or repair the roads down which we drive our gas-guzzlers behind the tinted windows of oblivion. Meanwhile, the peace and justice crowd does most of its work online, sending indignant but soulless petitions to indifferent politicians and then retreating into walled neighborhoods to gorge themselves on the very luxuries that are the real spoils of war.

If the church has converted the subversive wisdom of Jesus into the neutral energy of the Christ (blessing whatever it is we are up to), it is because we have lost the essential quality of Christianity as a *way of life*. The healer is now the dealer, and the assignment of faith has been replaced by a certificate of salvation. We have no choice now but to attempt our own ecclesiastical "back to the future" move, stepping over Constantine as if the centuries were sidewalk squares in a game of reverse "Mother May I." Before we vote to move another church to the distant suburbs or build a new Family Life Center instead of feeding the homeless, we should slip into the basement of the early church and take a look around.

It did not take long for the men who served others to become the bishops whom others served. Entitlement is the scourge of this and every age, and men of God still recline at the feast of power like Dives, belching their way through a meal to which

Lazarus is not invited. Orthodoxy's front door is gilded, but the rusty back door of the early church remains ajar—the one leading to the kitchen behind the creedal looking glass. There sits Jesus, cross-legged, amid the steam and misery of the world. He has not moved. He has no new marketing plan or quarterly mission emphasis. He is not a "new hermeneutic" or a cognitive physician who makes house calls with a bag full of answers to life's toughest questions. He is a movable feast, complete with bony knees and a matted beard. His message is a nonjudgmental presence. Without saying a word, the crowd gets it: we all matter; no exceptions.

TO FEEL WITH, NOT SORRY FOR

In many American churches, Jesus still comes "as one unknown"—or perhaps as one so well known as to be unrecognizable. He was penniless and itinerant, yet his gospel is now attached to some of the richest and most powerful people on earth, and the good news is really bad news for the poor. Captives are not released; they are warehoused. The blind do not see; rather, the sighted wear blinders. The oppressed are not liberated; they have become the new scapegoats. Sermons are no longer dangerous; they are simply adapted to the appetites and anxieties of the audience. Conservatives rail against sins of the flesh, as if to exorcise their own demons, and liberals baptize political correctness at the expense of honesty.

One crowd is reminded that some out there are sicker than they are, while the other is seduced into thinking that the problem is not enough thinking. Each, in its own way, is being called out of the wilderness of freedom and back to the dark but seductive slavery of an Egypt to which we cannot return. *The peddling of fear in any form as incentive to faith remains the most egregious sin that can be committed in the name of Jesus.* It feels very good to name the enemy and thank God that you are not like "those people." But if Christianity is to survive, someone needs to stand up in the middle of one of these hapless sermons and quote the comic-strip character Pogo: "We have met the enemy, and he is us."

From twenty-four-hour cable news stations to pulpits that duel over "much ado about nothing," everyone has climbed on the condemnation bandwagon. We enjoy being right so much that we have forgotten just how little this has to do with being a follower of Jesus. In our time, the land is full of culture warriors and their indignant disciples. What we lack are statesmen and -women. What we hunger after is kindness, patience, and an antidote to ego, instead of its sanctification. Worshiping Christ keeps us locked into theological battles over who is right and who is wrong. But following the example of Jesus liberates us to imitate rather than judge. What's more, the means to measure such imitation is utterly simple. The ministry of Jesus was, and is, and will always be about *compassion*—pure, unbridled, reckless compassion.

Indeed, when we choose a muscular form of locker-room Christianity, we are rejecting Jesus in favor of John the Baptist. But if we turn the gospel into an argument, no matter how elevated, we are the equivalent of those Pharisees who "tithe mint and rue and herbs of all kinds, and neglect justice and the love of God" (Luke 11:42). Perhaps this is the hardest lesson of the faith, next to forgiveness: "Do not judge, and you will not be judged; do not condemn, and you will not be condemned" (6:37).

In the earliest strands of the Christian tradition, followers of Jesus moved decisively away from God as apocalyptic judge and practiced instead a gospel of present healing. When Jesus called out demons and lifted curses from the afflicted peasants before him, he did so for one reason: he was filled with compassion. He was not trying to follow the law (indeed, he broke it by healing on the Sabbath), get elected to office, or establish a rogue medical practice outside the jurisdiction of the Temple.

He did it to try to relieve suffering. He did it to restore broken human beings to wholeness. He did it to help those bent over by their own feelings of worthlessness to stand up. There were apparently no preconditions, no theological requirements; not even a form of proper Jewish I.D. was required. Gentiles were welcome, female and male, slave and free, rich and poor. The consequences of such radical hospitality were as unacceptable in the first century as they would be in this one. True equality terrifies those who depend on hierarchy to run the empire.

One can only wonder what caused Jesus of Nazareth to become a follower of John and then get in line with all those other sinners to be baptized. According to Luke, he's not even at the front of the line (3:21), and undoubtedly the dove and the voice are descriptive fictions of the faith, like the virgin birth and the twelve-year-old genius in the Temple. But perhaps it was the execution of John without apocalyptic consummation that gave Jesus the sign he was looking for, and a new voice. Perhaps the storm god from Sinai, the lawgiver and judge, was not the last word. Perhaps faith is not a transaction at all, but a *covenant* of compassion with only one requirement—it obligates the recipient to become a "healed healer" taking the reign of God to others.

As for Jesus, he was not the kingdom's patron, and the disciples were not its brokers. The benefits of the reign of God would be freely given to anyone. The only debt owed for hospitality and healing would be for the clients of the kingdom to turn around and "heal likewise" in the name of the open table and a God of pure compassion. The movement of ministry for Jesus was threefold: question, action, and assignment. What do you want me to do for you? Go; your faith has made you well. Now "pay it forward."

What did this compassion look like? One scholar described Jesus as looking like a beggar, "yet his eyes lack the proper cringe, his voice the proper whine, his walk the proper shuffle.

He speaks about the rule of God and [the peasants] listen as much from curiosity as anything else. They know all about rule and power, about kingdom and empire, but they know it in terms of tax and debt, malnutrition and sickness, agrarian oppression and demonic possession."[3] Even so, they had heard would-be messiahs before, and poverty has a way of turning one into a cynic. "What, they really want to know, can this Kingdom of God do for a lame child, a blind parent, a demented soul screaming its tortured isolation among the graves that mark the village fringes?"[4]

One of the earliest and probably most authentic utterances of Jesus is: "Be compassionate as God is compassionate" (Luke 6:36). This is his *imitatio Dei,* the way to imitate God. Unfortunately, Matthew uses the word "perfect" (which makes faith an impossible ideal; 5:48), and in many English translations the word is "merciful," which has a very different connotation. In Hebrew as well as Aramaic the word usually translated as "compassion" is the plural of a noun that in its singular form means "womb."[5] As a woman feels compassion for the child in her womb, so compassion (*passion,* from the Latin word meaning "to feel," and the prefix *com,* "with") is a quality of vicarious, even visceral, empathy. This happens at a level "beneath" the brain, in biblical terms, for a man in the bowels, for a woman in the womb—in other words, deep within.

The problem comes when the Hebrew term is translated as "mercy" or "merciful." More than just "lost in translation," something is altered. Mercy has connotations of pity, especially between people of unequal status, or a response to wrongdoing. A person "chooses" to show mercy (or feel pity) toward someone even though he or she has the right to act otherwise. There is an implied, if not an explicit, quality of condescension. The concept of a God who chooses to show mercy is very different from that of a God who is, "to coin a word that captures the flavor of the original Hebrew, 'wombish.'"[6]

One's view of God determines one's view of faith, and thus to say that God is compassionate is different from saying that God is merciful. A compassionate God is one who models compassion for us, which is not the same thing as a God who may or may not extend mercy to us for something we may or may not have done wrong. Indeed, much of the liturgical "pleading" that dominates prayers of confession, to "take pity on me and have mercy on me a sinner," is a manifestation of this crucial difference. This is faith as a bargain, struck between a worshiper who is weak and helpless and a God who has the power to show mercy or turn away. Thus when we pray, we are not moving toward a transcendent Mystery, drawing on an ocean of compassion, but entering into a kind of private divine small-claims court, hoping for a favorable verdict.

In what was metaphorically a move down from the sky god of primitive religion to what Paul Tillich would one day call the "Ground of Being," Jesus shifted the thinking of his disciples away from a God who is remote, angry, unapproachable, and judgmental—to a God with earthy and distinctly feminine characteristics. This is a God who births us, feels with us (not sorry for us), and is nurturing and caring and protective. Luke portrays Jesus as reversing all the normal metaphors of power and gives us, instead: "How often have I desired to gather your children together as a hen gathers her brood under her wings, and you were not willing" (13:34).

One can only wonder how the world would have been different if Constantine had painted a mother hen on the helmets of his soldiers, wings spread to protect a brood of helpless chicks, instead of the cross. How strange that a symbol of nonviolent resistance and redemption ends up becoming part of a military uniform or is worn around the necks of inquisitors. Today the cross is quite literally wrapped in the American flag, as if there were no contradictions between the world's only superpower and the symbol of God's power made perfect in weakness.

Writer and teacher Barbara Brown Taylor ponders the image of a mother hen with her customary eloquence:

> Given the number of animals available, it is curious that Jesus chooses a hen. Where is the biblical precedent for that? What about the mighty eagle of Exodus, or Hosea's stealthy leopard? What about the proud lion of Judah, mowing down his enemies with a roar? Compared to any of those, a mother hen does not inspire much confidence. No wonder some of the chicks decided to go with the fox.[7]

This unbridled compassion, which is never an abstraction, but always a way of *being* in the world, would later be spoken of in the New Testament as "love." Again there is something lost in translation, because the word "love," like the word "freedom," has a thousand meanings. Just as the word "faith" has morphed into a synonym for a set of beliefs, rather than a deep and abiding *trust,* the word "love" is elastic beyond belief. It runs the gamut from a tenacious and self-sacrificing covenant to the squeal of an adolescent in the mall. But compassion (again, "feeling with") is the authentic religious move—to move beyond the life of the self and into the pain and possibility of another life. It does not mean to take pity or catch a whiff of one's own superiority, but to take action. To care is to make a difference in someone's life.

Today we seem surrounded by Christians who are long on condemnation and short on compassion. They identify the enemy and then hunker down armed with blessed assurance and an arsenal of rhetorical invectives. In so doing they have reversed the parable of the Pharisee and the publican by forgetting which one went home justified. It was *not* the one who said, "God, I thank you that I am not like other people: thieves, rogues, adulterers, or even like this tax collector" (Luke 18:11).

When Paul says, "Remember those who are in prison, *as though* you were in prison with them; those who are being tortured, *as though* you yourselves were being tortured" (Heb. 13:3, emphasis added), he is appealing to the empathetic imagination. We are not just to feel sorry *for* those in need; we are to feel *with* those in need as if (and until) the burden has become our own. Just as the amputee has been known to feel a "phantom" pain in an arm or leg that no longer exists, so too are followers of Jesus to feel the pain of others as if it existed in their own bodies.

When Jesus makes it clear that the criteria for judgment will be ethical and not theological ("Truly I tell you, just as you *did* it to one of the least of these who are members of my family, you *did* it to me," Matt. 25:40), he is asking his disciples to "transpose" their love for him into every*body* they meet as if they are encountering him over and over again. This requires the most difficult, but most important single move in the life of faith— *to escape the prison of self*—the dungeon of self-absorption into which we are all born. Thus to be "born again" is not to repeat a mantra "accepting Jesus Christ as our personal Lord and Savior," but rather to accept the radical freedom that comes only when we are freed from the self. Then we can take the longest journey in the known universe—the trip from the head to the heart.

TOUCHING THE UNTOUCHABLES

One of the most helpful insights to come from recent historical Jesus research is a renewed emphasis on the difference between purity and compassion. Marcus Borg makes it clear that Jesus' attack on the purity system of his day was a self-conscious redefinition of "holiness." At the heart of the Jewish social world was the "holiness code" of Leviticus 17–26, which contained the purity laws and was grounded in the imperative: "Speak to all the congregation of the people of Israel and say to them: You shall be holy, for I the LORD your God am holy" (19:2).

For observant Jews, this meant that to imitate God was to be holy as God is holy. "Moreover, holiness was understood to mean 'separation from everything unclean.' Holiness thus meant the same as purity, and the passage was thus understood as, 'You [Israel] shall be pure as God is pure.' The ethos of purity produced a politics of purity—that is, a society structured around a purity system."[8]

Lest we think this is only an ancient phenomenon or peculiar to Judaism, consider that in every culture there are distinctions of class and race that form infinite varieties of the caste system, always distinguished by relative degrees of ritual purity or pollution and ordered by social status ranging from the royals to the untouchables. But in each case, a purity system establishes a social and cultural "map" that indicates "a place for everything, and everything in its place."

In first-century Palestine, the purity map showed a range from the inherently pure (priests and Levites), to "Israelites," to "converts," to "bastards," to those with damaged testicles and missing body parts, especially a penis.[9] Physical wholeness was thought to indicate purity, while those missing something—the maimed, the chronically ill, lepers, eunuchs, and so forth—were impure. One's behavior as well as one's economic status could render one more or less pure. The observant were more pure, the nonobservant, less so; the worst were "outcasts" like tax collectors and shepherds. No wonder Luke has these lowest of the low receive the birth announcement ahead of the *New York Times*.

Being rich was no guarantee of purity, but if you were poor, you were almost certainly considered impure. For one thing, following the labyrinth of purity laws was not possible (or affordable) if you lived on the edge of starvation. So the "righteous" were those who followed the purity system (or could manipulate it), and the "sinners" were those who did not (or could not). Psychologically, cleanliness has always been considered "next to godliness," and that is why sinners to this day, in Christian confessions, are referred to as "sinful and *unclean*." Isaiah says it plainly: "We have all become like one who is unclean, and all our righteous deeds are like a filthy cloth" (64:6).

It should come as no surprise that males were considered, in their "natural state," to be more "pure" than females (a fact that can only come as a kind of late-night comedic shock to women who actually live with men). The reason is both obvious and born of male fear and superstition: childbirth and menstruation rendered women "impure." They bled, but they did not die. In this state, they had to be impure, so they could not enter the Temple to worship God.

All Gentiles were considered impure by definition, and Palestine was occupied territory, controlled by the military force of a gentile oppressor. Add to the oldest and most vicious kind of hatred on earth (hatred of a foreign occupying army) the additional insult that such infidels were impure, and they thus quite literally contaminated every street corner on which they swaggered with the sword. When they raped a Jewish girl, the despoiling was complete, and the eternal question took on a dark urgency: "When will the messiah come?"

At the geographic and cultic center of Israel's purity map stood the Temple and the priesthood.[10] Not only were the priests required to adhere to the strictest purity laws; the income of the Temple itself was derived from charging taxes, or "tithes," on agricultural products, which were otherwise considered impure and unfit for purchase by the observant. Add to this kosher enterprise the business of selling sacrificial animals, and you've got a kind of one-stop purity market at the epicenter of the religious universe. Religion and commerce have always been mutually parasitic, of course, and separating them is perhaps the most dangerous part of being a prophet. But if God does indeed desire compassion and not holiness and sacrifice, as the Hebrew prophets tell us, then the purity system collapses, its coffers dry up, and its beneficiaries get angry—very angry.

This set the stage for a single confrontation that may have been sufficient cause to arrest and summarily execute a peasant revolutionary—the "cleansing of the Temple." But this should come as no surprise when we consider that attacks by Jesus on the purity system were numerous. His *imitatio Dei* ("Be compassionate as God is compassionate") could not be reconciled with the *imitatio Dei* of his day ("Be holy [pure] as God is holy [pure]"). These were not just two different ways of seeing God, but two entirely different social visions. It is no wonder they called him the "Great Offense."

In every age, religious ideas have been considered safe if they are private and personal, but dangerous if they are public and political. By "political" I don't mean party affiliation or policy, but political in the Greek sense of *polis,* or "the city." This broad definition of politics seems largely forgotten but needs to be recovered. Who has the power? How is it exercised? Who wins and who loses?

The existing politics of purity was not merely an individual matter, as in "different strokes for different folks." It was a sociopolitical paradigm, and any attack upon that system was an attack upon the religious homeland. His numerous and direct attacks upon that system go to the core of what was offensive and dangerous about Jesus. He saved his white-hot anger for the sin of religious hypocrisy. This fact alone should make every religious professional nervous. When he called Pharisees "unmarked graves" that people walk over "without realizing it" (Luke 11:44), the criticism can seem rather obscure. That is, until we remember that corpses (and thus graveyards) were sources of severe impurity. To call Pharisees, who wished to expand the purity system, "unmarked graves" is tantamount to declaring them to be the *source* of impurity. When Jesus claimed, "There is nothing outside a person that by going in can defile, but the things that come out are what defile" (Mark 7:15), he was attacking a central tenet of Mosaic dietary law.

Even the familiar beatitude "Blessed are the pure in heart" (Matt. 5:8) can be understood in the context of the politics of purity. Although we often interpret this to mean that we must be as clean on the inside as we are on the outside, it may well be an ironic statement about the one-sided obsession with purity in the time of Jesus. The dominant religious culture stresses outward purity and external boundaries, but Jesus reverses this emphasis and thus critiques it.

Perhaps the most stunning example, however, is the parable of the good Samaritan. It is often used to stress the importance of being a good neighbor, but the message is much more explosive. The two religious professionals in the story (the priest and the Levite) may have felt *obligated* to remain pure, and contact with the dead was a major source of impurity. The wounded one is described as "half dead," so noncontact was a religious requirement. The Samaritan, who was considered impure to begin with, is described as the one who acted "compassionately." The parable sets listeners up to expect a Jewish hero, only to have that expectation shattered.

In healing lepers, a woman who was hemorrhaging, and a man possessed with a "legion" of unclean spirits and living in a graveyard near a herd of unclean swine, Jesus doesn't just trespass on forbidden turf but seems to act deliberately and provocatively in the breaking of social and religious boundaries. He ate with sinners and outcasts, thus violating the sacred tenets of table fellowship. In some instances, the guests were said to "recline," marking such an occasion as a banquet or celebration, which only added to the offense. This "open commensality" was one of two unforgivable sins according to John Dominic Crossan. The other was "free healing," which undercut the established doctors of religion.[11]

The open table would later be symbolized by the sacramental meal known as the Eucharist or Holy Communion, in which the breaking down of all barriers that exclude and separate human beings from one another and from God is dramatized. Unfortunately, it has become such a sterile affair, with grape juice and snow-white dice-sized cubes of bread sans crust, that we forget what it stands for: a real meal with real outcasts! Try imagining Communion with homeless people, for starters.

At the time of Jesus, women, considered a source of impurity, were second-class citizens; they were the property of males, forbidden to learn Torah, testify in court, initiate divorce, go out in public unveiled or unaccompanied by a family member, or attend meals unless they were courtesans. The inclusion of so many women in the early Jesus movement is yet another stunning example of the radical vision that is the reign of God. Jesus defends women against attack from indignant males, is hosted by Mary and Martha, and is taught by a Syro-Phoenician (gentile) woman. Women were part of the itinerant group from the beginning, were disciples, and are remembered as present at his death. In the early church, women played a prominent leadership role.

As today's church is torn asunder over the issue of homosexuality and quotes passages from the Leviticus holiness code to support discrimination against gays, we would do well to visit again the most neglected New Testament text with direct relevance to this issue: the story of the Ethiopian eunuch in Acts 8. Desexed in order to serve the queen (or not serve her, as the case may be), eunuchs were obviously "defective" and thus unclean. But this multilingual eunuch sits in a chariot reading a nonnative text from the prophet Isaiah, and Philip approaches him to ask if he understands what he is reading. This decision to approach and "sit beside" the eunuch is telling, and Philip's question is poignant when it comes to the vital task of interpretation, as is the eunuch's answer ("How can I unless someone guides me?" v. 31). Philip expounds on the meaning of the life of Jesus, and the eunuch recognizes that the prophet speaks to him—even to *him,* who bears a stigmatizing mark and will never have children. At that moment, he asks the most urgent question of our time when it comes to all those who have been left out: "What is to prevent me from being baptized?" (v. 36). The answer is *nothing*. The joyous conclusion of the story says it all. He is baptized and goes on his way "rejoicing."

I'M COMPASSIONATE, AND I VOTE

In the struggling and often stagnant mainline church, there is one constant refrain from those who have abandoned the pews to take up fishing, reading the paper, or just sleeping in on Sunday morning: *don't mix religion and politics!* I cannot imagine any preacher today who tries to interpret the gospel in ways that are faithful and relevant who has not heard this warning more than once. I've heard it many times myself: "Reverend, just deal with 'spiritual' issues, and leave politics out of the pulpit."

At one level, I am sympathetic to this argument; on another, adamantly opposed. First of all, this complaint is almost always directed at a "liberal" preacher by a conservative layperson, even though the Christian Right wrote the book on how to mix religion and politics. A more honest version of the complaint might sound like this: *don't mix religion and politics in ways I don't agree with.* This really means, don't mix religion and politics in ways that threaten my way of life—which really means, in ways that might require me to surrender power, money, or status. Not all preaching can be a healing balm. If we are true to the gospel, some of it will disturb, disorient, and even distress listeners.

In the sectarian world of politics, we should not let the gospel be co-opted by any party or politician. It is patently absurd to refer to God as a Democrat or a Republican, but it is nothing short of a mortal sin to suggest that all political decisions are neutral with regard to the life of faith and the ways of compassion. As long as politics is broadly conceived as the exercise of power and its moral consequences, then the church should never separate the body, soul, and body politic. Furthermore, it would be an abdication of the prophetic role of ministry to stop caring about political decisions that affect the lives of the people we have been ordained to care about. There is a difference between partisan politics and the politics of compassion. When asked to explain when he would stop being political from the pulpit, William Sloane Coffin Jr. responded, "When politicians stop making decisions that affect the lives of those for whom Jesus died."

Having said this, I am keenly aware of the delicious feeling that preachers get, on the right and on the left, by condemning the "mad hypocrisies of our time." We all wish to be thought of as "prophetic," but the definition of a prophet is sometimes so slippery as to be nonexistent. Fundamentalists condemn individual misdeeds, especially sexual ones, to the almost complete exclusion of collective sin and systematic discrimination and oppression. Liberals condemn collective sin and systematic oppression to the almost complete exclusion of individual misdeeds, especially sexual ones.

The essential premise of conservative religion is that we change the world one saved soul at a time; more progressive traditions stress the responsibility of individuals to acquire wisdom through reason and use it to change the unjust structures of society. To justify and perpetuate our own identity, we often make a cartoon out of the "other" and stress the merits of our tradition while neglecting the truth that our "opponents" possess. The red-state, blue-state dichotomy is true of religion as well and even drives much of the political division.

Unless one believes in a universe of equally true assertions (if this is postmodern, then I'm not), then the universe must at least have some things in it that are more true than other things—and for the church, more or less faithful to the gospel. We don't get to make it up as we go. The reason that serious biblical scholarship is so important is that we can indeed "recover" a message that more accurately represents Jesus as a teacher of wisdom and discipleship as a process of imitation, not conversion. We can indeed glimpse the Jesus of history and not be blinded by the Christ of faith. We can indeed deconstruct the high Christology of the church that obscures the politics of compassion and then *reconstruct* a church based on rejecting the politics of salvation.

For example, if one believes that Jesus rejected a politics of purity for a politics of compassion, then antigay forces in the church today must be subject to the critique not of "liberals," but of the gospel itself. Until we have homosexuality all figured out, shouldn't we practice radical hospitality? As long as we see "through a glass darkly," isn't it wise to err on the side of inclusion and compassion, rather than condemnation? Perhaps we cannot even admit to what is most difficult about this issue— that it is not what gays *are,* but what they *do* that is repulsive to so many. Does it not strike many heterosexuals (and perhaps some who do not live comfortably inside their own sexual skin) as "unnatural" and therefore impure?

To find scriptural support for what strikes them as "dirty," some cite the very holiness passages that their Lord later challenges. Under his imperative of radical hospitality, surely we can assume that even Paul would widen the circle today, saying, "There is no longer Jew or Greek, there is no longer slave or free, there is no longer male and female, *there is no longer gay or straight;* for all of you are one in Christ Jesus" (Gal. 3:28, amended).

If it is true that Jesus lifted up women in obvious and extraordinary ways, then the continued second-class citizenship of women in the church comes under the judgment of the gospel, not just Protestant reformers or feminists. If Jesus invited those on the margins of society to take the best seats at the banquet of the kingdom, then what has the church to say about a culture that continues to reward narrow, stylized versions of beauty, while creating a "reality" entertainment subculture that thrives on humiliation?

The question for the church of the future is not, "Have I provided dogmatic information sufficient for salvation?" but rather, "Have I shown compassion to those who need it and the love of God to those denied it?" In all honesty, we still operate by purity codes, and this is why we could not discuss AIDS for years after the outbreak of the disease, at the cost of thousands of lives. The most powerful, but unarticulated, objections to homosexuality are grounded in the idea that some things don't "belong together." Our halting response to the implosion of Africa is tied up in the ancient prejudice against "unclean" natives.

When the church preaches prosperity theology and gives divine aid and comfort to a society already paralyzed by rampant individualism, what word has the "body of Christ" to offer that brings hope to a world that desperately needs to value community again and restore the quaint but essential early American concept of *covenant*? If Jesus was indeed a "free healer," then how can anyone say that all health-care options are equally "Christian"? If the healthy will not pay to help the sick, just as the strong refuse to help the weak, then what are we saying about being our brother's or sister's keeper?

A church entirely devoid of political engagement is a living contradiction. Churches are political even when they refuse to act politically, because silence is a form of complicity and thus an endorsement of the status quo. The church is political the moment that it determines that one way of treating human beings is more compassionate than another way and then sets out to do the right thing. The church is political because it is a "city-state" whose citizens are under very strange and countercultural orders to live as resident aliens in a world gone berserk. When Britney Spears's navel gets more media coverage than millions of uninsured children, the church is not called upon to serve tea and wring its hands. It is called upon to speak truth to power.

It was Martin Luther King Jr. who recognized the difference between comforting the poor and confronting the people and systems that cause poverty. Of course we should be good Samaritans, but we should also consider doing something to make the road to Jericho less dangerous for everyone. In the end, Dr. King knew that "you cannot set the captive free if you are not willing to confront those who hold the keys. Without confrontation compassion becomes merely commiseration, fruitless and sentimental."[12]

SEVEN

DISCIPLESHIP AS OBEDIENCE, NOT OBSERVANCE

When he was saying this, a woman in the crowd raised her
voice and said to him, "Blessed is the womb that bore you and
the breasts that nursed you!" But he said, "Blessed rather are
those who hear the word of God and obey it!"

—*Luke 11:27–28*

In the Mediterranean world of the first century, a woman's
greatest achievement was to give birth to a famous son. Not
only does Jesus reverse this patriarchal notion, but he shifts
blessedness itself away from human objects to divine obedience. In his vision of the reign of God, one could be "blessed"
regardless of sex or gender, infertility or maternity. Every
obstacle blocking access to God is removed by making discipleship about call and response, not about inheritance or
accomplishment.

To be honest, the concept of discipleship today requires
little, if any, sacrifice—not to mention submission. Mostly, the
church-growth crowd makes joining a church as easy as possible. With so many churches struggling to survive, the process
of becoming a member is reduced to a kind of ecclesiastical
dating game. Perhaps this is the church you have been looking
for? Here are the services we provide (in an attractive physical
package no less), and if you will tell us something about your

needs, then maybe we can arrive at a mutual decision as to compatibility.

Don't worry, we say, it's not like getting married. If you will agree to fill an empty spot in the pew and make a pledge, we can move in together. Then, after the flush of our initial infatuation has faded and we start quarreling, you can decide whether to keep any of the promises you didn't make. It is all fairly reminiscent of that familiar airline script: "We know that when it comes to church attendance you have a choice, and we appreciate your choosing [your church name here]. It's been our pleasure serving you today, and when your future plans again call for collective worship, we hope to see you again on another [your church] flight."

Just once I wish the script could be real. What if we warned people against joining a church because turbulence in the pews is not "occasional and unexpected," but routine? What if more sermons could move beyond what pilots call "light chop," and more preachers would fly people right into the storm, instead of around it in search of "smooth air"? What if those oxygen masks dropped down almost every Sunday, and people had to grab them gasping, instead of hearing our standard rhetorical charade that advises otherwise terrified people to "continue breathing normally"?

Annie Dillard comes to mind; she advised us all to pray with our eyes open. She not only went into the woods looking for God, like her literary compatriots Henry David Thoreau, Ralph Waldo Emerson, and John Muir, but she also went to church. "I know only enough of God to want to worship him, by any means ready to hand. . . . There is one church here, so I go to it."[1] The church of which she speaks is a white frame Congregational church on Lummi Island in Puget Sound. On a good Sunday, only twenty others joined her there, and she confessed to feeling as if she was "on an archaeological tour of Soviet Russia."[2] She was not looking for perfection and had to stomach what she called the "dancing bear act" that is staged in Christian churches, Protestant and Catholic alike, week after week. Even so, she refused to consider the life of faith to be about convenient parking, calling it instead "an expedition to the Pole." Wherever we go, to the Pole or to church, "there seems to be only one business at hand—that of finding workable compromises between the sublimity of our ideas and the absurdity of the fact of us."[3]

Whatever else Annie Dillard thought of going to church or becoming a disciple, she didn't think it should be easy. She went in search of the Mystery, the inaccessible Absolute that compels us even as it eludes us, like those dignified explorers who set out to find the Pole and froze to death clutching backgammon boards and table silver sets. The equivalent to the Pole in worship is based on the metaphysical idea that the Absolute is the most inaccessible point of all, the point of spirit farthest from every accessible point of spirit in all directions. Dillard called it the "Pole of the Most Trouble. It is also—I take this as a given— the pole of great price."[4] Her way of describing the expedition, however, is priceless:

> Why do we people in churches seem like cheerful, brainless tourists on a packaged tour of the Absolute? . . . On the whole, I do not find Christians, outside the catacombs, sufficiently sensible of conditions. Does anyone have the foggiest idea what sort of power we so blithely invoke? Or, as I suspect, does not one believe a word of it? The churches are children playing on the floor with their chemistry sets, mixing up a batch of TNT to kill a Sunday morning. It is madness to wear ladies' straw hats and velvet hats to church; we should all be wearing crash helmets. Ushers should issue life preservers and signal flares: they should lash us to our pews.[5]

Despite worship services that she considered less polished than most high-school stage plays, Dillard marched off to worship week after week, knowing somehow that one does not get to God alone, any more than one gets to the Pole alone. She is describing the staid pilgrims of my Congregational heritage, what a friend of mine calls "the frozen chosen." But today there is another variety of amateur explorer, packed by the thousands into the metal-sided megachurches on Christian "campuses" in the mall-speckled suburbs. Underneath banners that look like ads for radio stations (the Buzz, the Rock, the Edge), the band is playing, the hands are swaying, and the hymn lyrics sound more like courtship than discipleship.

Worship consists of high-tech, high-volume, effusive praise and tearful thanksgiving for what God has done on behalf of each and every one of us—followed by preaching that circles the wagons of what is falsely assumed to be a besieged and righteous minority doing battle against the forces of secular humanism. The rhetoric is that of a western movie, the "last stand" between the chosen but misunderstood and legions of depraved liberal heathens whose worldly logic has led them to worship false gods (mostly in the temple of the flesh) and who are out to destroy the only true religion by removing it from the public square.

If this is too sentimental and too electric, what recourse does a Christian progressive have today? For those who would never think to raise their hands in worship (because they sit on them), mainline and liberal churches offer something as tedious as many evangelical services are self-centered: a dull and droning list of politically correct announcements that go on interminably. No detail is too minor and no story is too trivial to escape the sentimental displays of communal therapy. The hymns are often contorted by a preoccupation with inclusion at the expense of meter and particular power, and the sermon continues in the same vein—offering enlightened ways to cope with the aches and pains of daily life, instead of submitting to a vision so compelling as to redeem suffering and death itself.

In a world that is desperate for something real, many mega-churches today are like Disney World plus God, while too many mainline churches are serving up bits and pieces of the Great Books Club. One wonders which fiction is most cruel, that all your dreams can come true if you pray the "Prayer of Jabez" or that discipleship is the same thing as enlightenment. Odd as it may sound, we need to recover something as old and dangerous as it is transformative: following Jesus.

If the church is to survive as a place where head and heart are equal partners in faith, then we will need to commit ourselves once again not to the worship of Christ, but to the *imitation* of Jesus. His invitation was not to believe, but to follow. Since it was once dangerous to be a follower of The Way, the church can rightly assume that it will never be on the right track again until the risks associated with being a follower of Jesus outnumber the comforts of being a fan of Christ. Until we experience Jesus as a "radically disturbing presence,"[6] instead of a cosmic comforter, we will not experience him as true disciples. The first question any churchgoer should be asked and expected to answer is: *What are you willing to give up to follow Jesus?*

To recover this understanding of discipleship, however, we must confront an enormous obstacle in Western culture: the idea that to "obey" is to lose personal identity and become intellectually and spiritually oppressed. Notice what happens in Luke 11 when the woman in the crowd starts praising Jesus as the object of adoration and his mother as blessed? Being made the focus of attention and adoration makes him nervous, perhaps even belligerent. He is the signpost, not the Sign, and so he shifts the notion of "blessedness" from object to objective. "Blessed rather are those who hear the word of God and *obey* it."

Notice that he did not say blessed are those who hear the word of God and *believe* it. Nor did he say blessed are those who hear the word of God and *enshrine* it as doctrine. Nor did he say blessed are those who hear the word of God and *co-opt* it for a particular religious or political agenda. He said blessed are those who hear the word of God and *obey* it. That is, blessed are those who give up their old way of being in the world and willingly surrender to a new way. Blessed are those who are willing to take *new orders*—by marching to the tune of a different drummer and taking the road less traveled.

Can you feel the hair on the back of your Western neck standing up? Obey? Didn't we proudly remove that word from our wedding ceremonies (as in wives "obeying" their husbands)? Don't we seek to abolish all forms of servitude, whether physical, spiritual, or intellectual? Isn't the whole idea of growing up to escape our obligation to obey our parents, and isn't personal freedom about escaping our obligation to obey anyone or anything? This may be the church's ultimate equal-opportunity myth—plaguing liberals and conservatives alike. The way of Christian discipleship conforms to nothing and to no one.

THIS YOKE IS NEITHER EASY NOR LIGHT

Biblical scholars have long been fascinated with Matthew 11:28–30,[7] which contains the well-known and very comforting text: "Come to me, all you that are weary and are carrying heavy burdens, and I will give you rest. Take my yoke upon you, and learn from me; for I am gentle and humble in heart, and you will find rest for your souls. For my yoke is easy, and my burden is light."

When contemporary Christians hear these words, they receive them as a balm for weary souls, an invitation to lay down the cares and stresses of the world and let Christ shoulder them instead. But an intriguing case can be made that this is by no means what Matthew had in mind, and his audience would have gotten a very different message. Some scholars have argued that Jesus speaks here of the yoke of wisdom and equates it with his particular revelation of the Torah. Others contend that he is offering the yoke of himself, the one whose words and deeds reveal God's purposes and demands. Others see the words as referring to the eschatological "rest" that will come at the end of time.

A less-known, but very plausible argument, however, is made by scholars who argue that words like "labor," "carrying heavy burdens," "rest," and "yoke" are frequently associated with the exercise of power, especially imperial and political rule. Warren Carter, in *Matthew and Empire,* says: "Jesus, the one who proclaims and demonstrates God's reign or empire, issues an invitation to those who are oppressed by Roman imperial power to encounter God's empire now in his ministry in anticipation of the time when God destroys all empires including Rome's."[8]

Those who are "weary and are carrying a heavy burden" may well include not just the disciples but all those who struggle to support the wealthy. "Those who labor" may well refer to the 95 percent of the population that is just trying to survive; the verb "labor" comes from a Greek word that is frequently concerned with life under imperial rule, whether Assyrian, Babylonian, Persian, or Hellenistic. "Carrying a heavy burden" refers to those who "labor wearily" and are systematically oppressed by those who perpetuate unjust social structures. The rich can never get enough of or enjoy "the fruit of their toil," in which they have "crushed and abandoned the poor, they have seized a house that they did not build" (Job 20:18–19).

The promised "rest" in its most common usage denotes a very political reality, rest from one's enemies (Deut. 12:10), or the absence of war. Although it is most common to assume that the "yoke" is the burden of the Pharisees and their legalism, its historical meaning designates imperial rule imposed by a greater power over a lesser "against the latter's will and for the former's benefit."[9] Jesus may have been speaking ironically when he referred to what is "easy" and "light," or he may have been assuming that the present situation would not last forever because Rome's days were numbered. This is consistent with the idea that the kingdom is *immediate,* a present reality and a future totality. The rest he promises is not merely physical, but existential. God's reign can be experienced *now* as an alternative to Roman power.

As for the phrase "learn from me," it is a familiar call to establish a community of alternative commitments and social practices. What is revealing, and for our time critical, is the social and theological challenge of this text to Roman oppression. Serious biblical scholarship reveals a consistent message: *the gospel is a stunningly political document buried under centuries of sentimental interpretations.* The often-heard lament about mixing religion and politics is a symptom of this complete misunderstanding.

Even so, the call to take on this yoke is the call to service and sacrifice, not domination. This community will be constituted not by wealth, gender, status, or ethnicity, but by a radical egalitarian principle: *everyone* is a child of God. There will be a new economic order based on need, not oppression in service to conspicuous consumption. Violence is to be totally rejected, not by complete passivity, but by the use of nonviolent resistance, and all social divisions of the imperial world are to be rejected by a God whose love is beyond race, class, creed, and character.

The popular interpretation of this text as a private, apolitical balm for those who are weary and yet still loyal to the empire is but one of many examples of the way the teachings of Jesus have been altered or neutralized by what Crossan calls "the drag of normalcy." Indeed, this "yoke" is neither easy nor light. Before the church was adored and brought like a bride to a marriage of convenience with empire, arranged by Constantine in the fourth century, the gospel of Jesus of Nazareth represented an alternative reality that constituted an unacceptable threat to that very same bridegroom. The very empire that killed him would in short order offer him a place at the banquet of Roman power.

The alternative community he founded was eventually absorbed into the dominant culture, bearing the sword of doctrine. The Galilean sage, who tended to the poor and attacked the abuses of the Temple, was now given "reclining" rights at the feast of all male bishops. They had met in lakeside Nicea to hammer out their theological differences and forge Christianity into the official religion of the empire. The open commensality of Jesus was now formally replaced by the episcopal banquet of Constantine. William Sloane Coffin Jr.'s lament could be that of the whole church:

> Law is not as disinterested as our concepts of law pretend; law serves power; law in large measure is a recapitulation of the status quo; it confirms a rigid order designed to insulate the beneficiaries of the status quo from the disturbances of change. The painful truth—one with a long history—is that police are around in large part to guarantee a peaceful digestion for the rich.[10]

How, then, are we to be followers of Jesus today, when Christ is reclining at the banquet of the Pax Americana? To be a disciple today requires both a recovery of the original meaning of that word and the capacity to surrender oneself to the path of greater resistance. To "obey" is to recognize that the gulf between concept and capacity is so vast that, left to our own devices, we will almost always do what we feel like doing, even as we espouse noble thoughts about the need to do more. True discipleship is about obedience, because it is about *not* being in control all the time, but rather trusting that to act under love's obligation is to be more free, not less so.

The alternative is what we have now: the gospel as neutral energy blessing the world as it is. But make no mistake; this is easier than resisting such a world. To resist puts all disciples in the position of being denied the worldly benefits we enjoy. When Martin Luther King Jr. said that "unearned suffering is redemptive," he was talking about the essential wisdom of the gospel. We can suffer because of our own mistakes, of course, and this can produce wisdom as well. But when we suffer because we have submitted ourselves to a cause greater than private ambition or on behalf of someone who has no claim on us except common humanity, then the suffering that comes is charged with a redemptive power that can change the world.

To be a disciple today requires that we seek the wisdom of Jesus and then transpose that wisdom into metaphors that speak as wisely and as courageously to our time as he did to his. A disciple "obeys" not by literalizing first-century myths but by carrying forward the wisdom of biblical metaphors and creating new metaphors as powerful and as disturbing as those that gave birth to the church. The wisdom of Jesus was a spiritual insurgency in an occupied land. Today, the church itself is occupied by the gospel of the marketplace, and sacred space is increasingly indistinguishable from secular space. To generate sales and attract customers, the church and the mall are now common-law partners. We can listen to a sermon on conspicuous consumption and then shop on the premises right after the benediction.

PULLING THE TEETH OF THE GREAT OFFENSE

It does no good to tell people to follow Jesus if you are not able to explain what this would mean today. You cannot explain what it would mean today if you do not understand what it once *meant*. The great preacher Joseph Sittler once said that preaching is not about telling people what the Bible *said*, but fearlessly sharing with the congregation what the Bible has caused you to *say*.

For this reason, intellectually honest biblical scholarship is not to be feared by the church; neither should the church, however, feel beholden to every scholarly fad. What needs to be addressed without apology, however, is the virulent strain of anti-intellectualism that still plagues much of the church. During the first wave of historical Jesus research, German scholars rose with the sun, and on bitterly cold mornings they broke the ice that sealed their ink pots with the point of their quill pens and set about the task of doing exhaustive and meticulous work to reconstruct an honest vision of the most important figure in human history. They did this in service to the church, not to destroy it. The greatest threat to Christian discipleship, then as now, is a supernatural vision of a Jesus that one can only worship, but never follow. Rudolph Bultmann "demythologized" the gospel not to destroy faith but to make the radical message of Jesus even more accessible.

Today's third wave of historical Jesus research has a reputation for complete indifference to the church (which it deserves). But even this is changing, because pastors from Berkeley to Omaha need the fruits of biblical scholarship to counter enormous misconceptions about the message and ministry of Jesus. Writer and activist Jim Wallis describes how, as a young man growing up in an evangelical church, he never heard a sermon on the Sermon on the Mount. All the focus was on the epistles, especially Paul's contention that Christ died for our sins. Barbara Brown Taylor teaches a university course called "Introduction to World Religions" and confesses that her students have heard so much inaccurate information in church that they end up flunking Christianity—because they think they already know their own tradition. One student asked, "If Paul wasn't one of the disciples, where did he get his stuff?"

Even so, a deep and even paranoid suspicion continues to disparage higher criticism of the Bible, as if someone could publish a paper that would unravel God. One of the most gifted evangelicals, N. T. Wright, recently offered this scathing rebuke:

> The massive concentration on source and form criticism, the industrial-scale development of criteria for authenticity (or, more often, inauthenticity), and the extraordinary inverted snobbery of preferring gnostic sayings-sources to the canonical documents all stem from, and in turn reinforce, the determination of the Western world and the church to make sure that the four Gospels will not be able to say what they want to say, but will be patronized, muzzled, dismembered and eventually eliminated altogether as a force to be reckoned with.[11]

Methinks the bishop of Durham doth protest too much. Perhaps in light of both the astonishing reverence for and the equally astonishing ignorance about the Bible in our time, we might at least agree to the wise counsel of the Pharisee Gamaliel, who gave us the original version of "Let It Be": "So in the present case, I tell you, keep away from these men and let them alone; because if this plan or this undertaking is of human origin, it will fail; but if it is of God, you will not be able to overthrow them—in that case you may even be found fighting against God!" (Acts 5:38–39).

Scholars are not about the business of bringing people to faith, nor can their work, by definition, take faith away. At the very least, however, it can keep faith from being based on false premises or formed around an uncritical and oblivious intellectual dishonesty. Uneducated clergy can be as dangerous as quack physicians, and for this reason my spiritual forebears founded Harvard and Yale for the sole purpose of training pastors to think. Even so, not a single one of them would have presumed that their thinking alone could save people.

Today the edgy and even offensive work of historical Jesus scholars can help us to understand, for example, how the process of softening and altering the words of Jesus began as soon as the church began to market the messiah. Knowing this means that we can *reverse* the process and begin to recover what was, and still is, both astonishing and dangerous about that message.

Those first disciples who had been forever changed by their encounter with Jesus did not set out to domesticate it. But with the passage of time and the inherent pressure to market the message for a larger audience, the second and third generations of disciples felt compelled to turn the Galilean sage into the Son of God. Like advertisers today who must "break through the clutter," the early church wanted and needed to get the world's attention. The audience was largely Jewish, and the message was so counterintuitive as to appear ludicrous—especially the notion that God's power is "made perfect in weakness" (2 Cor. 12:9).

After several decades in which no written records are produced, the writings of Paul and his imitators begin to shift the focus from "the vision that mesmerized Jesus to Jesus the visionary."[12] By the time Mark writes the world's first gospel and Matthew and Luke follow suit a decade or so later, the marks of redaction have become obvious. The most offensive passages are softened to appeal to a broader audience. To "propagate," after all, is the root of "propaganda," and this was missionary propaganda.

Perhaps the most obvious change is a change in tense. The kingdom was an immediate and luminous reality to Jesus, even though it had a future dimension as well. But gospel writings began to segregate present and future tense again, projecting the kingdom once more into the future, rather than celebrating it as a fact of the present. An apocalyptic mentality returned, as surely to explain the continued existence of evil and the delay in the second coming as to cover what appeared to critics to be Jesus' naive sense of time.

The rhetorical strategies of Jesus are altered as well, so that their ambiguity and tension are reduced, and redactors begin "helping" listeners to get the "point" by adding material in front of and at the end of otherwise baffling parables. In Luke's account of the Beatitudes, drawn from the Q gospel, the poor are congratulated for possessing the kingdom (6:20), but this makes no sense. So Matthew adapts the same material to make it a more spiritual, less literal statement: "Blessed are the poor *in spirit,* for theirs is the kingdom of heaven" (5:3, emphasis added).

When Jesus prays in Matthew, "Give us this day our daily bread" (6:11), he displays absolute confidence that God will provide for our immediate needs. But Luke is unsettled by this and wants to portray God as providing on the installment plan, so he changes it to "Give us each day our daily bread" (11:3).

When Matthew's Jesus teaches that parents may be expected to give their children bread rather than a stone, it is real bread he is talking about (7:9, 11). But when Luke seeks a broader audience, one that is not so concerned about where its next meal is coming from, he changes the emphasis to a more spiritual one: "If you then, who are evil, know how to give good gifts to your children, how much more will the heavenly Father give the *Holy Spirit* to those who ask him" (11:13, emphasis added).

By the time John's gospel is written, the daily bread that can be depended on has morphed into eternal bread and a permanent end to hunger: "Jesus said to them, 'I am the bread of life. Whoever comes to me will *never* be hungry, and whoever believes in me will *never* be thirsty'" (6:35, emphasis added). Now the allegorical spiritualization of Jesus is complete, and his trust in the daily providence of God to provide bread one day at a time has evolved into a community that regards faith in Christ as a *substitute* for bread. Last, the bread becomes a symbol for the sacrificial body of Christ that, when eaten, will save us not from daily hunger but from our sins for all eternity.

Countless examples of how the early sayings of Jesus were softened and changed are available in the detailed work of New Testament scholars. But just a few examples will make the point and shed light on what it might mean to be a disciple of Jesus today. Take the simple and completely unambiguous command in the Sermon on the Mount: "Give to everyone who begs from you, and do not refuse anyone who wants to borrow from you" (Matt. 5:42).

I know of no one who follows this command. I have yet to attend a conference for clergy at which, walking down the street with my colleagues, ministers of the gospel emptied their pockets for every beggar. And further, I know of no one who would agree to make a loan to anyone who asked. To the contrary, even the prohibition against charging interest has long since ceased to be a Christian imperative.

A second example involves a familiar text that is all but absent from today's prosperity gospel pulpits: "It is easier for a camel to go through the eye of a needle than for someone who is rich to enter the kingdom of God" (Mark 10:25). This seems fairly straightforward, but what about the church budget? As an institution, the church depends on the generosity of its wealthy contributors, and they find this teaching to be another example of "soaking the rich." Instead of being honest about the Jesus message, that wealth is not a sin but can be spiritually debilitating, exegetical apologists go to work doing creative reinterpretations until they find what they went looking for—something that will pull the teeth of this inconvenient truth:

Fabric softeners have been applied. Some, for example, have imagined a narrow pass called the needle's eye, where it is difficult but not impossible for a loaded camel to pass through. Other compromisers have suggested a gate in the walls of Jerusalem called the needle's eye: at this gate a camel was required to squat down and wriggle through. Still others have argued that "camel" is a misunderstanding of a similar-sounding word meaning "rope." All such softening ploys are uncharacteristic of Jesus and subvert both the style and content of his wisdom.[13]

And so it goes. Riddles are moralized, and radical parables are softened or reversed. It is strenuously argued that the oral tradition allowed for countless changes that can never be tracked and that the original utterances of Jesus cannot be known with certainty—only as more likely or less likely. This is no reason to give up, however, because we are still obligated to pursue the "more likely." The leap of faith is still required, but we should only leap after reason has taken us as far as it can. The clues are always the same. Earlier material should be considered more trustworthy than later redactions, and when there are multiple sources, inside the church and out, and the offense has remained mostly intact, then we may be "getting warm" with regard to authenticity.

Such serious Bible study can no longer be confined to the academy or debated at conferences to which only hyperintellectuals are invited for tedious debates that often seem like much ado about nothing. Bible study has become essential to our survival, just as thoughtful, candid, and informed Christian education is essential to the future of the church. We live on a planet that is only a turn or two away from oblivion, and nuclear weapons are soon to be in the hands of everyone—those who are deluded as well as those who have deluded themselves into thinking that they are not.

Fundamentalism of every kind is surging, and its goal is nothing short of a return to a pre-Enlightenment world where everyone knows his or her place and stays in it—especially women, minorities, gays, and scientists. No amount of Madison Avenue magic can hide the bitter truth any longer. As much as we might like the idea of a gated world, fortified by private security contractors and dedicated to the idea that might makes right, the rope of civilization is now frayed to the breaking point. Paradoxically, this is, quite literally, a "come to Jesus moment."

MY KINGDOM IS NOT OF THIS WORLD

To be a disciple is to "obey" something that requires more than the life of obligatory religious observances ranging from those guilt-laden trips to church on Christmas and Easter to the annual charity baskets providing the illusion that the church is practicing year-round compassion. Disciples today are called to rebel against the rampant individualism of American culture and to reconstitute and then empower communities of "dignified indignance."[14]

These are communities not of the saved and the unsaved but of those learning how to be Jesus-wise and not Roman-foolish. They are *beloved* communities, where the strong support the weak and the healthy sacrifice to cure the sick. Their members care for the earth, for the life of the spirit, and for each other. Because they refuse to make ostentatious displays of wealth or form hierarchies, they will appear positively "peculiar," as we say in Oklahoma. As they grow in numbers and influence, they will be labeled "un-American." Some will even take the American flag out of their sanctuary, proclaiming it a "house of prayer for all people."

To be a disciple now requires not the embrace of a particular ideology but the resolve necessary to live by a new *ethic*. Jesus certainly made this much clear: ritual observances are not to be confused with living faithfully. For Israel, the most important questions were never theological, but always ethical. How goes it in the land with the widow, the orphan, the stranger? What would a just society look like, and how would the earth's resources be distributed? What does it matter if you keep every Sabbath law but neglect to care for your neighbor? It is not what you *believe* that matters ultimately, but what you *do*.

The Church of the Followers of Jesus will teach Jesus wisdom, not doctrine. It will focus on ethics, not theology. It will prosper only to the extent that it becomes the beloved community again, bound to Jesus as the reflected face of God and to all other wise ones. It will seek the truth wherever it may be found and practice faith as the most radical kind of freedom—the freedom to serve something higher and more important than oneself.

It seems only fair, for example, to ask that the members of the body of Christ look and act differently from those who are not part of the beloved community. They should seem like "resident aliens," according to authors Stanley Hauerwas and William H. Willimon, a part of a "colony" more than a congregation.[15] The Christian community should not feel at home in the world, as if it is a "voluntary organization of like-minded individuals."

Willimon once described the true meaning of "countercultural" behavior as going to see someone in a nursing home. You can't do anything more radical than that, he said. The response of the audience to his comment was a bit underwhelming, as if perhaps they were hoping for something a little more Hollywood—something that might turn into a documentary starring each one of them as a mad prophet decrying the hypocrisies of our time.

I hate going to nursing homes. I hate the way they smell. I hate to hear the Muzak of crazy babbling, the mad soliloquies of demented souls reliving their childhoods or insisting that I speak to the brown bear at the foot of their bed. The common dining area is the worst. All those wheelchairs pushed together and then abandoned, forming a circle of cloudy eyes and trembling hands. Everyone seems to be looking far off, as if dementia makes everything part of the background and nothing a part of the foreground. Ambulances arrive daily to pick up the dead, and the only thing that changes is the color of the Jell-O.

Once I went to a nursing home to visit a man I'd never met and lost his room number. Knowing that I wouldn't recognize him, I decided to stick my head into room after room while calling out his name. If there was a man in the bed, and he was not asleep, I would ask, "Are you Jack Burns?" On just my third try, a gentleman with a great shock of snow-white hair pulled himself up off the bed and looked at me smiling. My question had brightened his face, so I repeated it. "Are you Jack Burns?"

He said, "I am if you want me to be."

What followed was a conversation that would never have happened if I had not reluctantly "obeyed" my own job description. Likewise, we should tell anyone who joins a church that they have just entered into a strange and bewildering covenant of blessed inconvenience. We are all, of course, too busy to sit on another committee. They meet at inconvenient times, but we go because we are under orders. Yet time and time again we come home feeling that it was worth it, that we are better for having shared time with friends in the work of something more important than ourselves.

To be honest, we almost always try to think of reasons not to do something collective and "other-oriented." But invariably we come home from those experiences believing that we have done a good thing—a new program for the kids or an organized effort to meet with the city council about a living wage. It turns out to be a good way to spend Tuesday evening—even better than TV. We look one another in the eye, ask about our children, laugh, and toss a small stone of hope in the ocean of misery that is the world. Someone has to take minutes, of course, because "they also serve" who sit and take minutes.

To be a disciple is to submit to something uncertain and impractical, like not doing exactly what one feels like doing at any given moment. We are not called together in church to remind ourselves, one more time, what we "believe." It is a strange and peculiar American spectacle, this standing up, week after week, to proclaim, "This is my belief." Even stranger is the postmodern zeal with which we pretend that this is a God-given right, that others must respect our belief, and that it need not make sense to be legitimate. It must only be "sincere." This passes for the orthodoxy of pluralism, while constituting, in fact, the ultimate heresy: that we can be religious in isolation from one another, sacrificing nothing.

Instead of reflecting on the meaning of being a "beloved community under new orders," as I have grown fond of describing the church, Americans prefer, as one writer put it, "to be left alone, warmed by our beliefs-that-make-no-sense, whether they are the quotidian platitudes of ordinary Americans, the magical thinking of evangelicals, the mystical thinking of New Age Gnostics, the teary-eyed patriotism of social conservatives, or the perfervid loyalty of the rich to their free-market Mammon. We are thus the congregation of the Church of the Infinitely Fractured, splendidly alone together."[16]

Sacred covenants, on the other hand, actually make us all less free—at least when freedom is narrowly and selfishly defined. We don't have the luxury of pretending that we can live and act in isolation from one another. Marriage restricts us when it comes to having other sexual partners. Parenthood nearly obliterates personal time and lays waste to a lifetime of energy. Agreeing to the role of a citizen in a democracy shackles the voter with such unpleasant and time-consuming tasks as knowing the voting record of candidates and where they stand on the issues.

A woman approached me one day to talk about joining my church. "What brought you here?" I asked.

"I want to be less free," she responded.

Another man in his late fifties began attending regularly, always sitting in the back and listening intently to the sermons. For months he came, listened, scratched notes on the bulletin, and then left without speaking to anyone. Finally, he began to engage me in theological conversations over coffee, and he seemed remarkably informed about church doctrine, Christian practice, and the requirements of the life of faith. He was exceptionally well read, and I began to anticipate that he would join—delighted by the thought.

I was surprised, therefore, when he approached me after the service one Sunday and informed me that he had decided not to join the church. Obviously disappointed, I sought to encourage him by complimenting his remarkable knowledge of the gospel and the teachings of Jesus. "You probably understand the Christian faith better than 99 percent of the people who join this church. What's holding you back?"

He stared at the floor, and after an awkward silence he responded, "I'm a military man, and I know how to take orders. Therefore, my level of understanding is not an advantage. It might even be grounds for a court martial."

I must have still looked confused. That's when he made it as plain as possible.

"Reverend, I get it. I just can't do it."

EIGHT

JUSTICE AS COVENANT, NOT CONTROL

The arc of the moral universe is long, but it bends toward justice.

—*Martin Luther King Jr.*

Polite society counsels us to keep the peace by "not discussing religion or politics." When I ask my students to explain this folk wisdom, they get it right every time. "Somebody will get their feelings hurt." Religion and politics are volatile subjects when talked about separately, because they touch on what psychologist Abraham Maslow calls "core values." But when they are put together, especially as a political tool to divide and conquer, the situation can be explosive.

The problem, however, isn't that religion and politics are part of the lively dialogue of democracy, but how *one-sided* that conversation has sounded since the rise of the Christian Right. No so long ago, many evangelical Christians lobbied on behalf of public, or "common," education, worked to eliminate slavery, and then helped to expand women's rights—and they did this from religious conviction. Most took the separation of church and state for granted, believing that it was the best bargain for both entities. But they also participated in the covenant that is required of all citizens in a free society, pushing not for government endorsement of sectarian religious issues but for laws that would make the nation more compassionate and all its citizens more equal.

Prior to the establishment of the Moral Majority in the 1970s and 1980s, most evangelicals believed that partisan political involvement would compromise the gospel, and they knew that joining the gospel to any political party would hamper the freedom of that gospel to speak to all people. Deep religious conviction was an affair of the heart and not for show. As for seeking power, Christianity is a faith that was born at the margins of society, and it has always been most effective when it speaks from the margins.

What this generation has forgotten is that some religious communities used their faith as the basis for social transformation in the face of injustice. Mahatma Gandhi, Dorothy Day, Desmond Tutu, and others petitioned their governments for "redress of [moral] grievances." They shared a fundamental conviction that God cares about the suffering of *all* people, and this led them to propose alternative social structures. Many of them gave their lives for that vision. Base communities and liberation theology movements sought to dismantle oppressive systems and were thus inescapably political. Roman Catholic priests have been warned (and continue to be warned) that their work is to save poor souls, not to protest the domination systems of the Third World. Such an impossible dichotomy led Archbishop Dom Helder Camara to pen his famous complaint: "When I give food to the poor, they call me a saint. When I ask why the poor have no food, they call me a communist."

But all this changed in the late twentieth century. On the Catholic side, bishops went from issuing calls for a nuclear freeze and an end to poverty to debating whether pro-choice Catholic candidates should be offered Communion. On the Protestant side, high-profile public voices of the church became narrow, ugly, and retributive. One could be either a Christian or a Democrat, but not both. Judges were demonized for rulings that protected the separation of church and state or hindered attempts to impose sectarian beliefs through the force of law or in the public schools. A handful of emotionally volatile issues, especially abortion and gay marriage, dominated the public discourse to the exclusion of issues like poverty, war, and the destruction of the environment. Only recently has this begun to change, as thoughtful evangelicals like those in the Sojourners community have worked to reintroduce their members to their own history. This is both hopeful and exciting.

It also comes at a crucial moment in the history of the church. For a number of reasons, the church has become widely viewed as either irrelevant, the object of contempt, or both. The situation is complex, but two factors stand out. First, a narrow approach to the idea of salvation, as expressed in the blood atonement and with Jesus as the exclusive divine Savior, has played into the hands of a church seeking political power at the expense of the inclusive wisdom of its own gospel. "Getting saved" not only is a static and highly individualistic phenomenon but narrows and domesticates the redemptive activity of God in ways that conform all too conveniently to the worldview of the new American empire. In a land of entitled bargain hunters, salvation becomes the ultimate bargain.

Second, the notion of covenant as a collective expression of gratitude and mutuality has been trampled beneath a culture whose real devotion is to private ambition. The religious impulse, born in epiphanies that awaken us to our responsibilities to and for one another, is fundamentally corrupted when it is reduced to an individual balm. Faith is always supposed to make it harder, not easier, to ignore the plight of our sisters and brothers. In short, the church must make a crucial choice now between wisdom theology and salvation theology—between the Jesus who transforms and the Christ who saves. One is the biblical ethic of justice; the other is a postbiblical invention that came to fullness only after the Protestant Reformation.

Salvation theology reinforces the notion that religion is a *transaction,* rather than a covenant of compassion. God has done something for *me,* and the rewards belong to *me.* For others to reap the same eternal rewards, they must convert to *my* way of thinking in order to be similarly rewarded by *my* God.

As for suffering, it is commonly considered to be a form of divine punishment, not part of the journey toward wisdom. God's "justice" is often seen as the opposite of God's "mercy." Marcus Borg comments: "Given the choice, we would all prefer God's mercy and hope to escape God's justice. But seeing the opposite of justice as mercy distorts what the Bible means by justice. Most often, in the Bible, the opposite of God's justice is not God's mercy, but human injustice."[1]

Wisdom theology, on the other hand, is not to be confused with what is commonly called "enlightenment." Wisdom is not about crystals, channeling, or thinly disguised self-absorption. Wisdom is the unifying object of *all* religious faith, and suffering as part of the process of transformation is present in every faith tradition. The biblical story is the story of light overcoming darkness, scales falling from the eyes of those who could not (or would not) see. It's the story of the journey from a narcissistic and tribal understanding of faith to a death-defying embrace of the universal worth and dignity of all life—including creation itself.

Salvation theology, however, cannot be collectively understood by definition. It is a zero-sum game that cuts us off from the unsaved and often causes us to be arrogant and judgmental. The religious "loop" closes down upon itself; by making an *exclusive* claim, it becomes essentially *irreligious.* Human beings draw circles because we want to be inside them. Jesus kept expanding the circle to include more and more of us. A Christian covenant is therefore, by definition, a covenant of *inclusiveness*—or it is not Christian.

This idea, that we are to bear one another's burdens and sacrifice something in order to contribute to individual wisdom and collective transformation, is now so foreign to the American mind that, for example, no modern politician can even suggest that taxes might need to be *raised* without committing political suicide. The appeal is always to selfishness and greed, reminding us that it's "our money" and that the government (the enemy) is really stealing it from us. The result is the society we now inhabit, in which we worship at the altar of "whatever the market will bear." The government serves private interests at the expense of public assistance, and life is reduced to a game. A recent sermon title said it simply, but well: "I Win, We Lose."

The reason we should never *stop* talking about religion and politics is that our view of God shapes our view of how society ought to be ordered and what constitutes that vague but powerful concept known as *justice*. Christianity may be the dominant belief system in America, but there is hardly anything "biblical" about our understanding of justice. Today, the concept of covenant is legalistic, spelling out the consequences of breaking the covenant. Sin is entirely the fault of the sinner, not the consequence of a series of collective social failures. As for rehabilitation, how nineteenth century!

Today we see our religious and governmental relationships (as well as our interpersonal ones) in largely *contractual* terms. Mutuality and shared sacrifice are out; individual rights and unrestrained freedom are in. America has no controlling metaphor now, except the unholy trinity of Me, Myself, and I. "Every man for himself" may be a good theme for a western movie, but for the future of civilization, it's a recipe for disaster.

WHAT IS BIBLICAL JUSTICE?

"Where there is no vision, the people perish" (Prov. 29:18, AMP). Without a unifying metaphor, a grand plan, a model for the shape of the future, human beings begin to atrophy in a self-absorbed soup of gamesmanship and greed. In America's brief history, we have had a number of visions that unified the nation, from the convulsions of our own independence, to the abolition of slavery at great price, to fighting militant fascism abroad, to social movements that sought to end discrimination and injustice against our own citizens. The question is, What is our unifying vision *now*? Is it to defeat terrorism? Is it to get rich? Is it to maintain a lifestyle, regardless of the cost, to which we believe we are entitled?

The biblical vision, though tainted with human folly, violence, and sin, is a vision of *shalom*. When this Hebrew word is translated as "peace," something of its richness and complexity is lost. More than just the absence of war, *shalom* is a pervasive well-being that reflects the absence of oppression, anxiety, and fear and is characterized by health, wholeness, prosperity, and security. It is God's dream made manifest "on earth as it is in heaven." But it belongs to *everyone,* just as it is everyone's responsibility.

Despite the Bible's variety and breath, not to mention its tribal violence and chauvinism, there is a unifying vision in scripture—a "plot," if you will. Expressed in metaphor and myth, it begins with paradise for two people who destroy what was given to them and ends with a new paradise—the city of God, as all the nations are healed in the vision of Revelation. In between there are nightmares, of course, but the dream recurs again and again, on the lips of prophets and in the radical wisdom of Jesus:

> They shall beat their swords into plowshares,
> and their spears into pruning hooks;
> nation shall not lift up sword against nation,
> neither shall they learn war any more. (Isa. 2:4)

This dream of God is constantly set before the people of God, and they find ways to ignore it, pervert it, or simply forget it altogether. It is truly a "tale of two kingdoms," and the tension between the two animates scripture from start to finish. But it is *never* merely an individual or private vision. It is never about just "getting right with God" and then resting in the assurance of personal salvation. It is a *collective* vision, lived out in covenant with a God who is depicted as an Aggravator, not just a Comforter. Israel's very identity is bound up in the story of Jacob wrestling with an angel in the middle of the night on the banks of the Jabbok River (Gen. 32:22–32). Faith is a mortal struggle, and God is a divine Adversary.

What's more, because this biblical tale of two kingdoms was lived out in the midst of a world of wrenching rural poverty and oppression by urban elites, it was a dream that was continuously dashed by the realities of everyday life. The well-known beatitude "Blessed are you who weep now, for you will laugh" (Luke 6:21) is most often heard today in the context of a funeral. But it was originally a word spoken to peasants living with *daily* grief as constant and dark as any vision of hell on earth—dying children, life on the edge of starvation, death from common diseases, and hopelessness.

What's more, then as now, religion functioned to legitimize the social order. Its practitioners, the scribes and priests, maintained the system on behalf of the elites and thus gave divine sanction to social structures that were exploitative and politically oppressive. The message was: "This is how God wants it to be." Then against this deadly fiction came Jesus preaching: "This is *not* how God wants it to be."

Getting this message across might have been an impossible task except for one thing—Israel's memory of its own deliverance. This defining story, of what it believed to be a God-assisted exodus from the bondage of slavery in Egypt, was kept alive in song and story. Granted, one can argue that this is "tribal religion," and that the story would have been written differently if told by the Egyptians, but this important fact remains: Israel's foundational narrative was a story of *liberation* from the domination system operating in a peasant society.

At the heart of this story is a message about the nature of God. Unimpressed by the trappings of the royal court and the rituals that sought to appease and sanctify inequity, God is portrayed as being moved by compassion for the Israelites' misery and suffering and is believed to have liberated them from Egypt under the leadership of Moses. But this liberation was not without obligation. It was followed by a covenant delivered at Sinai that spelled out their responsibilities to God and to one another. Just as the original oppression was political, the liberation was also political, because it ended in a new kind of "bondage"—a religious covenant.

For several hundred years, the Israelites sought to live out this covenant in a way that reversed their experience in Egypt. There was no central government, no monarchy, and no elites. Instead, God was king. As a way to prevent power from accumulating in a few hands, each family was given a portion of land that belonged to them forever, according to the accounts in Joshua and Judges. Just imagine such a plan today as part of a political campaign: free land in perpetuity! Is this not socialism?

The experiment did not last, of course, and Israel soon established its own domination system through kings and their subsequent elites. But the model of joining religious ideas with political structures under the dictates of a covenant endured. Eventually the prophets and the peasant class would see themselves as being in bondage once more—not to Pharaoh, but to a new domination system. The classical prophets of ancient Israel—Amos, Isaiah, Micah, and Jeremiah—raised their "God-intoxicated voices of protest"[2] against the human suffering caused by unjust social systems. God's covenant with Israel had been broken, and one form of domination had been traded in for another. Then the three-step process of liberation, covenant, and alternative social structure would repeat itself. Over time, that structure would break apart, giving way to the reestablishment of power, the loss of covenant, and the return of yet another domination system.

It is no accident that the passion and preoccupation of Jesus should be something called the "kingdom" of God—an inherently political term. We tend to attach a fantastic quality to the word "kingdom" (as in Disney's magic kingdom), but for those who heard the words of the Galilean sage, a kingdom was their *everyday* reality—it meant living under a system of ruling elites. There was Herod's kingdom and Caesar's kingdom. So when Jesus spoke of the kingdom of God, the meaning would have been immediate and unmistakable. The kingdom of God is what life would be like if God sat on the throne instead of Caesar.

COVENANTS MADE AND BROKEN

It is deeply ironic that every Sunday millions of Christians say in the Lord's Prayer, "Thy kingdom come, thy will be done *on earth,* as it is in heaven." The implied covenant here is that the two kingdoms should be reconciled by our faithful effort to make it happen. As one scholar put it, "Heaven's in great shape; earth is where the problems are."[3] Unfortunately, Matthew changed "kingdom of God" to "kingdom of heaven"—probably in reverential deference to the Jewish belief that one should avoid writing or speaking the name of God. The effect over the centuries, however, has been to *spiritualize* the notion of justice and make countless Christians think of the kingdom only in heavenly terms, or concerning just the afterlife.

This suits today's ruling elite just fine, for they fear one thing from religion above all else: *that it will disturb the commercial status quo.* Charity they love, because it fills bellies without changing public policy. Pastors are shamed into thinking that political action means "taking sides" and that this somehow compromises the purity of faith. But as William Sloane Coffin Jr. reminds us, "Not to take sides is effectively to weigh in on the side of the stronger. . . . Compassion and justice are companions, not choices."[4]

What is wrong with America is identical to what is wrong with the church, and the two are feeding off each other in a demonic way. If the gospel cannot compel us to recover the meaning of covenant and the political consequences of being responsible to and for one another, then perhaps Karl Marx was right when he said religion is "the opiate of the masses." Though this saying has been misunderstood as a call to abolish religion, Marx did believe that religion was illusory and played a role in the oppression of the working classes. If Jesus is now a free-market capitalist who worships private property and favors fair skin over fair trade, then we should drive whatever we want, live wherever we want, and let the last woolly-headed liberal turn out the lights.

But if we want to survive, if we want peace, and if we still believe in justice, then we must change more than administrations. We must recover a theology of *conscience* and reject the dominant and heretical theologies of personal "victory." This cannot occur in our time without a renewed understanding of the meaning of covenant, and it cannot occur entirely outside of political action. Covenants are freely made agreements between persons. They function as residuals of trust, not as instruments of fear.

We enter into such agreements all the time in daily life, every time we hand over money as a "promissory note," stop on red, or go on green—we do so assuming that this covenant will be kept by others as well. There are legal consequences, to be sure, but we often feel bound by more than mere compliance. Consider, for example, sitting at a red light in the wee hours of the morning with no one around. Why not go? Because we live by the ethical force of our mutual covenants, and society itself is made possible by voluntary compliance with the unenforceable.

We drop our kids at school and thus participate in a covenant of trust with teachers, administrators, and other students. We come home each day to partners whom we love in a different way by virtue of our vows and promises. We are, as philosopher Martin Buber put it, promise-making, promise-breaking, and promise-remaking creatures. We are defined by how we relate, one to another, and how well we keep our promises.

When a covenant is a religious one, another dimension is added to the idea of an agreement, even one that is freely entered into. That dimension is a *transcendent* quality based on religious values. A religious covenant is not a contract, which we enter into and follow mostly for self-protection or to force compliance. In contracts, if one party fails to live up to the agreement, the agreement is voided. Not so with religious covenants. They are bound by the parameters of forgiveness and patience and characterized by a kind of transrational tenacity.

The covenant itself and what it makes possible are considered larger and more important than the benefit to either party. What's more, religious covenants are future-oriented; they are grounded in faith and are entered into in the belief that reciprocity and mutuality are transformational. Religious covenants are long-term voluntary commitments in which some of the individual's autonomy is lost—surrendered on behalf of the covenant itself. Ask any married couple who have worked through a crisis and saved a marriage to explain religious covenant, and the words will come easily.

Covenants by nature *restrict* freedom and lift up the notion of "duty"—which is precisely why they aren't very popular today. Freedom is widely misconstrued in Western culture as the freedom to do as we please unencumbered by a concern for the consequences of our actions. We assume that we are not our brother's or sister's keeper, and we like it that way. The good life is thereby widely confused with unrestrained indulgence made possible by nonempathetic self-absorption.

To the contrary, the biblical covenant we claim to honor is, in fact, *social, communal,* and *egalitarian.* Our dream, however—indeed, the American dream—is individualistic. In fact, we live in probably the most individualistic culture in human history.[5] We are told in a thousand ways that it's "all about me." It's about how I look, how much I own, how much power and status I have attained compared with others. We live under an astonishing barrage of mass-media messages that target individual insecurities in order to sell products. Our real national motto belongs to the maker of York peppermint patties: "You can't be too rich or too thin."

TOWARD A COVENANT OF TRUST, NOT TREPIDATION

Sociologist Robert Bellah and his colleagues have been telling us for years that every "good" society needs two things: opportunity and community.[6] Although we hear a great deal about opportunity in America, especially from politicians, we hear very little about community, except in very nostalgic ways. We hear stories of remarkable individual successes, like Horatio Alger, but a cruel fiction is thus perpetrated—that we are all "self-made" human beings. Not only is this patent nonsense, but it also constitutes a pernicious lie. It allows us to ignore the fact that without vital communities and institutions, like decent public schools, for example, many people are not even equipped to take advantage of the opportunities. The most twisted but perennial of American myths is that everyone has an equal opportunity to succeed.

Now we have come to the end of three decades of stressing opportunity and free markets as the magic bullet in a capitalistic society, while paying only lip service to communities and the sacrifices that they require. But without a balance between opportunity and collective social obligation the country is spinning out of control. A politics of individualism with no community counterbalance and no collective covenant will produce wave after wave of ethics scandals, a tsunami of disposable interpersonal relationships, and the preposterous theater of the rich claiming to be the overtaxed, overregulated victims of society. Sound familiar?

What has all this got to do with Jesus, and Christianity as wisdom, not salvation? The death-dealing politics of individualism is being *facilitated,* rather than corrected, by a church that caters to the individual soul and individual success, rather than to building the beloved community and practicing the politics of compassion. Popular salvation theology saves the *individual* ("without one plea, but that my savior died for *me*"). Saved individuals then join communities of other saved individuals, where they remain, as individuals, imperfect but forgiven. There they celebrate their salvation and look after largely individual spiritual matters—especially how to claim what God wants them to have (riches) and how to overcome bad habits and negative thoughts.

In what is perhaps the ultimate irony, the Christian Right professes to yearn for a return to America as a "Christian nation," without stopping to consider that the original covenants, like a "city set upon a hill," to quote the stirring religious language of Puritan colonist John Winthrop, were not "contracts on America," threatening divine punishments for specific moral sins. They were collective social visions of a more just society in the New World. Although far from perfect (they embraced slavery and second-class citizenship for women, among other things), these early American covenants were never about the individual, nor were they sectarian in nature. They "bound" people together, rich and poor, in order to pursue justice for the religious and nonreligious alike. This collective commitment was ultimately reflected in early American architecture (the grandeur of schools and libraries), the criminal justice system (a model for the world by the nineteenth century), even gathering places (the commons). It was all about what citizens of a young nation could do *together,* as long as they never forgot that beautiful, but now forgotten, concept: *the common good.*

Contemporary Christians have declared war on individual immorality but seem remarkably silent about the evil of systems, especially corporate greed and malfeasance. Sermons on greed have all but disappeared from today's pulpits, when only a hundred years ago congregations could expect to hear thundering judgments against the robber barons. How often in our wealthiest churches does anyone hear a sermon from Luke 12:48, "From everyone to whom much has been given, much will be required; and from the one to whom much has been entrusted, even more will be demanded"?

In late-twentieth-century America, the cult of the individual reached its zenith. With the help of willing corporate media, citizens became consumers. The news of every systemic failure, whether by government, industry, the schools, or the churches, was distilled down to the level of an individual failure—like a welfare mom or a clueless bureaucrat. It is always someone else's fault, and if you want further comment, you can speak to my attorney. In fact, we know so little about collective responsibility that we often hear: "Don't talk to me about racism—I never owned any slaves."

By directing all our anger at individual failures or scandals, we gradually forget that we are not called to shop and gossip, but to make, keep, and renew collective covenants in the quest for social, political, and economic justice. As the gospel got narrowed down to fervently held positions on a handful of culture-war issues, Christians who claimed to hear fetal screams turned a deaf ear to the postfetal screams of "enemy combatants" (most of whom were innocent) whom a reputedly Christian nation was torturing. Then they lied about it. Most pro-life Protestants did not lobby to end the death penalty, and divorce as a sin was out, while homosexuality as a sin was in. Where Jesus spoke, they were silent; where he was silent, they condemned.

While pushing endlessly, and by stealth, the teaching of "intelligent design" as a tribute to the Creator, these same Christians have been slow to join the environmental movement, which seeks to save that very handiwork—not to mention all of us, conservatives and liberals alike. All of this has been a calculated attempt to secure political power not for the sake of the poor, but to establish "biblical law" in a theocracy. These are covenants not on behalf of the poor but on behalf of power. That power is secured, now and always, through appeals to fear, even though a central tenet of the gospel is "Fear not."

We are all in competition with one another now and dedicated to that vacuous ideal "the pursuit of happiness." Would that the founding fathers had called it "the pursuit of contentment," because we have traded collective security for hyperindividualistic insecurity. We are not our brother's or sister's keeper. We are 300 million self-help projects warned by investment firms not to "outlive our money" (before they can gamble it away). A recent TV ad showed people walking around in public, at work, at the store, in the park, and so on, with giant numbers attached to their backs, revealing to the world exactly how much they had saved for retirement. As Social Security faces insolvency and Wall Street reels under the weight of its own greed and corruption, we have become little more than account balances competing with other account balances. Show me your number.

Once, early in my ministry, a young woman said in the midst of premarital counseling that she had taken advantage of her position in a local bank to hack into her fiancé's financial records. "Before I married him," she confessed, "I needed to know what he was worth."

The problem with most of our contemporary covenants is that they are not biblical—that is, they are not about the strong helping the weak, which is the central ethic of scripture. Instead, they protect the strong from the weak and comprise rules meant to reward and punish—hence they are instruments of *control*. Truth be known, a great deal of religious doctrine is born of a desire to control those around us (especially women). God's edicts must be simple, direct, and unequivocal—like those of a strict father. It's almost as if all that stands between us and moral chaos is too much love and forgiveness!

In everything we do these days, there is a certain *frantic* quality. In the way we shop, the way we travel, even the way we worship. Compulsiveness is always a sign that human beings are compensating for something and not living what Parker Palmer in *A Hidden Wholeness* calls the "undivided life."[7] At the heart of this social dis-ease is a basic lack of *trust*. We don't trust others; we don't trust God; we don't even trust ourselves. To secure ourselves against our own insecurity, as Kierkegaard put it, we set out to become masters of the universe and to hold chaos at bay for one more day.

Because we are dying, we find the idea of eternal life irresistible. Because we fear losing someone we love, we find the restrictive covenants of marriage very comforting. Because we are weak and vulnerable, we like to surround ourselves with symbols of strength and protection—walls, guards, guns, and very large vehicles. But most of all, because we fear utter *insignificance,* we attach ourselves to institutions or to human beings that flatter us and tell us we are indispensable, noteworthy, irreplaceable. The doctrinal manifestation of this need to be singled out, recognized, and loved beyond measure is not a two-way covenant at all, but a one-way transaction—the belief that God sent his only son to die for *my* sin and purchase *my* salvation. I followed the formula, and I've got mine. I pray that you will get yours.

That such a deity would devise and execute such a plan is, at its heart, an example of cosmic mistrust. On the other hand, to follow a teacher of wisdom named Jesus means submitting to an entirely different ethic—that we must lose ourselves in order to find ourselves. But in our culture, we are always urged to do exactly the opposite—to "find ourselves." We all want our fifteen minutes of fame. What's more, the religious covenant that we are invited to make by prophets and wise ones requires not knowing but *trusting* in some distant, unnamed, mysterious equilibrium we call God.

Faith itself is better understood as trust, a trust so deep as to baffle those who count only what can be weighed and measured. In the future liturgies of the church, the word "trust" should replace the word "faith" as often as possible. The word "wisdom" should replace the word "salvation." "Blood" should disappear altogether—along with all military metaphors and images. Bloody liturgies in church only encourage and sanctify the bloodletting of the battlefield. Please, for God's sake—no more "Onward Christian Soldiers."

The church must now make a pledge to correct its most recent heresy: teaching faith as a belief system characterized by certainty. Instead, we must recover faith's original impulse. It was never an intellectual assent to implausible assertions that could be traded in for improbable favors. It was a deep and abiding trust in the "arc of the moral universe" and the redemptive power of the beloved community. Ministry to mistrustful human beings can therefore never be a matter of substituting one illusion for another. Offering guarantees, for example, about the survival of personal identity after death is not about trust, but just the opposite. The church should tell the truth, which is that no one knows what happens to us after we die, and thus invite us all into a mystery requiring more trust, not less. Hate-filled preaching that instills in human hearts the fear of the "other" may be an effective way to seize and hold power, but in the end it's a covenant of mistrust. It's the antigospel.

When politicians and presidents refuse to talk to the enemy or consider apologies to be a sign of weakness, it is not a sign of principled leadership, but mistrust masquerading as resolute faith. When the world is divided up into the good guys and the evildoers, it is not Realpolitik in action, but a failure to trust that there is any goodness in others, just as it reveals a crippling blindness on our part to the evil in which we are complicit.

When Christians make the claim that only through Christ can one be saved, they display a fatal lack of trust in the power of other religious traditions to enlighten, edify, redeem, and transform. They mistrust ultimately the power of God to gather followers into the ways of wisdom and to reveal multiple levels of reality and consciousness. In the end, fundamentalists of any religious persuasion mistrust the very premise underlying the title of William James's classic work *The Varieties of Religious Experience*. To admit to "varieties" is to lose the monopoly of one's own experience.

But the truth is, one can embrace one's own tradition, deeply and unapologetically, without invalidating the religious tradition of another. Until we correct this most pervasive of illusions, we have no hope for peace. Fundamentalism of all kinds is the enemy of peace.

A Christian asked the Dalai Lama once whether she should become a Buddhist. His response was to tell the woman to become more deeply Christian and live more deeply in her own tradition. Huston Smith makes the same point by using the metaphor of digging a well. It is better to dig one well sixty feet deep than to dig six wells ten feet deep.[8] This is an act of trust and represents a covenant of trust. Come to think of it, marriage is only possible as an act of trust. Parenthood is a covenant of trust, and an achingly irrational one at that!

Years ago, I listened to Holocaust survivor and Nobel laureate Eli Wiesel speak to a group of Protestant ministers in Detroit. He had come to teach us the book of Job, and before he began his lecture he said something that I have never forgotten. He sat down, this small man with thinning hair, and opened up his Bible to one of the most enigmatic and fascinating of all biblical stories. Then with a sigh he paused, looked up, and said, "Let me be clear about something. I'm not going to try to convert anyone here to Judaism, and I would appreciate it very much if you didn't try to convert me to Christianity. What I am trying to do is to be the best Jew that I can be, so that you can be the best Christian that you can be. Let's study together."

NINE

PROSPERITY AS DANGEROUS, NOT DIVINE

It's the non-economic uses of money that make money so
complicated, even demonic. Jesus saw the demonic side
when he saw money as a rival god capable of inspiring great
devotion. "You cannot serve God and mammon." Note that
only money is put on a par with God, not knowledge, not
family nobility, not reputation, not talent: only money is
elevated to divine status. No wonder Jesus talked more about
money than any other subject, except the kingdom of God.

—*William Sloane Coffin Jr.*

If someone stopped me on the street and asked, "What is the
greatest threat facing America?" I would not hesitate to answer—greed. If the question were phrased differently to inquire
about the greatest threat facing the church, I would have a hard
time responding differently. Two heresies seem dominant in
our age. One is the heresy of docetism, the belief that Jesus was
not human at all, but God masquerading on earth as a human
being. The second is the so-called prosperity gospel, the heresy
of believing that God wants believers to get rich and that material abundance is proof of God's love.

Strangely, these two heresies are directly connected. The do-
cetic heresy at its heart reveals a kind of doctrinal greed, taking
the metaphysics of the incarnation to its most selfish extreme.

The literal consequences of such a heresy would suggest that during the earthly ministry of Jesus the heavens were empty, so to speak. When Jesus prayed to God, he was really praying to himself. When he spoke in God's name, it wasn't really blasphemy, but the original Source. Thus it was God who died on the cross, and God who raised Himself, returning to the "right hand of Himself," until He returns again Himself in disguise. Quite literally one could thus argue: if you don't know Jesus, you've never met God—or vice versa.

The prosperity gospel, on the other hand, hardly blushes when it comes to the object of faith. Never mind that it turns the Bible's teachings about wealth upside down. It is spreading like wildfire in our time, crossing over from white evangelical megaministries to black Pentecostal churches and sweeping the continent of Africa itself. Its defining proof-text requires a hermeneutical contortion. Preachers tell their flocks that when Jesus said, "I came that they might have life, and have it abundantly" (John 10:10), it was material wealth he was talking about, and the Bible is like a map that guides us to buried treasure. And it's all for us.

While channel surfing one day I happened to come upon a broadcast from the Crenshaw Christian Center in Los Angeles. Striding across a stage devoid of religious symbols (crosses are seldom visible in megachurches) was the Reverend Frederick K. C. Price. He is a dashing symbol of wealth and all its trappings. The suit was tailored silk; the rings and the Rolex caught and reflected the studio lights. He waved a Bible above his head, its gilt-edged pages sparkling like his cuff links, conferring scriptural link to his personal success. The message was obvious: I have made it, and this is why; you too can make it, and this is how.

He looked out upon an audience of thousands and asked: "When you read that Jesus says, 'I came that you might have life and have it more abundantly,' what does 'abundantly' say to you as an individual person? What?"

The congregation roared back the answer: "A whole lot of stuff!"

Price responded, "A whole lot of stuff. Talk to me, brother. A whole lot of stuff."

When asked recently to explain his defense of the prosperity gospel, Price responded, "God gives us the power to get wealth. Does that sound like he wants you to be on welfare? That's in the Bible! He gives you power or the ability to get wealth. Notice what it doesn't say. It doesn't say God will make you wealthy. It says he'll give you the power to get it."[1]

I can at least admire the apologetics here. Not even Reverend Price wishes to claim that God alone will make people wealthy. Such claims are absurd on several levels, not the least of which is Mary's song, the Magnificat (Luke 2:46–55). In the great reversal of the reign of God, the hungry will be filled with good things, and "the rich he has sent away empty." Price also assumes that when Jesus speaks, God is speaking, yet the claim that God *causes* wealth makes him a bit uneasy. For one thing, since "with God all things are possible," then why are we not all rich now? Certainly, it would not be for lack of praying.

Stranger still is the remarkable distortion of the meaning of "abundant life" as having to do primarily with material wealth, an interpretation that must, for the sake of this preacher's own "abundant" life, turn a deaf ear to a chorus of warnings issued by Jesus of Nazareth concerning the dangers of wealth. At precisely the moment in American history when there is a growing consensus that we are living unsustainable lives because of unsustainable appetites, the church has lost its own voice. Once considered a deadly sin, greed has been made over into a sign of divine election and blessing.

The creative exegesis this requires is breathtaking. The aforementioned Reverend Price, however, gives us an example. He says, confidently:

Jesus had plenty, and then he was always giving to people, always giving to the poor, and so he had plenty from a material point of view. He was responsible for 12 grown men—their housing, their transportation, their food, their clothing—for a three and a half year period of time. He had to have something. This concept of Jesus being physically poor is not biblically true; it's traditionally true.[2]

There you have it. Everything you have ever been told about the poverty of Jesus—his counsel to his disciples to take "no bread, no bag, no money in their belts" (Mark 6:8); his challenge to the rich young ruler to sell all he has, give the money to the poor, and follow him; the liturgies of his death on a cross with a robe as his sole possession—has been not just adapted but *reversed*. The "tradition" that brought us this misconception, according to Price, has distorted the true facts. But that very scripture, including those passages that speak of "abundant life," is the tradition!

From the earliest writings of Paul to the last line of John's Revelation, there is nothing in or out of the Bible that even hints that Jesus was wealthy. To the contrary, although he is systematically deified by the early church, he is never elevated socioeconomically. He lives and dies a peasant, and although there were obviously wealthy patrons in the early church from the beginning, the relationship between the Jesus community and material possessions was downright Marxist: "All who believed were together and had all things in common; they would sell their possessions and goods and distribute the proceeds to all, as any had need" (Acts 2:44–45).

The transformation of the social gospel into the prosperity gospel (also called the "name it and claim it" or "blab it and grab it" gospel) did not occur in a vacuum. It is the inevitable devolution of the power of positive thinking movement that became a mainstream movement in America with the sermons of Dr. Norman Vincent Peale. The idea that God wants individuals to be successful, as opposed to socially responsible, and that faith itself is a success strategy had its roots in nineteenth-century existentialism. Even in the Great Awakening, the emphasis in religion began to undergo an experiential shift from surrender of the self to transformation of the self—and now, sadly, to self-aggrandizement.

GOD THE COSMIC BELLHOP

A tectonic shift has occurred in Western Christianity, mostly in the past century. The chasm now separating Christians from their own gospel concerning wealth is so wide and deep that when someone shouts across it we think they are talking nonsense. But before faith got wrapped seamlessly in the garb of the good life, followers of Jesus used the gospel wisdom to lance the boils of ego. The enemies of the spiritual life were pride and vanity. Worshiping earthly power, or failing to see that all blessings belong to God and should be managed on behalf of the less fortunate, was a sin.

The gospel and the community that formed around it provided the possibility that by grace one might escape the prison of self. They taught the virtues of humility, generosity, and compassion. God's power had been "made perfect in weakness," said Paul (2 Cor. 12:9)—an idea that to this day is so radical and counter-cultural that it deserves the scorn heaped upon it. Nevertheless, a follower of Jesus would never have considered the covenant of faith to be an *individual* covenant, much less a strategy for success. Jesus had names for religious leaders who cloaked themselves in piety in order to acquire status and power and wealth—a "brood of vipers" is just one example (e.g., Matt. 3:7).

This "humility rule," if you will, prevailed as the ultimate test of any claim to religious faith until the purpose of religion itself began to shift—away from a way of life that required sacrifice and service to a sanctified form of private ambition. The preaching of the church reflected this shift in a consumer society in ways that dulled the damnation of greed and brought God on board as a kind of spiritual Retailer. To sharpen this point by a comparison, consider this line from the renowned preacher Charles H. Spurgeon, uttered just over a hundred years ago to what was then the largest congregation in all Christendom:

> I believe that it is anti-Christian and unholy for any Christian to live with the object of accumulating wealth. You will say, "Are we not to strive all we can to get all the money we can?" You may do so. I cannot doubt but what, in so doing, you may do service to the cause of God. But what I said was that to live *with the object* of accumulating wealth is anti-Christian.[3]

The meaning here is unmistakable and conforms to numerous scriptural warnings about the love of money as spiritually debilitating. In the twentieth century, however, a New York City preacher who went by the name of Reverend Ike turned this teaching on its head by saying, "The lack of money is the root of all evil!" and "If you have trouble handling money, send it to me."[4]

When John Wesley preached his famous sermon "On the Use of Money," he said that if you make and save all that you can honestly, but do not give all you can away to relieve poverty, feed the hungry, and heal the sick, you may be a living person, but a dead Christian. Our luxuries, according to Wesley, should always come after someone else's necessity. What's more, before we die, we should have given *all* our money away.

Now let's be honest. Most of us don't plan to give all our money away before we die. Most of us plan to leave most of it to our kids. As for the seductions of wealth, we should begin by stating the obvious: about nothing are human beings more hypocritical than sex and money. In the case of the former, we enjoy reserving for ourselves the right to engage privately in what we condemn publicly. In the case of the latter, we love to hate the rich people we secretly long to become!

It doesn't take a genius to figure out that the letter of James was written in and on behalf of a poor congregation: "Come now, you rich people, weep and wail for the miseries that are coming to you. Your riches have rotted, and your clothes are moth-eaten. Your gold and silver have rusted, and their rust will be evidence against you, and it will eat your flesh like fire" (5:1–3). Take that! Now let's go buy a lottery ticket.

Since confession is good for the soul, let me begin with myself. Because none of us are immune from the seductions of stuff, I recently found myself secretly lusting after one of those flat-screen high-definition television sets. But I knew perfectly well that as a minister I am supposed to at least temper my consumer impulses, especially when it comes to such an obvious status symbol. After all, people brag about the size of their flat-screen TVs the way some people speak about the number of vintage labels in their wine cellar. When you tell someone you bought a flat-screen TV, the next question is guaranteed—"How big?"

Even so, I had to admit that watching programs in high definition was quite wonderful, and increasingly I felt like a dinosaur with rabbit ears in a world of megapixels and liquid crystal displays. Then along came my teenage son to help me out of my dilemma. We connect as father and son around our mutual love of college basketball (especially our beloved Kansas Jayhawks), and so right in the middle of March Madness, Cass came to me one day with a proposal specifically designed to assuage my guilt.

"Dad, we need a high-def TV to *really* enjoy the tournament. You know you want one, so what better time? Think of all the fun we'll have watching it together."

This was the sign from God that I'd been waiting for! I went out immediately and bought one, although I debated in my own mind what was "big enough" versus what was "too big." Come to think of it, that is a debate that goes on every day on this shrinking planet. But in the end we find ways to rationalize what we want, and we want a lot.

The largest church in America is now led by Joel Osteen. It meets in the Compaq Center in Houston and regularly draws twenty thousand people to worship. Osteen's approach is more sophisticated than that of Reverend Ike, but the message is essentially the same. Not only does God want us all to be rich, but the down payment required is a level of giving to Osteen's church that corresponds to the prosperity gospel formula: one can expect to be rewarded in ways that are *commensurate* with one's giving.

Giving, in other words, is not really an act of devotion without strings attached. It is an investment. Joel's wife, Victoria, put it this way in a recent worship service: "He not only wants to enrich you, but do things for you you know nothing about. Let him breathe the breath of life into your finances, and he'll give it back to you bigger than you could ever give it to him." The congregation says "Amen" and the buckets go around.[5]

If we can step back a moment, after admitting to our own culpability, there is still something remarkable going on here. This is no small step away from the biblical ethic of how the strong treat the weak. The gifted preacher Ernest Campbell put it this way. Consider the fact that much preaching today revolves around telling people, "Invite God into *your* story!" But the message of the Bible is entirely different. The invitation of scripture is to ask, "How can you be invited into *God's* story?"

The former is egocentric and selfish. It assumes that God, as Campbell put it, is a kind of Cosmic Bellhop. Where would you like your bags? It reverses the subject-object order of faith itself. To be invited into God's story is the true meaning of covenant.

It means sacrificing what all partners in a covenant are required to give up in order to effect transformation and redemption—as individuals, as families, as communities, and as citizens of the world. Christians are not independent contractors. To assume the posture of a God who exists to meet *our* shameless desires in a world that begs for bread is only possible in this culture for two reasons: "First, Christianity is the dominant faith tradition; second, the nation permits and rewards extraordinary inequalities of wealth and power."[6]

Once again, we see that the present crisis is not just political but theological. The heresy that makes all other heresies possible today is the idea that one can make the Bible say whatever it is that one wishes it to say, and that refusing to participate in such postmodern nonsense is a sign of intolerance or insensitivity to a gospel of "different strokes for different folks." People mistakenly call this religious freedom. It's not. According to author and essayist Curtis White:

> Religious freedom has come to this: where everyone is free to believe whatever she likes, there is no real shared conviction at all, and hence no church and certainly no community. Strangely, our freedom to believe has achieved the condition that Nietzsche called nihilism, but by a route he never imagined. For Nietzsche, European nihilism was the failure of any form of belief (a condition that church attendance in Europe presently testifies to). But American nihilism is something different. Our nihilism is our capacity to believe in everything and anything all at once. It's all good![7]

At one level, thoughtful people will ask, so what's wrong with Osteen's gospel of kindness to others, positive self-esteem, leaving past mistakes behind, and material blessings? Don't we all want these things, however we seek them or justify them, and isn't much of the critique of the prosperity gospel tinged with simple envy at its remarkable success? So what if he never mentions sin, suffering, or self-sacrifice? Isn't that what turns people off about organized religion?

The answers to these questions depend upon what one believes about the meaning and purpose of religion to begin with. If it is truly about getting saved and then getting rich while you wait to die, then the prosperity gospel is the natural result of our collective theological amnesia. But if the message is not infinitely malleable, if it really is about wisdom, selflessness, peace, and social justice, then our way of being the church cannot escape critique. When two ways of being in the world are diametrically opposed to each other, the claims of equal validity for each cannot be made so long as they are both called the same thing! It would be more honest for Osteen to call his enterprise the Osteen Institute for Positive Thinking and Material Prosperity. Calling it a church begs the question of whether all manifestations of the church are equally valid. Can any institution selling any product or behaving in any manner still call itself a church?

"YOUR BEST LIFE NOW" VS. THE SERMON ON THE MOUNT

Few would argue with the assertion that the Sermon on the Mount is the Constitution of the Christian faith. Although clearly part of the "emerging tradition" of the early church and subject to obvious redaction, the essence of the Sermon on the Mount, like the parables, stood a better chance of remaining reasonably intact because of its form. It consists of condensed aphorisms that reverse conventional wisdom and thus could be memorized as part of the oral tradition. The following should therefore give all prosperity preachers pause, including Osteen, author of the bestseller *Your Best Life Now*:

> Do not store up for yourselves treasures on earth, where
> moth and rust consume and where thieves break in and
> steal; but store up for yourselves treasures in heaven,
> where neither moth nor rust consumes and where thieves
> do not break in and steal. For where your treasure is, there
> your heart will be also. (Matt. 6:19–20)

One of the convenient truths about the prosperity gospel is
that it either attracts people who are already wealthy but want
more with less guilt (our name is legion) or promises a miracle
for those who are in desperate straits and on the verge of financial ruin. Either way, it plays on *anxiety*. There are plenty of both
these days (guilt and anxiety), as the rich get richer and the poor
get poorer. But consider how odd this message is compared to
Jesus' follow-up on living a simple life: "Do not *worry,* saying,
'What will we eat?' or 'What will we drink?' or 'What will we
wear? . . . For tomorrow *will* bring worries of its own. Today's
trouble is enough for today" (Matt. 6:31–34, emphasis added).

Jesus goes on to say that we should seek *first* the kingdom of
heaven, and the basic necessities of life will be provided. This
cannot possibly have anything to do with wealth or riches,
since he prayed only for enough bread for the day. The emphasis is upon the kingdom, with its open table and social justice,
which comes *before* daily bread. When he is reported to have
said, "Ask for whatever you wish, and it will be done for you"
(John 15:7), he cannot have meant that we should pray (as in
the popular revision of the "Prayer of Jabez") for riches, since
this is inconsistent with the way he taught his disciples to pray.
The emphasis is always "other-oriented," and this produces "just
enough." The early church was, on the whole, a gathering of the
poor. If there can be any doubt remaining about the dangers of
wealth, Jesus goes on to say, "No one can serve two masters; for
a slave will either hate the one and love the other, or be devoted

to the one and despise the other. You cannot serve God and wealth" (Matt. 6:24).

To use Paul Tillich's phrase, this has to do with "ultimate concern." Whatever becomes your ultimate concern *is* your god. So you cannot pretend to worship both without being a hypocrite. What lesson can be learned from Jesus' statement "Blessed are the poor" and from the parable of Lazarus and the rich man, except that those who prosper in this life while ignoring the poor will get their just reward?

In the parable of the rich man who foolishly stockpiles his wealth, building larger and larger barns, only to die suddenly without anything of true value (Luke 12:16–21), the wisdom of Jesus runs counter to the premise of the prosperity gospel itself. God does not exist to bless anyone's standard of living, and there are indeed "no pockets in a shroud." This unconventional wisdom would be a threat to every investment firm on Wall Street—mocking the idea of retirement anxiety and counseling that we should live in the moment with reckless generosity. In the letter of James is this counsel: "You covet something and cannot obtain it; so you engage in disputes and conflicts. . . . You ask and do not receive because you ask wrongly, in order to spend what you get on your pleasures. Adulterers! Do you not know that friendship with the world is enmity with God" (4:2–4).

Prosperity gospel preachers have even defended their appeal to material wealth by grounding it in the covenant with Abraham. They interpret his blessings as primarily material in nature and then extend those blessings to Christians. Televangelist Kenneth Copeland argues: "Since God's covenant has been established and prosperity is a provision of this covenant, you need to realize that prosperity belongs to you now!"[8] To defend this position, prosperity preachers appeal to Galatians 3:14, but only to the first half of the text, which says that "in Christ Jesus the blessing of Abraham might come to the Gentiles . . ." The second half reads, "so that we might receive the promise of the Spirit through the faith." Obviously, these are not material blessings that Paul is talking about.

Some prosperity preachers even distort orthodox views of the atonement, especially 2 Corinthians 8:9: "For you know the grace of our Lord Jesus Christ, that though he was rich, yet for your sakes he became poor, so that by his poverty you might become rich." Ironically, Paul was teaching the Corinthians that since Christ accomplished so much for them through his death and resurrection, then how much more ought they to empty themselves of their riches in service to him.

A final example is 3 John 2: "Beloved, I pray that you may prosper in all things and be in health, just as your soul prospers" (NKJV). Prosperity preachers like Oral Roberts have used this text as a carte blanche approval of the gospel of prosperity. But this is merely a greeting by John, and the Greek word translated as "prosperity" is only used four times in scripture and does not mean to prosper in the sense of gaining material possessions. Rather, it means "to grant a prosperous expedition and expeditious journey" or "to lead by a direct and easy way."

Where there is a capitalist will, however, there is almost always a nonbiblical way. So many of us desire material wealth, and our culture offers so few other ways to measure success, that the prosperity gospel is the inevitable result of a faith tradition now completely assimilated into the dominant culture. The appeal is irresistible: *you can have all this and Jesus too.* Whether it's Joel Osteen or the Reverend Creflo Dollar (his real name), who brags about the number of Rolls Royces God has given him, there is now a whole generation of high-powered, influential, attractive preachers who are peddling a dangerous myth. They are "drunk with the wine of the world," to use poet James Weldon Johnson's phrase. The fact that the prosperity gospel is growing so rapidly in the African American community may be because more blacks have moved into the middle class, and this is a way to justify upward mobility without feeling guilty, according to Professor Michael Dyson of Georgetown University. "The civil rights movement said, 'You are responsible for your brother and sister. You ought to bring them along.' The prosperity gospel says, 'Your brother or sister is responsible for him- or herself, and what they should be doing is praying right, so that God can bless them, too.'"[9]

This "gospel of bling," as Robert Franklin calls it, represents what he calls "the single greatest threat to the historical legacy and core vales of the contemporary black church tradition." It has placed the church in the posture of "assimilating into a culture that is hostile to people living on the margins of society, such as people living in poverty, people living with AIDS, homosexuals, and immigrants."[10]

When the church moves away from the work to which it was called and commissioned, the poor will have lost one more ally in a world where we shop with a religious frenzy and step over homeless people on our way to the next clearance sale. Just when we desperately need a gospel that can critique our madness, a "Christ against culture" to use H. Richard Niebuhr's phrase, we have preachers telling us how to serve *mammon* by *using* God.

The church can no longer afford preachers who fail to take a stand when they know that the church is facilitating evil, whether it's a war based on lies, cruelty toward gays based on fear, or a distortion of the wisdom of Jesus as fantastic as the prosperity gospel. It's time we faced the hard truth. Selling Jesus as an investment strategy is a sin, and anyone claiming to be a Christian who does not practice simplicity and generosity is engaged in self-deception. After all, the best seats at the banquet mean nothing if, at the final banquet, God starts serving at the back of the line.

BEYOND THE SENTIMENT OF SIMPLICITY

There is a warm and fuzzy movement in the land today whose adherents wink at Thoreau, adore St. Francis of Assisi, and preach the virtues of "green" while parking two Range Rovers in a three-car garage and leaving a carbon footprint the size of Alaska. The verdict is in, and humanity itself faces a challenge to its very existence. The science we say we trust (unless it threatens our way of life or our religious beliefs) has spoken clearly, and our way of being in the world has become unsustainable. The way we consume, the way we farm, the way we go to war over oil—they have all come home to roost, and we are now at the end of our planetary rope.

As Al Gore described global warming recently, "The earth has a fever."[11] We are the major cause of that fever, and after we are gone the fever will eventually break and the earth will eventually repair itself without us. Perhaps this is our fate. Perhaps we are arrogant to assume that we are destined to remain the dominant species on this gorgeous globe. But in the meantime, what on earth is the church doing to save a perishing planet, instead of just our imperishable souls?

The answer is, almost nothing. As writer and critic Wendell Berry puts it, "The certified Christian seems just as likely as anyone else to join the military-industrial conspiracy to murder Creation."[12] Here and there, pockets of religiously inspired conscience are bubbling up, and although they face rejection and condemnation, some brave and thoughtful evangelicals are joining in the call to care for the earth. Mainline and liberal churches ought to do more than just applaud this fact. They should join hands and hearts to do battle with all the enemies that we all agree on: global warming, poverty, and the continued degradation of women. There's nothing wrong with having a "personal relationship to Jesus," as long as you know something about the company you are keeping. Liberals and conservatives could actually come together now over what it would mean to follow Jesus on a dying planet. Just think of the numbers.

To save ourselves, however, we will first have to *save Jesus from the church*—break him out of the stained-glass window in which he is frozen as a two-dimensional superhero without depth, flesh, or breath. We need to turn away from the institutional forgeries that constitute orthodoxy for millions: the blood atonement, fear-based fantasies of the afterlife, "vertical" notions of heaven and hell, selective providence based on human ignorance, and a God who pimps for us on the battlefield. Whatever else we think we know about the Great Mystery that goes by many names, this one fact is true: God's thoughts are not our thoughts, even on our best days.

A consistent chorus of voices today is rising across what used to be considered impossible divides—political, economic, racial, sexual, and religious. The message is that what Dietrich Bonhoeffer called a "religionless Christianity" is not a new gospel at all, but the recovery of the original. Our faith was not born as a belief system; it was turned into one. We need not fear science, just because we have learned to understand time and space differently. It is not even a scandal now to call oneself an "atheist" (a nontheist) who still believes in the transcendent mystery that we call God. What's more, a nontheistic understanding of God is what actually makes interfaith dialogue and mission possible. If God is the "Ground of Being" and not a Cosmic Dealer, then faith must be a journey toward wisdom and compassion and not a system of human creeds with divine consequences. This is a journey we can all take together, regardless of our specific prophets, teachers, or revelations. This is our hope.

Since survival itself now depends upon living in sustainable local communities, and the church at its best is a model of such community, it offers more hope than any other institution in our society for leading the way home. It cannot do this, however, if it remains a salvation club, dedicated to the "very strange enterprise of 'saving' the individual, isolated, and disembodied soul . . . as an eternal piece of private property."[13]

The resources of creation must be more fairly distributed, and the church at its best could be a kind of fire-breathing dragon of conscience. If not, these growing inequalities will spark the kind of revolution that destroys the good with the bad. Revolution has never come except where conditions were revolting and the veneer of civilization thin. As history has proved with monotonous regularity, when the food finally runs out, the have-nots will grab whatever weapons are available and head straight for the suburbs.

The eminent Old Testament scholar Walter Brueggemann said once that to "do justice" is to "sort out what belongs to whom, and to return it to them."[14] This assumes that the prosperity gospel has it exactly backwards, or Moses would have said, "Let my people prosper!" What biblical justice does is *restore* what is denied, whether it's freedom, human dignity, or the essentials of existence itself. Whether it is David's rape of Bathsheba and his murderous cover-up or the death-dealing invasion of Iraq under false pretenses, we commit injustice when we take what doesn't belong to us in order to enrich ourselves.

Perhaps the time has come for all of Christendom to sit at the feet of the Quakers and the Mennonites again. Perhaps we should all try to emulate the Friends and other nonviolent groups like them and practice simplicity and integrity as a *lifestyle,* not just as a politically correct sentiment. I have come to believe that of all those attempting to recover the essence of New Testament Christianity, the Quakers may have been the most faithful to the wisdom of Jesus. Believing that everyone has the ability to experience the love and leadership of God and that no ecclesiastical authority has to mediate or direct that experience, they live and act in ways that seek to remove anything that fosters pride or compromises one's relationship to God—wealth, striving after success, or fashionable dress.

"Live simply so that others may simply live" is often thought to be just a standard liberal bumper sticker, but it has taken on an apocalyptic urgency. There is, quite simply, no hope for survival if we do *not* simplify. The church should take the lead by explaining that in the upside-down world of the reign of God, there are actually blessings to be found in "downward mobility."

In what has become a prophetic statement about the sickness of the age, Emma Lapsansky framed the Quaker imperative this way: we must "dampen the noise of everyday life" in order to be open to the voice of the Inward Teacher.[15] Contrary to the prosperity gospel, "plainness" becomes a personal virtue, and individual excesses are considered unethical because, as William Penn put it, "what aggravates the evil [of adherence to fashion] is that the pride of one might comfortably supply the needs of ten."[16]

It has been our habit of late to separate the causes of war from our lifestyle, when in fact the seeds of war are planted there. A Quaker teacher and antislavery advocate, writing over two centuries ago, argued in one of the earliest analyses of the structural roots of poverty that the accumulation of wealth was itself a form of violence. "May we look upon our treasures, and the furniture of our houses, and [our] garments, and ask whether the seeds of war have any nourishment in these our possessions."[17]

If the rest of the church could recognize this as the ancient concept of *stewardship* and rescue that word from its narrow application to fund-raising, we might discover that simplicity is not just practical, but liberating. It is, after all, the lesson of every enlightened teacher that material possessions beyond what is necessary for survival and simple pleasures should be disowned. The cycle of always wanting and acquiring more—and then storing, insuring, maintaining, and protecting all this stuff from theft—is expensive, time-consuming, and idolatrous and gets between the soul and life itself. To choose what is "plain and sober," as Robert Barclay put it, is to battle vanity.

There is another way, and in the present crisis might lie the seeds of a different future. Expensive gas may actually help to bring back the joys of walking and bicycling, the socialization of mass transit, even the underrated beauty of just staying home. Americans may give up, finally, one of the most debilitating myths of Western culture: that there can always be more and more of everything. Besides, less is not just inevitable; it can be redemptive.

If you have ever lived in a house where nothing was ever discarded, you know that clutter closes in on the soul—as if you will eventually be found dead in the only space left free of knickknacks. To become a *minimalist,* therefore, is not just to express an architectural preference. Rather, it is to sweep the inane thieves of perfectly empty space out with the trash and gaze in astonishment on the forgotten beauty of a bed, a lamp, and a book. Austerity intensifies everything left standing.

More is not more, and excess may yet become the tattoo we regret from the weekend when we tried, but failed, to purchase happiness. It may become fashionable again to repair something, rather than to replace it, and to send away the chemical truck as it pulls up to spray poison on our yards in pursuit of the perfect lawn. For Jesus' sake, send those trucks back where they came from. You may have more weeds, but the chemicals won't all end up in mother's milk.

It is a foolish dream, perhaps, but it's mine—and faith is always against the odds. In my dream, people will plant vegetable gardens again and sit outside, watching the sky. They will learn to sew on buttons and make something with their own hands. The will take their own shopping bag to the store, and they will recycle everything as if the earth depends on it. Nothing will seem stranger than an "all you can eat" restaurant, and nothing will bring more shame in the future than to sport a grossly distended belly in a world of skeletal children.

Remember, in the church we should know what community means. Our bodies are part of the Body, and our open table is an exercise in sublime absurdity. The elements of bread and wine are so minuscule that we appear to be daring God to satisfy us out of all proportion to their size. Perhaps—even only *maybe*—we will begin to slow down, breathe deeply, dig in the dirt again with our own fingers, and save a small enough slice of the world to become contagious, even beautifully corrupting, "like yeast that a woman took and mixed in with three measures of flour until all of it was leavened" (Matt. 13:33).

TEN

RELIGION AS RELATIONSHIP, NOT RIGHTEOUSNESS

Are you jealous of the ocean's generosity?
Why would you refuse to give this love to anyone?
Fish don't hold the sacred liquid in cups!
They swim the huge fluid freedom.

—*Rumi*

I know a couple who begin each day with a brief ritual they call "canopy." Married many years, this husband and wife engage in a simple, wordless, predawn ritual. They sit facing each other, legs entwined, hands clasped behind each other's back, their foreheads lightly touching. In silent meditation, they stagger their inhaling and exhaling so that, quite literally, they take *in* and then breathe *out* each other. No prayers are spoken; no requests of God are made; no human professions of any kind are offered. There is just silent, sacred *proximity*—the resting of heads together and the exchange of breath. If "canopy" is forgotten, the day does not go as well, I'm told.

This simple act bears witness to more than just a couple's desire to stay connected to each other. The deeper truth is one that could save the church from its own preoccupation with sin and salvation: it is *relationships,* not transactions, that hold the key to human happiness. We are as we relate—not as we possess, control, believe, or conquer. The most sacred space in all of creation is the space *in between*.

Such a truth is easy to verify, for indeed life itself provides all the evidence. Our deepest misery, as well as our most sublime moments, are the result of our relationships. Beginning with children and parents, the Little gods observe the Big gods in the temple of the home,[1] and daily domestic liturgies create meaning, value, order, and often a most insidious form of competition. Broken covenants between children and parents underlie much of the dysfunction in the world, and the unfinished business between fathers and sons has launched wars, deceived nations, and even led to madness.

In the West, we speak of happiness in quantifiable terms as it relates to accomplishments and possessions. But when love is new, lovers seem to need nothing but each other, and they often remember the times when they were poor as the happiest times. The wealthy are just as often miserable beyond belief and so consumed with the objects that separate them from one another as to suggest an inverse relationship between wealth and happiness. Too much stuff can clutter the space "in between."

Aristotle noted that of all the most prized possessions in the world (including health and wealth), humans end up prizing *friendship* above all—especially old friends.[2] There is not a human joy that is not *relational* at its core, whether it is the mystery of love between lovers, between a child and a best friend, between a musician and the epiphany of sound, between an athlete and a respected opponent, between an artist and the created work, between a reader and a book, between a disciple and a teacher, or between a seeker of wisdom and the Ultimate Mystery. Real wisdom is never achieved in isolation or by objectifying the other. Wisdom is the by-product of the mystery of human communion with the nonobjectified other, met with humility and vulnerability in the sacred space that appears when one is asked to dance.

Faith itself is a relationship, and scripture cannot be objectified without destroying that relationship. We continue to speak of a "battle for the Bible," when in fact the Bible is a *conversation*. We overhear it at a great distance, translated (and corrupted) from foreign tongues, and spoken by those who never imagined us as the intended audience. It is always wise to remember that not a single word of the Bible was written for you or for me—so how can we be having a "battle" over it? One only competes for what one wishes to possess, yet how does one "possess" a conversation? We can only listen carefully and thoughtfully and in the posture of one who, in search of wisdom, is listening through a keyhole to the distant echoes of a love affair.

Those who use the Bible as a weapon or as a kind of "holy encyclopedia in which one may look up information about God"[3] have turned the conversation into an object and then into an idol. The relationship no longer has integrity. Metaphors get demoted to the rank of reports, and then people argue over whether they are "true." The scriptures are songs of wonder and amazement over the birth of a new relationship to God, but we have turned them into a test for true believers—as if you can give lovers an exam and then assign a grade to the accuracy of their passion.

When the sacred conversation we now call the New Testament conversation first began, it was between an itinerant Galilean teacher and his peasant-class student entourage. By the time it ended, he was divine, and every great Judaic theme had reputedly been reinterpreted and completed by his coming. At first, he was spoken of as the son of Adam, who would return at the end of the age as messiah and whose resurrection was a sign that God had vindicated a righteous servant. Then the conversation began to change—and with it, of course, the relationship changed.

As his followers grew in number and the second coming did not occur, the point on the time line at which Jesus became the

Christ was moved back. For Paul, it happened at the resurrection, when he was "adopted" as the Son of God. For Mark, it was moved back to his baptism, when a voice from heaven announced the verdict. Matthew and Luke moved it back farther, from a grown man standing waist-deep in the muddy waters of the Jordan to the miraculous conception of an infant with only one human parent. Finally, as the second century dawned, the last gospel of John was written in the heat of the Christian-Jewish divorce, and the divinity of Christ was moved back as far as possible—to the beginning of time, where he is preexistent and fully divine, begotten of no human parent, except as he chooses to "humble himself" and assume the form of a servant in a plot to save the world.

By the time the bishops gathered at lakeside Nicea in 325, it was clear that the only way to put the Christ above all other royal figures was to make him coequal with God, for "anything less would have put him on a par with other royal figures who could boast of one divine parent."[4] Half-human, half-divine lords were commonplace, so the bishops sealed the transaction with the Nicene Creed, and the sage became the Savior. He is the "only begotten Son of God, begotten of the Father before all worlds, God of God, Light of Light, Very God of Very God, begotten, not made, being of one substance with the Father by whom all things were made; who for us men, and for our salvation, came down from heaven, and was incarnate by the Holy Spirit of the Virgin Mary, and was made man, and was crucified also for us under Pontius Pilate."

Notice what happens to the life of Jesus of Nazareth in this most formative of all creeds. He "came down, . . . was made man, and was crucified." The gospel is reduced to a cosmic loop with eternal consequences. Gone and rendered superfluous are the Sermon on the Mount, the maddening parables, the open

table, the boundary-breaking mission to the Gentiles, the eleva-
tion of women, the touching of the untouchables—and not a
word of the creed testifies to the redeeming power of unconditional love to cure and to restore.

Why should we be surprised? The earliest creed, the Apostles' Creed, had already eliminated the life and message of Jesus.
Countless Christians have mouthed these lines in worship for
centuries: "Who was conceived by the Holy Spirit, born of the
Virgin Mary, suffered under Pontius Pilate . . ." Look carefully
at what separates the birth of Christ from his death. The world's
greatest life is reduced to a comma.

Strange as it sounds, we must *demote* Christ now and recover
him as Jesus once more, if we are to enter and survive the new
age that is upon us. As long as the relationship remains one
between a fearful and ignorant people looking for favors in
exchange for beliefs and an alien invader who swoops out of
heaven and back again to recruit and claim believers, we will
worship passively from a distance, instead of following closely
enough to smell his breath and be made wise. The church meant
well by its promotion, of course, but unwittingly sowed the seeds
of separation between all that is human and all that is divine. In
so doing, we have *reversed* the message of Jesus, who was trying
to arrange an unlikely marriage and then keep us together.

True religion is relationship, not righteousness. It must play
out "on earth as it is in heaven." For this we need clarity and
self-consciousness about the nature of our relationships and
what makes them authentic and life-changing—as opposed
to inauthentic and death-dealing. If a first-century Jew can
model a new relationship with God for his disciples, then a
twentieth-century Jew can define the true nature of the sacred
as a personal dialogue. The latter's name is Martin Buber, and
the church would do well to remember what he said.

I AND THOU

Martin Buber was a philosopher, a theologian, and one of the great minds of the twentieth century. He spelled out his essential belief that life at its depth is *dialogical* and that reality itself is defined by personal dialogue: "When two people relate to each other authentically and humanly, God is the electricity that surges between them."[5] Influenced by Kierkegaard, Nietzsche, Dostoyevsky, and the eighteenth-century Jewish movement called Hasidism, Martin Buber was an early Zionist but then became one of the leading proponents of cooperation with the Arabs. His tense, paradoxical, spiritual philosophy has influenced Christian theologians like Reinhold Niebuhr, Paul Tillich, and Karl Barth. His landmark work is entitled *I and Thou* (*Ich und Du*, 1923).

According to Buber, human beings may adopt one of two attitudes toward the world: either I-Thou or I-It. The former is the relationship between a subject and another subject and, as such, is a relationship in which human beings are aware of each other as having a "unity of being." Instead of thinking of the other as having specific, isolated qualities, in an I-Thou relationship human beings engage in a dialogue that involves each other's whole being and is thus a model for the divine relationship.

I-It relationships, on the other hand, involve a "dialogue" between a human being and an object. This subject-object relationship may involve another human being, but only if that person has been turned into an object—as when an employer treats employees as cogs in a machine or a predatory lover reduces the subject of seduction to an object and the union to a "conquest." Even when people appear to be in love, they may in fact only be attracted to a projection of themselves in the other, and thus the other is "objectified." In religion, when believers use God just for peace of mind, for special favors, or as a substitute Parent, the relationship becomes one of subject-Object.

William Blake's image of Nobodaddy, the punishing father in the sky, comes to mind.

For this reason, Buber rejected the idea that God was "wholly Other," as Barth believed, or the *mysterium tremendum,* as Rudolph Otto believed. "Of course God is the 'wholly Other,' but He is also the wholly Same, the wholly Present," said Buber. "Of course He is the *mysterium tremendum* that appears and overthrows, but He is also the mystery of the self-evident, nearer to me than my I."[6]

The distinction between I-Thou and I-It is more than just a philosophical curiosity. It is crucial for the recovery of Christianity as incarnate wisdom, not salvation. An I-Thou relationship is a direct interpersonal relationship that is not mediated by any intervening system of ideas or objects of thought. It is a direct subject-to-subject relationship, and thus it is an end in itself, never a means to an end. For Buber, I-Thou stood for the kind of meeting in which two beings face and accept each other as truly human. Thus, the relationship is not utilitarian or self-serving; rather, it is an ultimate relation involving the whole being of each subject.

Love, as a relation between I and Thou, is the supreme subject-to-subject relationship, characterized by caring, respect, commitment, and responsibility. It is a covenant in which both subjects find completion in a shared reality, a unity of being that is impossible if either party in the relationship is objectified. For Buber, God is the eternal Thou and, as such, represents the ultimate in a nonobjectified relationship, since God can never be known, investigated, or examined as an object of thought. Instead, God is Being Itself and transcends all attempts at objectification. The relationship with God is the foundation for all other I-Thou relations, and faith becomes a matter of dialogue, not fear or ritual conformity.

Buber never wavered in his belief that the ultimate compliment one could pay to God was to be in constant dialogue with

God, like his servant Job, as if God were like a member of the family to be submitted to, but nonetheless argued with: "See, he will kill me; I have no hope," says Job, "but I will defend my ways to his face" (13:15). Even when things seem hopeless, the dialogue must continue. Hope vanishes when we stop talking to one another.

It was Buber's study of Hasidism, which emphasized an awareness and celebration of holiness in everyday life, that led him to believe in a "worldly holiness." God was no remote abstraction but could "be seen in every thing, and reached by every pure deed." Because he was committed to an understanding that God was nonsectarian, irreducible, and never the "object" of thought, he resisted the Zionist goal of establishing a Jewish state and bitterly opposed what he called "the disease of nationalism." Instead, he promoted what he called "Hebrew humanism." Because both the Jews and the Palestinians had a common love for the land, he believed that a just and cooperative arrangement could be worked out. Instead, the war that accompanied the establishment of Israel in 1948 came as a bitter fulfillment of his worst fears.

It should come as no surprise that Martin Buber wrote extensively on Jesus and Christianity, even though he rejected Christian claims for the divinity of Christ. One can only wonder what he might have thought of a Christian who referred to Jesus as a misunderstood Jew and regarded the Bible as a conversation. Martin Buber believed that the Galilean sage had exemplified the highest ethical and spiritual ideals of Judaism and wanted most of all for the dialogue between Christians and Jews to continue. "Whenever we both, Christian and Jew, care more for God Himself than for our images of God," he wrote, "we are united in the feeling that our Father's house is differently constructed than our human models take it to be."[7]

The dogmatic tenets of the world's religions have turned God into an It, into a Lawgiver and Judge, and faith into a subject-

Object relationship. No wonder faith is a "product" now in a consumer culture, a vindication of war and a guilt-alleviating justification for lavish lifestyles. The creeds have offered us a deal instead of a dialogue, salvation in place of an encounter, a pension in place of a purpose. It was Buber who said, "Success is not one of the names of God."

When we enter into relationship with Thou, we perceive that we are now responsible for all those whom we once considered strangers, but in whom the Face of Thou resides. The echo of Jesus' disciples is unmistakable here: "Then the *righteous* will answer him, 'Lord, when was it that we saw you hungry and gave you food, or thirsty and gave you something to drink?'" (Matt. 25:37, emphasis added). This applies also to our enemies, the ones our former president refused to sit down and speak with (the ultimate example of an I-It relationship). Martin Buber profoundly observed that when we enter into an I-Thou relationship, we have "abolished moral judgment forever; the 'evil' man is simply one who is commended to him [or her] for greater responsibility, one even more needy of love."[8]

If Martin Buber's philosophy is taken seriously, then it represents a danger to all external authorities and institutions, because it assumes that people can enter into authentic relationships and live as free, mature, and independent adults. "Religious faith does not result from the mindless recitations of religious formulas or from the adherence to unintelligible liturgical routines, but from the total commitment of one's being and one's life to the eternal *Thou*."[9]

JESUS AS THE ANTI-IT

If the Bible is a conversation inspired by God, but not infallible, then what can we say is normative about it for either Jewish or Christian communities? And what does the voice of Jesus mean for Christians in that conversation? The answer lies in the distinction between a formative and a *final* conversation. We never have the last word, and the prophets urge us to go on listening and then go on speaking truth to power. The dialogue is always the dialogue of covenant, and the struggle is always about how to move beyond I-It relationships to authentic and transforming I-Thou relationships.

In the beginning, in the poetry to Genesis, God speaks the world into being and then pronounces it good. Not only is creation itself a rhetorical act, symbolized by speaking, but it is a *relational* act, born in the movement of the breath of Thou and its life-giving effect over what was a "formless void," dark and deep—a lifeless It. Creation unfolds in the relationship between each It (darkness, lack of separation, barrenness, lifelessness) and its opposite, a Thou (light, land, swarming creatures, and finally human beings). It may seem arrogant that humans should crown themselves as the final act of creation, the *imago Dei,* but in our world only humans have developed a consciousness sufficient to ask where creatures like us and everything else came from. As separated as we still are from Thou, we have taken our first tentative steps away from being an It.

Every creation story seeks to answer this question and to establish life as meaningful, as opposed to meaningless, by daring to imagine that the universe has *intentionality* and thus purpose. If everything is just a fantastic accident, then we can assume that we are little more than fantastic Its, participating in no way with a creator Thou. But if we exist because we were meant to exist, then our very *being* is a statement of value—it is better that we *are* than that we are *not.* This is the starting point for all theology. Why is there matter, and does it matter?

No one can, or should, try to answer this question for anyone else, but an affirmative answer has obvious consequences. It compels us to ask additional questions about our relationship to Thou, so that we will know something about not just our origins but also our responsibilities. The answer comes immediately in the Hebrew scriptures with the myth of the garden of Eden, where human prototypes display the innate ability to disobey, to be vain, to be victims, and to be tempted to believe that they might become as Thou—and end up relating to all creation as if it were an It.

Why does Cain kill Abel in the Bible's first murder? Because the ancient prejudices between farmers and shepherds rendered one offering acceptable and the other unacceptable—just as to this day one sibling often suspects that he or she is not the favorite and jealously renders the other an It. Abraham's wanderings are the supreme example of one who trusts Thou so deeply as to leave all comfort and wealth behind to act on the promise of fulfillment—the land of Canaan and a multitude of descendants. Sarah gives birth to Isaac against all odds, but this is not a biological miracle; it is wisdom—when dealing with Thou, we do not figure the odds. When Joseph's brothers sell him into slavery and leave him for dead, he ends up saving their lives and giving the credit to Thou. Jealousy can turn you into an It, but covenant can reverse the process and restore your relationship to Thou.

When the Israelites find themselves turned into an It in the land of Egypt, they are led out of bondage by someone who insists that a subject-object relationship is not the will of Thou. It turns out to be easier to escape one kind of bondage than to enter into the bondage of a covenant, however, and the rest of the Hebrew Bible can be read through this simple lens: keep the covenant, inherit the promise; break the covenant, lose the promise. Objectify the other, or turn God into a tribal deity who shares your superstitions and tribal bias, and the idea of faith itself is perverted and forsaken.

No one made this point more dramatically than the Jewish prophets, whose remarkable lives and writings are often overlooked by Christians who dismiss the entire "Old Testament" as the gospel of loveless legalism while holding that the "New

Testament" is the gospel of translegal grace. Also, because gospel writers used the prophets to "predict" things, like the circumstances of the birth of Jesus, it is easy to mistake a prophet for a clairvoyant. What they did, in fact, was demonstrate what an authentic I-Thou relationship looks like, sounds like, and acts like. By refusing to be made into Its for the king ("Tell me what I want to hear"), many paid with their lives.

As masters of oral speech, the prophets had a passion for social justice that was, in the case of Amos, "downright electrifying."[10] They did not just entertain radical thoughts; they embodied radical lifestyles to draw attention to their ideas. Hosea named two of his children Lo-ruhamah and Lo-ammi, which in Hebrew mean "Not pitied" and "Not my people." Isaiah named two of his children after Hebrew phrases that predicted what would happen to Judah and walked naked and barefoot through the streets of Jerusalem over a period of three years to symbolize that Judah should not enter a military alliance with Egypt against Assyria, for Assyria would conquer Egypt and carry the people off naked and barefoot as prisoners of war.[11]

Jeremiah was a prophetic performer, shattering a clay jug and announcing, "Thus says the LORD of hosts: So will I break this people and this city" (19:11). Once he wore a wooden yoke to symbolize what Jerusalem and Judah should do to bear the yoke of Babylon and not join an alliance against it. Another prophet, Hananiah, broke Jeremiah's wooden yoke to make the opposite point. Ezekiel was perhaps the "star of prophetic street theater"; just before the Babylonian conquest and destruction of Jerusalem, he was told by God to make a model of Jerusalem surrounded by a siege wall, camps, and battering ram (4:1–17):

> In a public place, he is to lie on his left side for 390 days, then on his right side for 40 days, to symbolize the number of years that Israel and Judah are to spend in exile. During all this time, he is to eat starvation rations

such as would be available in a city under a prolonged siege, and he is to bake bread using human dung as fuel. All of this would symbolize what was soon to happen to Jerusalem.[12]

And to think that today we arrest people for stepping over imaginary lines, or when they gather to protest war, or when they try to form a union. We shame dissident pastors into silence and warn them not to discuss "controversial" issues like immigration or equal rights for gays. The truth is, we have few pastors in the church today who qualify as outrageous for the cause of justice, and in fact the most common model for ministry now is someone who is well married (preferably with children), respected, pious, and doesn't "cause trouble." In this sense, the church has made an It out of the ministry—turning it into a profession demanding decorum, rather than recognizing it as a divine calling with disturbing consequences.

These God-intoxicated Hebrew prophets brought the abstract ideas of religion down to earth and fearlessly shared what they believed was wrong with the domination systems of the world. Abraham Heschel describes "their breathless impatience with injustice" and recognizes that they possessed *"sympathy with the divine pathos."*[13] They stood with the poor and against the elites as shamelessly as Hosea stood by his fallen wife and then claimed that it was never too late to go in search of her and bring her home, as if the porch light is always on in the kingdom of I-Thou.

Jesus was a product of this prophetic tradition, and he soaked up the wisdom teachings of Israel. He also stood in the tradition of "street theater," and he knew the value and the danger of "acting out" alternative social visions in public. He spoke intimately of God, incurring charges of blasphemy, and healed without credentials in a way that undercut the Temple and the business of religion. But in all things, from the beginning to the end of his memorable public ministry, he was, to put it in the paradigm of Martin Buber, the "Anti-It."

"It" was any and all dehumanizing objectifications—of God as lawgiver and judge, remote, inaccessible, angry, and in need of appeasement; of the Temple as a place of corruption and stifling legalism; of the poor as expendable ciphers; of the sick and insane as mad dogs to be chained up in graveyards; of Samaritans as untouchables; of women as invisible and inferior; of the rich as unredeemable; of common fishermen as incapable of wisdom; and of children as undeserving of simple patience and a loving touch. If the world defined anything or anyone as an It, Jesus demonstrated that it could be *redefined* in relationship to Thou. Even inanimate objects could become lessons about Thou: seeds, salt, wineskins, yeast, empty jars, hidden treasure, or stones that would cry out if the truth could find no other voice. Our artificial distinctions between secular and sacred did not matter to Jesus, because he was a mystic. He knew that the way we relate to anything ultimately determines how we relate to everything—including God.

Born in scandal, he redeemed scandal. A student of John the Baptist, he graduated from judgment to compassion. A member of the peasant class, he redefined royalty. A student of Moses, he instituted a higher law. A man of prayer, he expanded the practice to include every good deed done for the sake of an It that deserved to be in relationship with Thou. Enemies were to be prayed for, not killed; broken relationships with brothers and sisters were to be repaired before coming to the altar; anxiety about what to eat, drink, or wear is wasted energy, because in the kingdom of right relationships you get what you need, not necessarily what you want. Storing up treasures on earth is foolishness, asking for what you need is a good idea, and treating others as you wish to be treated is the signature of I-Thou. Religion is relationship, not righteousness, because love changes everything.

WAKING UP WORTHY AND WALKING

The last book in the Bible concludes with a famous warning: "I warn everyone who hears the words of the prophecy of this book: if anyone adds to them, God will add to that person the plagues described in this book; if anyone takes away from the words of the book of this prophecy, God will take away that person's share of the tree of life and in the holy city, which are described in this book" (Rev. 22:18–19).

Whether this describes a warning about adding to or taking away from the book of Revelation or the whole Bible does not matter now. The warning *itself* must be ignored. The page must be turned, and the conversation must continue. The voices in the Bible are like the major premise in a syllogistic argument. They launch the conversation with an assertion, but they are not self-evident. They are an invitation, not a pronouncement, the first words of an emerging community, but hardly the last word. The Bible is not literally the word of God but a collection of human words about God, inspired, but covered with human fingerprints. Taken out of context, scripture has been and continues to be used to defend the indefensible: slavery, anti-Semitism, and the degradation of women, minorities, and those outside the sexual, social, or economic mainstream.

It has been used to smear science, to sanction war, and to hide the abuses of its own priests. Instead of filling kings with compassion, it has been used to support the divine right of kings. As God has revealed new truth to each generation, the Bible has often been used to resist it, justify violence against its adherents, and divide creation into those who are saved by believing certain things and those who are lost and dispensable because they dared to question them. The very book that preserves the remarkable teachings of Jesus, the wise and enlightened one, is now the hammer of orthodoxy and thus betrays the spirit of the Galilean sage to whom it testifies. One can find nothing in the Sermon on the Mount to suggest that faith can be reduced to a tract, available at the grocery store, listing the eight rungs up the ladder of glory.

The old way of being Christian in the world cannot stand; and a new way cannot be avoided if the faith is to endure and the human race is to survive. Christianity requires no sacrifice of the intellect; it can withstand any question we dare to ask and any answer we are brave enough, in the service of truth, to offer. The belief that the Bible is the unique revelation of God, containing the literal words of God and defining faith as a set of beliefs that are required now for the sake of heaven later, is not only indefensible, but socially, politically, and now environmentally fatal. Fundamentalism in any form is the enemy of the future. Thus, when we model fundamentalism in any form, we are hypocrites to condemn it in others.

In her wonderful book *Christianity for the Rest of Us,* Diana Butler Bass confounds the common belief that all mainline churches are dying. Those that are thriving, in fact, may seem very different inside and out, but they have at least three characteristics in common. First, there is an embrace of *tradition,* but not traditionalism in a postdenominational age. Second, there is an emphasis on *practice* not purity among legions of churchgoers who are fed up with exclusivist Christianity. And third, the objective of the spiritual life is *wisdom,* not certainty in a changing world, where the questions are even more important than the answers. "Counter to the prevailing view that people want certain answers, mainline pilgrims rest comfortably with ambiguity. They resist dogmatism in favor of being part of a community where they can ask life's questions—a circumstance that they identify as necessary for the spiritual life."[14]

What is required now is a shift in human consciousness about the nature of faith and the object of religion itself. We should cease to ask, "Are you a *believer*?" and ask instead, "Are you a *follower* of Jesus?" We must not inquire, "Are you saved?"

but instead ask, "Are you able to drink of this cup?" And we must be ever vigilant about the meaning of discipleship, so that it does not turn into courtship. The operative question for the new age is not, "Do you love Jesus?" but, "Has Jesus ever been a radically disturbing and transforming presence in your life?"

This new Reformation, which is now in its infancy, will focus its attention not on the Trinity or justification by faith or works but on Christian *practice.* Grounded in the open table, forgiveness as reciprocal, and devotion as a private activity divorced from public acts of piety, it will look and sound a lot like the earliest strands of the Jesus tradition—because that's precisely what it is. Before disciples were called Christians, they were a collection of misfits who practiced radical hospitality by eating a sacred meal without a guest list or a bouncer. Now one can be called a Christian just by mouthing a creed. So how will we reverse this perversion and recognize a disciple in our time?

Here's how we will know. Access to God, the unnamed and unknowable One, will be *unbrokered* and therefore never denied to anyone outside of any religious franchise. Jesus may have started a new religion in spite of his true intentions, but we should base it on his teachings, not ours. The notion of "privilege" will be anathema to Christian practice. As John Dominic Crossan so pointedly puts it, "Jesus robs humankind of all protections and privileges, entitlements and ethnicities that segregate human beings into categories. His Father is no respecter of persons. Does that not include the label *Christian?*"[15]

In the emerging church, faith will be not a transaction (benefits for beliefs) but a beloved community in which the rewards of I-Thou relationships are *intrinsic.* Love will be its own reward, and the church will stand by its most sacred duty—to slay the self in service to Something More. Easter will be reclaimed as a spiritual, not a metaphysical, moment, and latter-day disciples will have an opportunity to be resurrected in this world, rather than the next. The myths that proclaim divinity and human sexuality to be mutually exclusive must be rejected, lest we continue to suffer a body-spirit duality that is death-dealing instead of redemption. If that means Jesus was a bastard, then perhaps the gospel becomes an even more miraculous story than if he is the preexistent Lamb of God. Otherwise, the claim that God meets us in our brokenness and suffering is a lie. For God so loved the world that he sent an alien?

In a world shredded by absent or emotionally crippled fathers, Jesus needs a real one—and if that was Joseph, so be it. I want to see his figure in the crèche as something more than a contrived and awkward "extra." I want fathers to consider what sort of man raises such a wise son, and women to consider why devotion is not limited to purity but encompasses faithfulness in the midst of uncertainty and ridicule. The false dichotomy created by "Mary the mother of God" and the "other" Mary, falsely portrayed as a prostitute, has made women in the church spiritually schizophrenic for centuries.

My beloved preaching professor, Fred Craddock, said once, "Perhaps people are obsessed with the second coming because, deep down, they are really disappointed in the first one." Christianity should be future-oriented to the extent that it works to build a world that is fit for children, but it should never play the role of apocalyptic racketeer. We must all stand up together now and tell the end-times preachers, "Methinks thou doth enjoy this fear-mongering too much." God is in it for the long haul.

Finally, the gospel is "good news" not for adherents but rather for *practitioners*. And the practice of Christianity is made possible not by intellectual assent to propositions but by an existential embrace of *worthiness*. Most of the harm done in this world is the result of people who are compensating for deep insecurities, who are trying to "prove" something to someone, but who always come up short. That's why the premise of the gospel deserves to be called "good news." It is a call not to accept a formula for salvation but to act on an unearned inheritance:

that we are *created* by God, *children* of God, *beloved* by God, and *accepted* by God.

It means that every morning, we can wake up worthy and walk. This is the grace that brings radical freedom and the end of striving. Faith is something we *do,* against the odds, in loving defiance of a world gone mad. We do not become a good person by believing in God; we become a good person by loving God, especially the God we meet in every living thing. For the prophet Micah, his successor Jesus, and all the rest of us who are praying for a new day in the church, the most important question we can ask now is not about what we believe. It is about how we relate.

"He has told you, O mortal, what is good; and what does the LORD require of you but to do justice, and to love kindness, and to walk humbly with your God?" (Mic. 6:8).

A PREACHER'S DREAM: FAITH AS FOLLOWING JESUS

During my seminary days, every student at Phillips Graduate Seminary was required to write a credo—a concise statement of what one *really* believed about God, Jesus, the Bible, and the church. As students, we joked about whether this was a legitimate academic exercise or a matter of quality control. Did they really want to know what we believed or were they just making sure we believed something before turning us loose on Christendom?

In those days (the late 1970s), three books in particular had been formative for me, giving me permission to consider an alternative vision of faith, not to mention a different way to conceive of parish ministry. One was Friedrich Schleiermacher's *On Religion: Speeches to Its Cultured Despisers*. Another was Bishop John A. T. Robinson's *Honest to God*. The last was Leslie Weatherhead's *The Christian Agnostic*. I had arrived at seminary with more than my share of doubts, but I was also pulled along by something I could neither name nor ignore. My graduate studies had done two things simultaneously—added to my doubts and made even more palpable the pull of that unnamed and unknowable Something.

So when I sat down to write my credo, I called it, after Weatherhead, "The Credo of a Christian Agnostic." I had significant doubts about the church as an institution, but I was also a child of the 1960s, and something in my heart hummed along when George Harrison sang "My Sweet Lord." I too really wanted to know him.

Looking back on my early days in the pulpit, I am ashamed to say that I often inflicted a self-righteous liberalism on people who did not deserve it. In my tiny student church in Marland, Oklahoma, I preached a sermon one Sunday that disassembled, for poor unsuspecting farmers, the theory of the blood atonement. They listened patiently, their calloused hands folded, their foreheads creased from driving rented tractors over rented fields. When I had finished explaining why, in my expert opinion, they were not "washed in the blood of the Lamb," they demonstrated amazing grace by inviting me to lunch!

I knew so little about their world that I once called on a farmer during wheat harvest in the middle of the day. He was asleep in the other room. I though maybe he was ill. When I appeared confused, the wife looked at me as if I was from another planet. "We don't cut wheat in the daytime, young man. It's too hot. He's asleep because he's been riding the combine all night."

It is good for ministers to be honest about how little they know and how poorly they hide the fact behind religious jargon and a desire for self-display. It is also good for ministers to remember that they are the keepers of an ancient secret, a radical gospel that is both a product of its time and timeless. And like it or not, we are all priests, no matter how thoroughly Protestant. It may frighten us, and we may not like the responsibility, but when people look at us, they see God's ambassador. They also see a confessor.

This lesson also came home to me early, on the high plains of Oklahoma, when I was called to the hospital in Ponca City to visit a dying member of that same student congregation. We hardly knew each other, but this elderly man had insisted that "the young minister come." I stood next to his bed, and he said, "Dying is hard. Last night I tried to suffocate myself."

I stood there absolutely mute, trying to figure out why none of my classes had prepared me to say anything in this situation (and thus, mercifully, I said nothing), when suddenly he changed the subject.

"Reverend Meyers," he said, "when I was young, we had a housekeeper, a woman who cleaned for us, and she was handsome." He emphasized the word "handsome" by making a curving motion with his weathered hand. Then he paused and looked out the window for a long time. Then he looked at me and said, "Reverend Meyers, I got too close to that woman once."

After a long silence, he pulled me down close to him and said, "Do you know what I mean?"

I said, "Yes, sir. I know what you mean."

The years rolled by, our children came, and after two years of postgraduate study at Drew University, I was called to the pulpit of Bushnell Congregational UCC in Detroit, the most racially divided city in America. I visited the Ford River Rouge plant, where raw steel went in one end of the plant and Model T's rolled out the other. I studied the legacy of Reinhold Niebuhr, whose only pastorate was in Detroit and whose memoir, *Notebook of a Tamed Cynic,* suddenly made sense to me. Just beneath the happy, but fading Motown sound, racism and the riots smoldered under every conversation. In a Detroit coffeehouse, I read *Moral Man and Immoral Society.*

When the chance came to return to Oklahoma, it was to become the pastor of Mayflower Congregational Church in Oklahoma City. It was small, made up mostly of three extended families, and politically conservative. On a good Sunday, sixty people showed up to worship and they wanted nothing to do with the UCC. "Too liberal," they said.

So began an adventure in ministry that has lasted twenty-five years and renewed my faith in the possibility of the church as a beloved community. Those early years were difficult, because trust comes slowly in parish ministry. Looking back, I realize that I grew up with the congregation, that some of the older members were very patient, but that through it all we did not turn loose of one another.

Seeking to build a liberal Protestant church fashioned after Riverside in New York without the cathedral, we attracted the attention of a Reformed Jewish congregation and a progressive African American church—and we entered into covenant with them. At the time, I was blissfully unaware of the existence of Muslims in Oklahoma City.

A generous member offered to put the sermons of the Mayflower pulpit on the radio, and people began to listen, because "faith comes by hearing." Our worship services remained simple, covenantal rather than creedal, and we resisted many of the changes in worship style and music that were emerging. We still prefer the human voice, live music, and the clear glass windows of a meetinghouse to high-tech auditoriums.

In the meantime, which W. H. Auden reminded us is the most important time of all, we pledged to reject only those people whom Jesus would have rejected and neither made claims of absolute authority nor offered assurance of personal salvation for the doctrinally "sound." The congregation took responsibility for its own ministry and mission and has evolved into a force for love in Oklahoma City that astonishes me to this day.

Ministers love to believe that when a church thrives, it is mostly their doing. Not so. Our job is to turn loose the community property that is the gospel of Jesus Christ and then remove obstacles that keep people from thriving in such a community. The success of Mayflower Church has come mostly from the irrepressible desire of its people to respond to the call of God. The church now feeds and clothes six hundred homeless persons a month. We've built a year-round medical clinic in the remote mountain town of Jinotega, Nicaragua, and an orphanage for deaf children. In Oklahoma City, we repair homes for the elderly, tutor public-school students who are falling behind in reading, and house the state's first comprehensive program for children with autism at no cost to parents. The level of monetary giving from our Benevolence board is remarkable for a church of seven hundred and fifty members, as are the number of candidates in our church who run for public office. We have been a center of resistance to the war in Iraq since before it began.

None of this occurred because we set out to be politically correct or intellectually self-righteous. We wanted to be, ultimately, followers of Jesus. The questions we asked ourselves were simple, but more radical than we knew. What would happen if we accepted original blessing over original sin and stopped trying to *prove our worthiness*—to a parent, to a spouse, to an employer, or to God? What if we took seriously Paul Tillich's counsel that we "accept the fact that we are accepted"?

What if we could pull off a modern-day miracle and persuade a whole community of human beings that faith is characterized by what I have called from the pulpit "the end of striving"? What if we could shift the idea of salvation from survival of personal identity to *radical freedom*? Not freedom *from*—obligations, promises, fidelity, commitment, and self-sacrifice—but freedom *to*—live beyond angst, be delivered from self-pity, escape the prison of self, grow old gracefully, master the ego, live in harmony with the natural world, and break the chains of fear itself, especially the fear of death? What if we followed Jesus, instead of just worshiping Christ?

We have certainly had our share of failures, and we are by no means a collection of saints. But somehow the power of the beloved community has triumphed over everything—and this is the miracle of parish ministry. Staying in one place a long time can be an astonishing incubator of grace. Instead of searching in vain for perfection, we need to stay put and harvest the joys of intimacy. It was Flannery O'Connor who said it best: "Somewhere is better than anywhere."

To begin this book, I told a true story in the Prologue about a nightmare that is not uncommon these days. Like lots of other people, I have wondered what it means to call oneself a Christian today. But not all dreams are nightmares. Indeed, my own congregation has ended up giving me hope in a world of despair, and for this I will never be able to repay them.

Mayflower Church, in fact, has become a different kind of dream, and it deserves to be shared also. It inspired a very different vision recently, as I drifted off to sleep on a Saturday night. The alarm was set for 5 a.m., and in what constitutes a luxury in my world, the coffee was already made, and all I had to do was push the button. As always, I woke just before the alarm went off, silenced it, slipped out of the bed where my beloved lay, and went down the hall past the room where my son slumbered in deep, adolescent oblivion.

The coffee gurgled, and the house filled up with the aroma of consciousness. I sat down at the computer to write my pastoral prayer and get ready for the early service. The house was dark, but the birds were stirring. They grow loud just as the day breaks, even through no human eye can see it—the instant when the dawn steals the night.

I cupped my hands around the steaming mug, closed my eyes behind my fogged-up glasses, and realized that I had been dreaming. In my dream I had seen a "surge" of a different sort—soldiers coming home, and sun-soaked markets in Baghdad where nothing explodes, and dark-eyed children flying kites again. In my dream I saw Americans stop their shopping long enough to pay their respects to every flag-draped coffin and to mourn every death, regardless of where, or how, it occurred.

In my dream, I heard the voices of a new generation of leaders who will one day restore dignity and honor to this land I love, and who, in humility, will know what they do not know. War will again be the horror of last resort, and peace will be waged at the highest level with the help of the church of Jesus Christ, the Prince of Peace. Fashions may change, but one thing will remain constant—the church can be counted on for an unwavering commitment to nonviolence. We will never again argue the case that violence saves.

In my dream, TV preachers had all retired to serve local parishes because preaching into a camera and asking strangers for money was not what Jesus had in mind. On Sunday morning, the inside of a church had become the only place where a millionaire could end up seated next to a homeless person living with HIV, or a church matriarch could sing hymns in harmony with a teenage runaway who joined the youth group just for the pizza. I woke up thinking: *if this is Christianity and these are Jesus followers, I want to be one.*

In my dream, I saw walls knocked down, built by nations that once condemned their enemies for building walls. Preachers got their nerve back and thundered: "Nothing advertises human failure like a wall, and no human being should ever be called an 'alien,' illegal or otherwise."

In my dream, no one had to choose between science and religion, as if the head and the heart cannot marry, and women took their rightful place around the open table, serving as well as being served. Sexual orientation was an identity, not a curse, and money was a form of portable power, not an instrument of oppression. I woke up thinking: *if this is Christianity and these are Jesus followers, I want to be one.*

In my dream I saw churches lead the way to protect the environment—conserving energy, recycling, preaching the virtues of organic farming and lawn care, and establishing community gardens. Sunday school classes were free and open forums in which adults could ask any question, and no one feared new ideas or new ways of being faithful.

In my dream, gays and lesbians were constituents of creation, not freaks of nature. In light of our incomplete knowledge about the mysteries of human sexuality, the church vowed to make up for human ignorance by practicing divinely inspired radical hospitality—in other words, to act like a church. Opponents of gay marriage like to say, "God made Adam and Eve, not Adam and Steve," but at Mayflower we have a follow-up question to ask: "So who made Steve?" As evangelicals are fond of saying, "At the foot of the cross the ground is level." I woke up thinking: *if this is Christianity and these are Jesus followers, I want to be one.*

That's when I remembered where the dream came from. The seeds of this vision had been planted by a sermon I heard years ago.[1] The story came out of Appalachia, from a place called Watts Bar Lake, where a certain preacher served a tiny rural mission among the poorest of the poor. It was their custom on Easter to have a baptismal service in the evening—by immersion of course—at sundown.

After the candidates for baptism moved into the water to be dunked, they waded across to the shore, where the congregation had gathered to sing and cook supper. The folks on the shore had built little booths for changing clothes out of hanging blankets. After those newly baptized had dried and changed, they formed a circle around the campfire to get warm, and then the rest of the congregation formed a larger circle around them.

A man named Glenn Hickey always did the honor of introducing the new people, giving their names, explaining where they lived and where they worked. Then the ritual would begin. One by one, each person in the outer circle would make an offer to those standing by the fire.

"My name is . . . and if you ever need somebody to do washing or ironing . . ."

"My name is . . . and if you ever need anybody to chop wood . . ."

"My name is . . . and if you ever need anybody to babysit . . ."

"My name is . . . and if you ever need anybody to repair your home . . ."

"My name is . . . and if you ever need anybody to sit with the sick . . ."

"My name is . . . and if you ever need a car to go to town . . ."

Around the circle it went, until those who had symbolically died and risen to Christ were officially "adopted." Then they all ate and had a square dance, and at the appointed time a man named Percy Miller, with thumbs in his bibbed overalls, would stand up and say, "Time to go."

He lingered to put out the fire, kicking sand over the dying embers. Then he looked at the preacher and said, "Craddock, folks don't ever get any closer than this."

When I first heard this story, it was from the mouth of the preacher himself. In the silence of the sanctuary, after a long pause, Fred Craddock looked out at all of us, peered over his spectacles, and let the story sink in. Then he said, "Once, when I told this story to a group of city folk, they looked amused, but confused. One of them said, 'Fred, what do they call that where you come from?'"

He replied, "I don't know what you call it where you come from. But where I come from we call it . . . church."

ACKNOWLEDGMENTS

This book would not have been possible without the invitation by Dennis Smith, professor of New Testament at my alma mater, Phillips Theological Seminary, to join the famous (or infamous) Jesus Seminar. It has been in the midst of such remarkable and fearless biblical scholars that I have found new ways to uncover, correct, and communicate the Good News. I hope this book helps to take the light of the Westar Institute out from under the bushel basket of animosity toward organized religion, and lets it shine for beleaguered pastors everywhere.

In the meantime, I continue to be amazed at my abundant life, made possible by the luminous web of family, friends, and colleagues. From the love of my parents, who are alive and well in Bellingham, Washington, to read this book and be proud; to my wife, Shawn, soul-mate and salvation; to my three children, Blue, Chelsea, and Cass, who tolerate their father's public life and preacher ways; to my mentor and example in the pulpit, Fred B. Craddock; to my colleagues and students at Oklahoma City University; and to the beloved community of Mayflower Congregational UCC Church in Oklahoma City.

Last, but not least, I want to thank those remarkably gifted people whose calling it is to shepherd books down the long and winding road that connects a good idea to something worth reading. To John Shelby Spong, who put in a good and timely word on my behalf; to Lisa Zuniga, production editor, who helped end my addiction to commas and misplaced modifiers; to Levan Fisher, whose cover design is superb; to Emily Grandstaff, publicist extraordinaire; and most of all, to my editor at HarperOne, Roger Freet, who pushed me in all the right directions. Without his perceptive prodding, the book would have been long on urgency but short on grace.

NOTES

CHAPTER 1: JESUS THE TEACHER, NOT THE SAVIOR

1. Marcus Borg, *Meeting Jesus Again for the First Time* (San Francisco: HarperSanFrancisco, 1995), chap. 2.
2. Albert Schweitzer, *The Quest of the Historical Jesus,* trans. W. Montgomery (New York: Macmillan, 1968), p. 403.
3. Borg, *Meeting Jesus Again for the First Time,* p. 21.
4. Bill McKibben, "The Christian Paradox: How a Faithful Nation Gets Jesus Wrong," *Harpers,* August 2005, p. 31.
5. Robert Funk, *Honest to Jesus: Jesus for a New Millennium* (San Francisco: HarperSanFrancisco, 1996), p. 2.
6. John Dominic Crossan, *Jesus: A Revolutionary Biography* (San Francisco: HarperSanFrancisco, 1994), p. xi.
7. For a more complete understanding of the breadth and depth of non-canonical gospels, see Robert J. Miller's *The Complete Gospels,* 3d rev. ed. (Santa Rosa, CA: Polebridge Press, 1995).
8. John Dominic Crossan, *Jesus: A Revolutionary Biography* (San Francisco: HarperSanFrancisco, 1994), p. xi.
9. John Shelby Spong, *Jesus for the Non-Religious* (San Francisco: HarperSanFrancisco, 2007), pp. 18–19.
10. Marcus Borg, *Reading the Bible Again for the First Time* (San Francisco: HarperSanFrancisco, 2002), p. 31.
11. Funk, *Honest to Jesus,* p. 2.
12. For an excellent study of Ricoeur's approach to scripture, see Mark Wallace, *The Second Naiveté: Barth, Ricoeur, and the New Yale Theology* (Macon, GA: Mercer University Press, 1990).
13. Crossan, *Jesus,* pp. 27–28.

CHAPTER 2: FAITH AS BEING, NOT BELIEF

1. Marcus Borg, *The Heart of Christianity* (San Francisco: HarperSan-Francisco, 2003), p. 26.
2. Borg, *Heart of Christianity*, pp. 28–37.
3. Borg, *Heart of Christianity*, p. 30.
4. To explore Jesus the Jew, Amy-Jill Levine, author of *The Misunderstood Jew* (San Francisco: HarperOne, 2006), suggests such titles as Geza Vermes, *Jesus the Jew* (Philadelphia: Fortress, 1973); *Jesus and the World of Judaism* (London: SCM, 1983); *The Religion of Jesus the Jew* (Philadelphia: Fortress, 1993); *Jesus in His Jewish Context* (Minneapolis: Fortress, 2003); Bernard Lee, *The Galilean Jewishness of Jesus* (New York: Paulist, 1988); Donald Hagner, *The Jewish Reclamation of Jesus* (Grand Rapids, MI: Zondervan, 1984); and the three volumes and counting of John Meier, *A Marginal Jew* (New York: Doubleday, 1991–2001).
5. Levine, *Misunderstood Jew*, p. 19.
6. Levine, *Misunderstood Jew*, p. 20.
7. John Shelby Spong, *Jesus for the Non-Religious* (San Francisco: Harper-SanFrancisco, 2007), p. 15.
8. See Marcus Borg's summary in *Meeting Jesus Again for the First Time* (San Francisco: HarperSanFrancisco, 1995), chap. 2, p. 40, n. 6.
9. John Dominic Crossan, *Jesus: A Revolutionary Biography* (San Francisco: HarperSanFrancisco, 1994), pp. 25–26.
10. Crossan, *Jesus*, p. 10.
11. Frederick Buechner, *Peculiar Treasures: A Biblical Who's Who* (Harper & Row, 1979), pp. 69–70.
12. The New International Version has become the most popular "contemporary English" translation of the Bible for evangelicals. Red-letter editions of the NIV are just as popular now as those of the venerable King James Version were for earlier generations.
13. Borg, *Meeting Jesus Again for the First Time*, p. 29.
14. The term "cognitive dissonance" was coined by Leon Festinger to describe a conflicted mental state in which one idea, usually an unexamined assumption, is brought into direct conflict with a new idea, creating dissonance. If a person believes, for example, that he or she values good health but is a smoker, the two ideas create cognitive dissonance that (as the opposite of harmony) needs to be resolved so that homeostasis (a state of equilibrium) can be restored. The person can give up smoking or give up the idea that it is unhealthy (retreat into denial about the dangers of smoking), but something has to "give." In the spiritual world, dissonance can be created by telling

stories in which people get more than they deserve or are too easily forgiven, stories that shatter conventional religious wisdom with subversive wisdom. When something "gives" here, listeners often learn new truths or a new way of seeing.

15. Borg, *Meeting Jesus Again for the First Time,* p. 77.
16. Robin Scroggs, *Paul for a New Day* (Philadelphia: Fortress, 1977), p. 10.
17. Some scholars have wondered about the significance of a camel. What could a beast that stores up fat and fluids to carry it through a long journey represent?
18. See Luke 10:12; Matt. 10:15; Luke 10:13–14; Matt. 11:21–22; Luke 11:31; Matt. 12:42; Luke 11:32; Matt. 12:41.

CHAPTER 3: THE CROSS AS FUTILITY, NOT FORGIVENESS

1. Martin Hengel, *Crucifixion in the Ancient World and the Folly of the Message of the Cross* (Philadelphia: Fortress), quoted in John Dominic Crossan, *Jesus: A Revolutionary Biography* (San Francisco: HarperSanFrancisco, 1994), p. 124.
2. Crossan, *Jesus,* p. 130.
3. John Shelby Spong, *Jesus for the Non-Religious* (San Francisco: HarperSanFrancisco, 2007), p. 97.
4. Spong, *Jesus for the Non-Religious,* p. 98.
5. Crossan, *Jesus,* p. 145.
6. Martin Kähler, *The So-Called Historical Jesus and the Historic, Biblical Christ,* trans. and ed. C. Braaton (Philadelphia: Fortress, 1964), p. 80.
7. Bart Ehrman, *Misquoting Jesus: The Story Behind Who Changed the Bible and Why* (San Francisco: HarperSanFrancisco, 2005), p. 10.
8. Crossan, *Jesus,* p. 146.
9. The complete and detailed explanation of this move from historical passion to prophetic passion to narrative passion can be found in Crossan, *Jesus,* pp. 145–51.
10. Spong, *Jesus for the Non-Religious,* p. 107.
11. See Walter Wink's trilogy, *Naming the Powers* (Philadelphia: Fortress, 1984); *Unmasking the Powers* (Philadelphia: Fortress, 1986); and *Engaging the Powers* (Minneapolis: Fortress, 1992).
12. Stephen Finlan, "Christian Atonement: From Metaphor to Ideology," *The Fourth R,* July–August 2007, p. 3.
13. Marcus Borg, *The Heart of Christianity* (San Francisco: HarperSanFrancisco, 2003), p. 95.

14. Robert Funk, *Honest to Jesus* (San Francisco: HarperSanFrancisco, 1996), p. 11.

15. Albert Noland, *Jesus Before Christianity* (Maryknoll, NY: Orbis Books, 1978), p. 117.

CHAPTER 4: EASTER AS PRESENCE, NOT PROOF

1. John Dominic Crossan, *Jesus: A Revolutionary Biography* (San Francisco: HarperSanFrancisco, 1994), p. 160.

2. Rudolph Bultmann, "The Primitive Christian Kerygma and the Historical Jesus," in Carl E. Braaten and Roy A. Harrisville, trans. and eds., *The Historical Jesus and the Kerygmatic Christ: Essays on the New Quest of the Historical Jesus* (New York: Abingdon, 1964), p. 42.

3. Crossan, *Jesus*, p. 95.

4. Crossan, *Jesus*, p. 163.

5. Robert Funk, *Honest to Jesus* (San Francisco: HarperSanFrancisco, 1996), p. 260.

6. Funk, *Honest to Jesus*, p. 263.

7. Crossan, *Jesus*, p. 179.

8. James M. Robinson, "From Easter to Valentinus (or to the Apostles' Creed)," *Journal of Biblical Literature* 101 (1982): 5–37.

9. Funk, *Honest to Jesus*, p. 270.

10. Funk, *Honest to Jesus*, p. 270.

11. Funk, *Honest to Jesus*, p. 267.

12. Elaine Pagels, "The Controversy over Christ's Resurrection: Historical Event or Symbol?" in Elaine Pagels, *The Gnostic Gospels* (New York: Random House, 1979), p. 6.

13. N. T. Wright has written extensively from an evangelical perspective on the various beliefs in resurrection, or life after death, in numerous works. For an overview of pagan, Jewish, and early Christian perspectives, see his McCarthy lecture, "Jesus' Resurrection and Christian Origins," delivered March 13, 2002, in the Faculty of Theology of the Gregorian University.

14. Crossan, *Jesus*, p. 197.

15. Crossan, *Jesus*, p. 190.

16. Crossan, *Jesus*, pp. 190–91.

17. John Shelby Spong, *Jesus for the Non-Religious* (San Francisco: HarperSanFrancisco, 2007), p. 118.

18. According to Robert Funk, "By the time the documents of the New Testament were written, belief in the resurrection of the body had become widespread. It seems to have been embraced by the Essenes at Qumran, by the Pharisees, and by the Jesus movement, but not

by the Sadducees. The motivation for entertaining the idea was that the human sense of justice demanded that somebody, presumably God or the gods, rectify the injustices perpetrated in this life. . . . The resurrection was a particularly congenial idea for the new Jesus movement. . . . Jesus' resurrection represented vindication for the persecuted and wrongfully executed man Jesus. It was compensation for his suffering. It also positioned Jesus as a cosmic judge who would return at the end of the age and preside over the resurrection of the righteous to eternal life and the resurrection of the wicked to eternal punishment" (*Honest to Jesus,* p. 275).

19. See Stanley Hauerwas and William Willimon, *Resident Aliens* (Nashville, TN: Abingdon, 1989).

CHAPTER 5: ORIGINAL BLESSING, NOT ORIGINAL SIN

1. G. K. Chesterton, *Orthodoxy* (Garden City, New York: Image/Doubleday, 1959, repr. ed.), p. 15.
2. "Literalized" is a term used often by John Shelby Spong to describe what happens when nonhistorical Bible stories, meant to communicate deep spiritual truths, are treated as historical accounts.
3. See Matthew Fox, *Original Blessing* (Santa Fe, NM: Bear, 1983).
4. Joseph Campbell, *The Hero with a Thousand Faces,* 2d ed. (Princeton, NJ: Princeton University Press, 1968), p. 3.
5. Augustine, *Confessions,* bk. V, p. 6.
6. William Shakespeare, *Macbeth,* Act 5, Scene 5.
7. Walter Wink, *The Human Being: Jesus and the Enigma of the Son of the Man* (Minneapolis: Fortress, 2002), p. 38.
8. Matthew Fox, *The Coming of the Cosmic Christ* (San Francisco: Harper & Row, 1988), p. 13.
9. Archibald MacLeish, "Bubble of Blue Air," *Riders on Earth Together, Brothers in Eternal Cold, New York Times* (Dec. 25, 1968).
10. Abraham Heschel, *Moral Grandeur and Spiritual Audacity* (Farrar, Straus and Giroux, 1997), p. 252.
11. Fox, *Coming of the Cosmic Christ,* p. 6.
12. Fox, *Coming of the Cosmic Christ,* p. 26.
13. Ken Wilber, "A Spirituality That Transforms," http://wilber .shambhala.com/html/misc/spthtr.cfm/ p. 9.

CHAPTER 6: CHRISTIANITY AS COMPASSION, NOT CONDEMNATION

1. Søren Kierkegaard, *The Parables of Kierkegaard,* ed. Thomas Oden (Princeton, NJ: Princeton University Press, 1978), p. 71.

2. Robin Meyers, "Virtual Virtuosity," *Christian Century,* November 1, 2000, p. 1109.

3. Crossan, *Jesus: A Revolutionary Biography* (San Francisco: HarperSanFrancisco, 1994), pp. 194–95.

4. Crossan, *Jesus,* p. 195.

5. See Phyllis Trible, *God and the Rhetoric of Sexuality* (Philadelphia: Fortress, 1978), chaps. 2–3.

6. Borg, *Meeting Jesus Again for the First Time,* p. 48.

7. Barbara Brown Taylor, "As a Hen Gathers Her Brood," *Christian Century,* February 25, 1986, p. 201.

8. Borg, *Meeting Jesus Again for the First Time,* p. 50.

9. See Jerome Neyrey, *The Social World of Luke-Acts* (Peabody, MA: Hendrickson, 1991), p. 279.

10. Neyrey, *Social World of Luke-Acts,* pp. 278–79.

11. See John Dominic Crossan, *The Historical Jesus: The Life of a Mediterranean Jewish Peasant* (San Francisco: HarperSanFrancisco, 1991).

12. William Sloane Coffin Jr., *Credo* (Louisville, KY: Westminster John Knox, 2004), p. 43.

CHAPTER 7: DISCIPLESHIP AS OBEDIENCE, NOT OBSERVANCE

1. Annie Dillard, *Holy the Firm* (San Francisco: Harper & Row, 1984), pp. 55, 57.

2. Dillard, *Holy the Firm,* p. 57.

3. Annie Dillard, *Teaching a Stone to Talk* (San Francisco: Harper & Row, 1982), p. 30.

4. Dillard, *Teaching a Stone to Talk,* p. 19.

5. Dillard, *Teaching a Stone to Talk,* p. 40.

6. This was a favorite expression of Dr. Ernest Campbell, former minister of the Riverside Church of New York City.

7. See Warren Carter, *Matthew and Empire* (Harrisburg, PA: Trinity Press International, 2001), chap. 7.

8. Carter, *Matthew and Empire,* p. 112.

9. Carter, *Matthew and Empire,* p. 122.

10. William Sloane Coffin Jr., *Credo* (Louisville, KY: Westminster John Knox, 2004), p. 151.

11. N. T. Wright, "Kingdom Come," *Christian Century,* June 17, 2008, p. 29.

12. Robert Funk, *Honest to Jesus: Jesus for a New Millennium* (San Francisco: HarperSanFrancisco, 1996), p. 241.

13. Funk, *Honest to Jesus,* pp. 245–46.

14. This is a notion developed in my last book, *Why the Christian Right Is Wrong: A Minister's Manifesto for Taking Back Your Faith, Your Flag, Your Future* (San Francisco: Jossey Bass, 2006).

15. See Stanley Hauerwas and William Willimon, *Resident Aliens* (Nashville, TN: Abingdon, 1989).

16. Curtis White, "Hot Air Gods," *Harpers,* December 2007, p. 14.

CHAPTER 8: JUSTICE AS COVENANT, NOT CONTROL

1. Marcus Borg, *The Heart of Christianity* (San Francisco: HarperSanFrancisco, 2003), p. 127.

2. Borg, *Heart of Christianity,* p. 130.

3. John Dominic Crossan makes this point in several books and his essay "Jesus and the Kingdom," in Marcus Borg, ed., *Jesus at 2000* (Boulder, CO: Westview, 1997), pp. 52–53.

4. William Sloane Coffin Jr., *Credo* (Louisville, KY: Westminster John Knox, 2004), pp. 50–51.

5. Robert Bellah, *Habits of the Heart* (Berkeley: University of California Press, 1985).

6. Bellah, *Habits of the Heart.*

7. See Parker Palmer, *A Hidden Wholeness: The Journey Toward an Undivided Life* (San Francisco: Jossey Bass, 2004).

8. Borg, *Heart of Christianity,* p. 223.

CHAPTER 9: PROSPERITY AS DANGEROUS, NOT DIVINE

1. "Prosperity Gospel," *Religion and Ethics Newsweekly,* August 17, 2007, http://www.pbs.org/wnet/religionandethics/week1051/feature.html.

2. "Prosperity Gospel."

3. Tom Carted, ed., *2,200 Quotations from the Writing of Charles H. Spurgeon* (Grand Rapids, MI: Baker, 1988), p. 216.

4. Ben Witherington, "What's Wrong with Prospering? The Gospel According to Joel Osteen," March 30, 2006, http://benwitherington .blogspot.com.

5. Ralph Blumenthal, "Joel Osteen's Credo: Eliminate the Negative, Accentuate Prosperity," *New York Times,* March 30, 2006.

6. Robert Franklin, "The Gospel of Bling," *Sojourners Magazine,* January 2007.

7. Curtis White, "Hot Air Gods," *Harpers,* December 2007, p. 13.

8. Kenneth Copeland, *The Laws of Prosperity* (Fort Worth, TX: Kenneth Copeland Publications, 1974), p. 51.

9. Michael Dyson, quoted in "Prosperity Gospel."

10. Franklin, "The Gospel of Bling."
11. Al Gore, in his acceptance speech for the Nobel Peace Prize, Oslo, Norway, December 10, 2007.
12. Wendell Berry, *Sex, Economy, Freedom and Community* (New York: Pantheon, 1993), p. 94.
13. Berry, *Sex, Economy, Freedom and Community*, p. 114.
14. Walter Brueggemann, *To Act Justly, Love Tenderly, Walk Humbly* (New York: Paulist, 1986), p. 5.
15. E. J. Lapsansky, "Past Plainness to Present Simplicity: A Search for Quaker Identity," in E. J. Lapsansky and Anne A. Verplanch, eds., *Quaker Aesthetics: Reflections on a Quaker Ethic in American Design and Consumption* (Philadelphia: University of Pennsylvania Press, 2003), p. 4.
16. William Penn, *No Cross, No Crown*, ed. R. Selleck (Richmond, IN: Friends United Press, 1981), p. 85.
17. John Woodman, "A Plea for the Poor," in Phillips P. Moulton, ed., *The Journal and Major Essays of John Woolman* (New York: Oxford University Press, 1971), p. 255.

CHAPTER 10: RELIGION AS RELATIONSHIP, NOT RIGHTEOUSNESS

1. This metaphor comes from a chapter on parenting in my earlier book *Morning Sun on a White Piano: Simple Pleasures and the Sacramental Life* (New York: Doubleday, 1998), chap. 4.
2. See Aristotle's discussion of friendship in his *Nichomachean Ethics,* especially bks. VIII and IX.
3. Karen Armstrong, in a lecture at Trinity Episcopal Cathedral in Portland, Oregon, February, 2002.
4. Robert Funk, *Honest to Jesus: Jesus for a New Millennium* (San Francisco: HarperSanFrancisco, 1996), p. 295.
5. Martin Buber, *I and Thou,* trans. Ronald Gregor Smith (New York: Scribner, 1958).
6. "I and Thou," *Time,* January 23, 1956.
7. David Novak, *Jewish-Christian Dialogue: A Jewish Justification* (Oxford: Oxford University Press, 1992), p. 82.
8. Buber, *I and Thou,* p. 109.
9. Martin Barich, "A Few Thoughts on Martin Buber's *I and Thou,*" http://www.rjgeib.com/barich/papers/martin-buber.html.
10. Marcus Borg, *Reading the Bible Again for the First Time* (San Francisco: HarperSanFrancisco, 2001), p. 118.
11. Borg, *Reading the Bible Again for the First Time,* p. 122.
12. Borg, *Reading the Bible Again for the First Time,* p. 123.

13. Abraham Heschel, *The Prophets,* 2d ed. (New York: Harper & Row, 1969), vol. 1, pp. 4, 26.
14. Diana Butler Bass, *Christianity for the Rest of Us: How the Neighborhood Church Is Transforming the Faith* (San Francisco: HarperOne, 2006), p. 51.
15. Funk, *Honest to Jesus,* p. 311.

EPILOGUE: A PREACHER'S DREAM: FAITH AS FOLLOWING JESUS
1. From a sermon by Fred B. Craddock and paraphrased from a collection of stories entitled *Craddock Stories,* ed. Mike Graves and Richard Ward (St. Louis, MO: Chalice, 2001), and used with Dr. Craddock's kind permission.